MIND-BODY INTER[ACTIONS] AND DISEASE

and

PSYCHONEUROIMMUNOLOGICAL ASPECTS OF HEALTH AND DISEASE

**Proceedings of a Conference Sponsored
by the Reunion Task Force of the
NATIONAL INSTITUTES OF HEALTH**

Edited by

Nicholas R. S. Hall, Ph.D.
Director
Institute for Health and Human Performance

Fred Altman, Ph.D.
Acting Chief
Basic Prevention and Behavioral Research Branch
National Institute of Mental Health

Susan J. Blumenthal, M.D., M.P.A.
Assistant Surgeon General
and
Deputy Assistant Secretary for Health

Health Dateline Press

ACKNOWLEDGMENTS

The chapters in this book are edited presentations made at a landmark public symposium on *Mind-Body Interactions and Disease* sponsored by the National Institutes of Health. The symposium and the preparation of this proceedings involved the efforts of many individuals not credited elsewhere in this volume. Space does not permit mentioning all their names, but the Editors are grateful to all those who contributed to making the symposium a success and to preparing these proceedings. However, there are two individuals whom we feel it necessary to acknowledge by name: Gerri Adams for handling the day-to-day administrative tasks involved in organizing a symposium, and E. Terry MacGillivary for making the arrangements and ensuring that the meeting ran smoothly.

Nicholas R.S. Hall, Ph.D.
Fred Altman, Ph.D.
Susan J. Blumenthal, M.D., M.P.A.

TABLE OF CONTENTS

SYMPOSIUM PARTICIPANTS

Robert Ader, Ph.D.
Professor and Director
Center for Psychoneuroimmunology Research
Department of Psychiatry
University of Rochester
300 Crittenden Boulevard
Rochester, NY 14642

Fred Altman, Ph.D.
Acting Chief
Basic Prevention and Behavioral
Medicine Research Branch
National Institute of Mental Health
5600 Fishers Lane, Room 10-104
Rockville, MD 20857

Michael H. Antoni, Ph.D.
Associate Professor
Department of Psychology
Behavioral Medicine Research Program
University of Miami
P.O. Box 248185
Coral Gables, FL 33124-2070

Sean Arkins, Ph.D.
Assistant Professor
Department of Biological Sciences
Illinois State University
MC4120
Normal, IL 61790-4120

Barry Arnason, M.D.
Director
Department of Neurology
University of Chicago
5841 S. Maryland Avenue
Room J209, MC2030
Chicago, IL 60637

Wendy Baldwin, Ph.D.
Deputy Director for Extramural Research
Building 1, Room 144
National Institutes of Health
Rockville Pike
Bethesda, MD 20892

Shamgar Ben-Eliyahu, Ph.D.
Department of Psychology
Tel-Aviv University
P.O. Box 39040
Tel-Aviv 69978
ISRAEL

Susan J. Blumenthal, M.D., M.P.A.
Deputy Assistant Secretary for Health
Assistant Surgeon General
Office on Women's Health
U.S. Department of Health and Human Services
Independence Ave., S.W., Room 730B
Washington, DC 20201

Dana Bovbjerg, Ph.D.
PNI Laboratory
Memorial Sloan-Kettering
  Institute for Cancer Research
1275 York Avenue
New York, NY 10021

Thomas Boyce, M.D.
Division of Behavioral and Developmental Pediatrics
University of California, San Francisco
P.O. Box 0314
400 Parnassus Avenue
San Francisco, CA 94143

Dedra S. Buchwald, M.D.
Associate Professor
Harvard Medical Center
325 Ninth Avenue, ZA-60
Seattle, WA 98104

Sheldon Cohen, Ph.D.
Professor
Department of Psychology
Carnegie Mellon University
Pittsburgh, PA 15213

Linda S. Crnic, Ph.D.
Associate Professor
Department of Pediatrics
Mental Retardation Research Center
University of Colorado Health Sciences Center
Campus Box C233
4200 East Ninth Avenue
Denver, CO 80262

Fawzy Fawzy, M.D.
Professor and Deputy Chairman
Department of Psychiatry and Biobehavioral Sciences
University of California, Los Angeles
Westwood Plaza, C8-861 NPI
Los Angeles, CA 90024-1759

David Felten, M.D., Ph.D.
Professor
Department of Neurobiology and Anatomy
University of Rochester Medical Center
Elm Street, Box 603
Rochester, NY 14642

Robert A. Good, M.D., Ph.D.
Distinguished Research Professor
Department of Pediatrics
All Childrens Hospital
801 Sixth Street South
Box 753
St. Petersburg, FL 33701-4899

Barry L. Gruber, Ph.D.
Weems Creek Medical Center
600 Ridgely Avenue, Suite 210
Annapolis, MD 21401

Nicholas R.S. Hall, Ph.D.
Director
Institute for Health and Human Performance
9757 Lake Nona Road
Orlando, FL 32827

Ronald B. Herberman, M.D.
Director
University of Pittsburgh Cancer Institute
University of Pittsburgh Medical Center
Kaufmann Building, Suite 201
3471 Fifth Avenue
Pittsburgh, PA 15213-3221

Margaret E. Kemeny, Ph.D.
Associate Professor
Department of Psychiatry and Behavioral Sciences
School of Medicine, Box 9
University of California, Los Angeles
760 Westwood Plaza
Los Angeles, CA 90024

Janice Kiecolt-Glaser, Ph.D.
Professor
Department of Psychiatry
The Ohio State University
West 12th Avenue
Columbus, OH 43210

Mary Jeanne Kreek, M.D.
Associate Professor
Rockefeller University
York Avenue, Box H28
New York, NY 10021

Mark Lyte, Ph.D.
Professor
Department of Biological Sciences
Mankato State University
P.O. Box 8400
Mankato, MN 56002-8400

Dominique L. Musselman, M.D.
Research Fellow in Neuroendocrinology
Department of Psychiatry and Behavioral Sciences
Emory University School of Medicine
1639 Pierce Drive, Suite 4000
Atlanta, GA 30322

John F. Sheridan, Ph.D.
Professor
Department of Oral Biology
The Ohio State University College of Dentistry
1159 Postle Hall, Box 192
305 W. 12th Avenue
Columbus, OH 43210-1241

George F. Solomon, M.D.
Professor Emeritus of Psychiatry/Biobehavioral Sciences
University of California, Los Angeles
19054 Pacific Coast Highway
Malibu, CA 90265

David Spiegel, M.D.
Professor
Department of Psychiatry and Behavioral Medicine
Stanford University School of Medicine
Stanford, CA 94305-5544

Esther Sternberg, M.D.
Chief
Unit on Neuroendocrine Immunology and Behavior
National Institute of Mental Health
National Institutes of Health
9000 Rockville Pike
Bethesda, MD 20892

Stephen A. Straus, M.D.
Chief
Laboratory of Clinical Investigation
National Institute of Allergy and Infectious Diseases
National Institutes of Health
Rockville Pike
Building 10, Room 11N228
Bethesda, MD 20892

Caroline Whitacre, Ph.D.
Professor
Department of Medical Microbiology and Immunology
The Ohio State University
2078 Graves Hall
333 W. 10th Avenue
Columbus, OH 43210-1239

Bruce Zwilling, Ph.D.
Professor
Department of Microbiology
The Ohio State University
Bioscience Building
484 W. 12th Avenue
Columbus, OH 43210-8120

PREFACE

The chapters in the first part of this book are edited presentations made at a landmark public symposium on *Mind-Body Interactions and Disease* held January 12, 1994 at the National Institutes of Health (NIH). Each article is preceded by an introduction prepared by the editors for the purpose of providing relevant information about the speaker as well as the topic. Many of our nation's top experts in what is called Psychoneuroimmunology (PNI) presented their findings from scientific studies that examined the biological mechanisms by which the mind and the body influence one another, especially with respect to the immune system. We hope that the information provided in this volume will provide a better understanding of the mind-body connection. The symposium was one of the activities sponsored by the NIH Reunion Task Force in celebration of the reunion of the former ADAMHA Institutes - National Institute on Alcohol Abuse and Alcoholism, National Institute on Drug Abuse and the National Institute of Mental Health - with NIH.

This preface incorporates the introductory remarks of Wendy Baldwin, Ph.D. and some of the remarks presented by Susan J. Blumenthal, M.D., M.P.A., who were Co-Chairs of the Reunion Task Force. The goal of the Reunion Task Force was to identify common scientific interests and to facilitate the institutes working together.

There was no shortage of topics, for behavioral research is an integral part of many of the institutes at the NIH. For example, at the National Institute of Child Health and Human Development there is a focus upon the normal development of children as well as the socio-behavioral aspects of fertility, infant mortality, and childhood diseases. At the National Institute on Aging, there has been a long-standing interest in studying the inter-generational effects upon the health and the well being of the elderly. The largest institutes - the National Cancer Institute, the National Institute of Allergy and Infectious Disease, the National Heart,

Lung and Blood Institute - each have programs that are predicated upon the premise that there are profound behavioral influences on the susceptibility and progression of the diseases in each institute's purview. The integration of the three behaviorally-oriented institutes enhances our ability to understand, treat, and prevent all diseases.

The Task Force identified a number of critical health issues of interest to multiple institutes in which to sponsor activities. Among the issues identified was Compliance and Adherence which has far-reaching ramifications. National surveys have revealed that after receiving specific medical instructions, up to 40 percent of the population fails to fill their prescriptions. We know that in clinical trials, where we are right at the point of testing an intervention, the extent to which people are able and willing to participate fully and to comply with that trial can greatly influence the outcome. Consequently, the NIH Reunion Task Force convened three seminars on this and related issues in the context of chronic disease, infectious disease, and addictive disorders.

Another was the role of the family in health care and maintenance. The role of the family is not only an interesting topic, but one that cuts across virtually all of the institutes' program areas. Indeed, when we examine where most health care is delivered we realize that the majority is delivered in the family. It is also within the family unit that many positive health behaviors that we all depend upon are learned. It was for that reason that eight institutes participated in formulating an agenda in consultation with the National Council of Family Research to promote research on the impact of the family on health and disease. This is an area of research that we hope will flourish, especially since the health-related behaviors learned within the family contribute in such a profound way to the prevention of disease. Celebratory activities focusing on other topics were also conducted.

The focus of the symposium reported in these proceedings - a better understanding of how the mind and body interact to facilitate or impair good health - is a critical issue for all of the institutes at NIH. PNI is an area of investigation which focuses on these relationships.

PNI is an unusual field of study. It is a scientific discipline concerned with elucidating the anatomical and chemical pathways via which the mind and body communicate with each other. It is also concerned with the impact of behavior upon immunity and the impact of immune status upon behavior. Its defining language is that of psychologists, psychiatrists, neuroscientists, and immunologists. Those who work within its bounds employ methodologies that probe systems extending from the gene to social support. The field has historical roots extending into the writings of ancient Greek, Chinese, and Indian healers. Modern day roots draw upon the successes of Western physicians as well as those of witch doctors. It is also a subject that is capable of eliciting contrasting emotional responses. There are those who embrace the most preliminary anecdotal data without question, and those who reflexively reject any claim that involves mental regulation of immunity. Neither outright rejection nor automatic acceptance is warranted. Instead, we need to examine data based on rigorous research to ascertain what is reasonable and use the results of well designed studies as a foundation for formulating clinical strategies. This proceedings of the NIH-sponsored conference on *Mind-Body Interactions and Disease* will provide that opportunity.

Susan Blumenthal, M.D., M.P.A., was responsible for developing the celebratory activities. She used working groups representing institutes with interests in the topics covered to assist her in planning and organizing these activities. The PNI working group was chaired by Fred Altman, Ph.D. from NIMH. The other members were Norman Braveman, Ph.D., National Institute of Dental Research; Lynda Erinoff, Ph.D., National Institute on Drug Abuse; Norman Krasnegor, Ph.D., National Institute of Child Health and Human Development; Francine Lancaster, Ph.D., National Institute on Alcohol Abuse and Alcoholism; Andrew A.

Monjan, Ph.D., National Institute on Aging; Susan Nayfield, M.D., M.Sc., National Cancer Institute; Ann Schluederberg, Ph.D., National Institute of Allergy and Infectious Diseases; Novera H. Spector, Ph.D., National Institute of Neurological Disorders and Stroke; Susan Spring, Ph.D., National Institute of Allergy and Infectious Diseases; Susana Sztein, Ph.D., National Institute of Arthritis and Musculoskeletal and Skin Diseases; Ljubisa Vitkovic, Ph.D., National Institute of Mental Health; and Andrew Mariani, Ph.D. (Secretary). The editing of the proceedings was done by Nicholas R.S. Hall, Ph.D. The Copy Editor was Cecilia Ferrer.

The order of the presentations in these proceedings has been slightly altered from the order at the symposium. A chapter has been added following this preface to acquaint the reader with the immune, nervous and endocrine systems. The Historical Perspective section presents an overview and history of the field. The section on scientific evidence presents the relationship between psychological variables such as stress and the onset and progression of various diseases. The final chapter in this section discusses neural-immune communication. A list of readings is presented for those who may wish to obtain additional information. Finally, a Glossary is included which readers are encouraged to use to facilitate their understanding of the material presented.

An additional 24 chapters have been added to this second edition of *Mind-Body Interactions and Disease*. They are based upon presentations made at a scientific conference called *Psychoneuroimmunological Aspects of Health and Disease* that followed the public workshop upon which the first section is based. The objective of the first meeting was to present research findings in a manner that would be readily understandable to the educated lay person. The objective of the second conference was to summarize key research findings that would enable policy makers and scientists to formulate priorities for future research strategies. Consequently, these chapters are of a more technical nature, but because they contain critical health-related information they are now included in this second edition.

The chapters in the second section are based upon a series of presentations directed to an audience of scientists. The intent was to briefly review existing data as well as to present new and provocative findings that could be used to shape the direction of future research in the field of Psychoneuroimmunology. This section of the book was originally written in the format of a monograph to assist in defining future research objectives at the NIH. While of a more technical nature than the chapters in the first part of this book, the information is clearly presented and extends some of the findings described previously. In the monograph prepared for the NIH, all of the chapters exist as a single document with a separate listing of the individual contributors. In this book, the editors chose to identify the primary presenter of a particular chapter. It is important to recognize, however, that virtually all of the participants contributed in a significant manner to many of the sections. For example, the recorded comments of working committees were used to compile the information that is found in the Introduction and Conclusion. For this reason, there is a listing of all of the participants even though some of them may not be directly identified with a specific chapter. In this second edition, the glossary has been expanded to include many of the terms that are used in the newly added chapters. There are also references with supporting data for all of the key concepts that are described.

OVERVIEW OF THE IMMUNE, NERVOUS, AND ENDOCRINE SYSTEMS

OVERVIEW OF THE IMMUNE, NERVOUS, AND ENDOCRINE SYSTEMS*

Nicholas R. S. Hall, Ph.D. and Fred Altman, Ph.D.

Introduction

Dr. Nicholas Hall is a scientist and pioneer in the field of mind-body research. He has been the recipient of two prestigious Research Scientist Development Awards, one from the National Institute of Mental Health, and one from the National Institute on Drug Abuse. Dr. Fred Altman is Acting Branch Chief of the Basic Prevention and Behavioral Medicine Research Branch at the National Institute of Mental Health. He served as the Chairman of the Psychoneuroimmunology Working Group, the group which organized the symposium upon which these proceedings are based.

The functions of the immune system are integral to our good health and play a critical role in our vulnerability to disease. A hyperactive immune system may lead to the development of autoimmune disease or allergies. With a depleted immune system, the body is at risk of being overwhelmed by invading bacteria and viruses. At several levels - and in markedly different ways - the immune system can be profoundly influenced by chemical changes subsequent to altered emotional states. The following discussion will not attempt to describe in detail the workings of the immune, nervous and endocrine systems - a subject that could easily warrant several volumes devoted exclusively to each topic. Instead, the emphasis will be upon those processes that provide the foundation for mind-body interactions.

---

* Portions of this chapter were excerpted from an article called "Thinking Well" by Nicholas R.S. Hall and Allan L. Goldstein, published in *The Sciences*, March, 1986, pp. 34-41.

Cells of the Immune System

Most of the cells that comprise the immune system can be placed into one of two categories based upon the target they are designed to attack: 1) those that are primed to eliminate distinct pathogens from the body, and 2) those that will respond to anything that is recognized as simply not being part of the body. Within the first category are the lymphocytes. Those that give rise to antibody secreting plasma cells are called B-lymphocytes (or B-cells), while those that directly attach to pathogens or release chemicals that regulate other cells are called T-lymphocytes (or T-cells). Both B- and T-cells respond in a highly specific manner when attacking pathogens. This is in marked contrast to the so called 'phagocytic' cells which respond to things that are recognized as not belonging in the body. While this distinction is convenient when teaching the subject of immunology, it is somewhat simplistic. In fact, all of the cell types interact with each other so that no single population of cells by itself is capable of effectively defending the body against disease-causing microbes.

The first cellular line of defense against viruses and bacteria that invade the host is the phagocytic cell. When the skin is breached, swarms of these scavenging white blood cells descend upon the scene and ingest the transgressors. The phagocytic cells include monocytes, macrophages, as well as neutrophils. They literally wrap their membranes around the pathogen, pull it into the cell, and then as a result of chemicals that become activated, the pathogen is destroyed. Those phagocytic cells that circulate in the blood are called monocytes and neutrophils. Some of the monocytes eventually end up in fixed tissues, where they become macrophages. These cells also provide signals enabling T-cells to respond more efficiently to the pathogen. For this reason, they are often referred to as 'presenting' cells. The antigen attaches to the membrane of the monocyte, and then it is presented to the T-lymphocyte along with a chemical signal which is interleukin-1 (IL-1). This enables the T-lymphocyte to then respond by secreting its own chemicals. In addition to producing chemicals that are capable of activating the T-cells, other chemicals which are very important in the inflammatory response are also produced by monocytes. These mediators of inflammation are called complement proteins which, by inflaming the afflicted area, create an inhospitable micro-environment for foreign tissues. Other chemical mediators of the immune response include histamine, which dilates blood vessels in preparation for the arrival of legions of lymphocytes; and prostaglandins and leukotrienes, substances that help start and stop the activities of macrophages and T-cells. This complex arrangement lends to the immune system the flexibility required to strategically orchestrate its responses to countless new and varied microorganisms that invade the body.

Organs of the Immune System

Lymphocytes function in a relatively specific manner when attacking disease-causing organisms. Like all white blood cells, lymphocytes derive from bone marrow; but whereas some remain in the marrow until they reach full maturity and are therefore designated B-cells, others, early in their development, migrate to the thymus - the master gland of the immune system - and for that reason are called T-cells. It is within the thymus gland and bone marrow that the T- and B-cells learn to distinguish between a person's constituent cells and entities that are foreign to the body. Both types of lymphocytes then circulate through the bloodstream before lodging in such lymphoid tissues as the spleen and lymph nodes, where they remain inactive until confronted with any of thousands of types of antigens (i.e., foreign substances such as organic waste, toxins, viruses, and bacteria). Lymphocytes are highly specific, responding to only one or just a very few related pathogens. So, a T-cell or a B-cell that is primed to attack influenza A will ignore the rhinovirus that causes common cold symptoms, the herpesvirus, or any number of other pathogens.

Function of the Immune System

T-lymphocytes exist in several different forms. There are some which play a regulatory role. These include the T-helper cells, which facilitate the production of antibody by B-cells and the activation of phagocytic cells. There are also effector cells within the T-lymphocyte population that can directly attack pathogens. Cytotoxic T-cells, for example, are those that have been associated with killing tumors. They do this by quite literally snuggling up to the tumor and injecting lethal chemicals which then destroy the proliferating cell. They also secrete chemicals called cytokines that are capable of regulating the various cells within the immune system. Certain of these cytokines, for example IL-1, are capable of acting within other biological systems including the brain.

In the presence of a particular antigen, B-cells become plasma cells which synthesize and release proteins called antibodies. An antibody is designed to destroy the specific pathogen that gave rise to its production. There are several different types of antibody or immunoglobulins (Ig) which are found in humans. These include IgM, IgG, IgE, IgD and IgA. Each is specialized to attack a specific type of antigen.

Some T- and B-lymphocytes become memory cells. Memory cells are capable of being stimulated months, even years later, by the same pathogen except they go into high gear much more quickly. So instead of taking days in order for an antibody to be produced, the memory cells can start producing antibody within about 48 to 72 hours. The production of memory cells is the basis of vaccinations. When a person is vaccinated, the purpose is not to enable the host to ward off and keep pathogens from entering the body. The objective is to produce memory cells, so that when the same pathogen subsequently enters the body, the immune system will respond more efficiently.

Two physiological events that contribute to our defense against pathogens are fever and sleep. They are so important that they can be induced by the immune system. A lot of microbes cannot survive when body temperature goes up even a few degrees. Furthermore, nearly all aspects of the immune system are boosted as a result of elevated body temperature. Several chemicals produced by the immune system are capable of inducing fever, although one of the best studied is IL-1 which was originally called T-cell activating factor. The name was changed when it was discovered that it was capable of doing many other things within the body. For example, it stimulates a fever response by acting within a part of the brain called the anterior hypothalamus and nearby regions. IL-1 is also capable of stimulating sleep. Not just any sleep, but slow wave sleep; that deep, restful stage of sleep which is the time when growth hormone is produced. Growth hormone is capable of boosting the immune system thereby increasing the probability that the invading pathogen will be successfully eliminated from the body. Thus, chemicals produced by the immune system construct a microenvironment within which the white cells can work more efficiently. When the system works in an optimal manner, infectious agents are swiftly eliminated with no or minimal symptoms.

When the immune system is impaired, pathogens that would normally be eliminated from the body without clinical consequences are able to proliferate. It is during the time consuming process that culminates in the production of antibody that symptoms occur. While protective, antibodies can also serve as a barometer of immune system activation. Some investigators interpret the presence of elevated antibody as an indication that the initial defenses have failed, requiring the activation of T- and B-cells. This is especially true of infectious agents that are always present but usually in a dormant state. It is when the first line of defense fails that such microbes are able to proliferate, causing symptoms and stimulating the production of antibody. The transition from a dormant to an active state is referred to as 'reactivation' and most often occurs when the immune system becomes impaired. In the following chapters, this concept will be discussed in the context of herpesvirus infection and tuberculosis.

Conversely, relatively high antibody titers following deliberate exposure of a person to an attenuated pathogen - as would occur following vaccination - are interpreted as a sign that the immune system is working efficiently.

The Nervous System

The nervous system is involved in the prevention and control of illness. It is composed of central and peripheral components. The central nervous system consists of the brain and spinal cord while the peripheral nervous system consists of the remainder. The peripheral nervous system itself consists of two parts, the somatic nervous system which controls movement and receives sensory information from the environment, and the autonomic nervous system which receives sensory information from and controls internal organs such as the heart, the stomach, the lungs, and other organs. The autonomic nervous system itself is composed of two branches, the sympathetic and the parasympathetic. The sympathetic branch is connected to the central nervous system along most of the length of the spinal cord and tends to activate the organism in preparation for flight or fight. In contrast, the parasympathetic nervous system is connected to the central nervous system at the brain stem and lower spinal cord (sacral) levels and tends to deactivate the organism in preparation for more vegetative functions such as digestion. Evidence to be discussed in this Proceedings will document the fact that the autonomic nervous system innervates all of the major tissues of the immune system and can directly affect the course of maturation as well as the biological activity of lymphocytes.

The nervous system is composed of cells called neurons. Information is transmitted within neurons by electrical activity referred to as nerve impulses. Neurons connect to other neurons and to every organ system in the body. However, there is not a physical connection between neurons or between neurons and other cells; there is a gap which is referred to as a synapse or synaptic cleft. Nerve impulses cannot cross synapses. Messages are transmitted across synapses by the release and uptake of chemicals referred to as neurotransmitters. Neurons receive information at the level of the cell body or processes referred to as dendrites. They respond by transmitting impulses along a process called an axon. Some axons are very short while others can wend their way all the way from the brain into the spinal cord where they relay their message to the peripheral nervous system.

A large number of substances can function as neurotransmitters. Families of compounds include the catecholamines, indolamines, as well as peptides. Specific examples of each of these families include dopamine, serotonin, and beta-endorphin respectively.

The Endocrine System

Many of the substances that can serve as neurotransmitters within the brain are also produced by cells that are not part of the central nervous system. Outside the brain, they may have a quite different function, including the regulation of the immune system. For example, epinephrine is a member of the catecholamine family and can function as a neurotransmitter within the nervous system. But it is also produced by cells of the adrenal gland where it is released into the blood stream. Chemicals that are released into the blood and that convey information at a distance within the body are referred to as hormones. Glands which produce hormones are referred to as endocrine glands. The discovery that autonomic nerves interlace lymph tissues has recast our view of the immune system. It now seems to resemble the endocrine system, and like all endocrine tissue possesses a direct anatomical link to the brain although it remains to be seen whether messages carried by that anatomical link flow in both directions as they do within the endocrine system.

The Hypothalamic-Pituitary-Adrenal (HPA) Axis

One of the major pathways by which the central nervous system regulates the immune system via the endocrine system is the hypothalamic-pituitary-adrenal (HPA) axis. In the hypothalamus at the top of the HPA axis, neurotransmitters - in particular, serotonin, acetylcholine, and norepinephrine - regulate the secretion of corticotropin releasing factor (CRF). CRF induces the pituitary to secrete adrenocorticotropin hormone (ACTH). This hormone, in turn, stimulates the adrenal glands to release steroid hormones (glucocorticoids) into the bloodstream. Ultimately, a build-up of glucocorticoids in the blood triggers neurons in the brain to cease the process that gives rise to this steroid. CRF release is inhibited and the release of ACTH and glucocorticoids stops. It is called a negative feedback loop and is a means by which the system regulates itself.

The major impact of this axis on the immune system is its affect on T-cells. T-cells are acutely sensitive to glucocorticoids. This is especially true of nascent T-cells, which represent about 90 percent of all T-cells present in the thymus at any time. Greatly elevated glucocorticoid levels will either damage or destroy these cells or prematurely induce their migration from the thymus to other immune tissues. The resultant shrinkage of the thymus is so pronounced that the gland's weight has been used in the past as an indirect way to assay the release of adrenal glucocorticoids. However, as was indicated, the effects of glucocorticoids are biphasic; in high concentrations they mute the immune response, whereas in small amounts they have been shown to activate it. Normally, the adrenal glands secrete glucocorticoids in a daily tidal rhythm, and the point at which lymphocytes respond most aggressively to antigens has been correlated with the interval during which the level of circulating glucocorticoids falls to its lowest point. Sometimes, the glucocorticoid, cortisol, is referred to as the body's 'stress hormone' because that is when it is most often released.

Psychology and Health

In this overview the function of the immune system in the control of pathogens to prevent and control disease has been discussed.

Further, the regulation of the immune system by the nervous and endocrine systems has been considered. What has not been mentioned is how psychological variables - particularly stress - affect health. Clearly, psychological variables are mediated by the brain. In turn, the neural activity corresponding to stress and other psychological states, conditions, and dispositions impacts the hypothalamus. Indeed, the release of glucocorticoids from the adrenals as a result of the cascade of activity in the HPA axis is an important marker of stress. The previous discussion indicates how hypothalamic activity can alter immune function and thereby health. Although the precise mechanisms whereby emotional distress can impair the immune system are not known, these interconnections provide a potential means by which psychological variables can influence health outcome.

Clinical practice cannot long remain unaffected by the research described during the course of the NIH-sponsored symposium that this book is based upon. The discovery of pathways that bind the brain and the immune system rescues the behavioral approach to studying disease from the shadowy practices of witch doctors and places it squarely within the rational tradition of Western medicine. Aware now of the complex physiological basis for behavioral modification of the immune response, physicians can spend less time fielding criticism and more time exploring which types of therapy are of the greatest benefit. We are witnessing the birth of a new integrative science, Psychoneuroimmunology (PNI), which begins with the premise that neither the brain nor the immune system can be excluded from any scheme that proposes to account for the onset and course of human disease.

HISTORICAL PERSPECTIVE

OVERVIEW OF MIND-BODY INTERACTIONS

Susan J. Blumenthal, M.D., M.P.A.

Introduction

An overview of some of the categories of evidence documenting that mind-body interactions are relevant to disease will be described by Dr. Susan Blumenthal. Dr. Blumenthal is a national leader in behavioral medicine, mental illness, and women's health issues. She serves as Deputy Assistant Secretary for Health, and Assistant Surgeon General in the U.S. Department of Health and Human Services. At the time of the conference, Dr. Blumenthal was Co-Chair of the NIH Reunion Task Force which organized the symposium called *Mind-Body Interactions and Disease*. The 33-member NIH Reunion Task Force had representation from all NIH Institutes, Offices and Centers and served to facilitate the 1993 merger of the National Institute of Mental Health, National Institute on Drug Abuse, and National Institute on Alcohol Abuse and Alcoholism into the NIH community. She was also Chief of the Behavioral Medicine and Basic Prevention Research Branch at the National Institute of Mental Health.

Recent Developments in Mind-Body Research

The effects of psychological states such as stress and depression, and the effects of events such as bereavement and job loss on health have been reported for centuries. In fact, Virgil, the Roman orator and poet wrote, "Mind moves matter". The Greek philosopher and physician, Aristotle, advised his fellow physicians, "Just as you ought not to attempt to cure eyes without head or head without body, so you should not treat body without soul". Sir William Osler, considered to be the father of modern medicine, wrote that when attempting to predict health outcomes from tuberculosis in patients, it is just as important to know what is going on in a man's - let's also make that a woman's - head as in his or her chest.

From Aristotle's time to our own, the medical literature contains a wealth of anecdotal information documenting the intimate and complex mind-body connection. From either our medical training or our personal experience, we are all familiar with stories of the cancer survivor whose cancer was in remission until their spouse died, or the daughter who in caring for an aged parent with Alzheimer's disease suffers a severe decline in her overall health, or on the positive side, the stories of breast cancer patients who joined a support group and lived longer than patients with similar medical prognoses who did not participate in this kind of intervention.

All of these stories ring true. They make sense to us on a human level, even if we haven't been able to make sense of them on a scientific level in the past. But in recent years, due to an explosion of scientific advances in our understanding of the brain, biology, and behavior, and the discovery and application of new tools and techniques from molecular immunology and the neurosciences, researchers have begun to unravel and to understand such stories on a scientific level by gathering evidence to document complex interactions among psychological states, life events, our biologic function, and our health.

One of the most significant and really unexpected findings that fostered this new field of PNI was that the immune system can respond to chemicals secreted by the central nervous system. In fact, the immune system's white blood cells, called lymphocytes, that are mobilized to fight infections in our bodies, become less responsive when they are exposed to the brain chemicals that the body secretes when we are stressed. Subsequent findings and studies demonstrated that stress does, in fact, increase our susceptibility to the common cold. Our mothers were right. Hostility can increase the likelihood of heart disease, while social support and strong relationships can prolong not only the life expectancy of patients suffering from breast cancer and heart disease, but also the quality of their lives.

Conversely, we also know that many physical illnesses can trigger certain psychological conditions. For example, six months before they develop any other clinical signs of pancreatic cancer, a significant proportion of men will develop a depression. Approximately ten percent of Acquired Immunodeficiency Syndrome (AIDS) patients will develop mood, behavioral, cognitive, and memory changes before they develop somatic signs of the illness. In both these cases, the NIH is supporting research designed to determine whether the immune system may be secreting powerful hormonal substances called cytokines that might in turn trigger these emotional and cognitive changes.

What has emerged in this new field of PNI is the understanding that there is a bi-directional interaction between the nervous, immune and endocrine systems. These complex interactions appear to powerfully influence our health and susceptibility to disease. Additionally, there is evidence that behavioral and lifestyle interventions such as support groups, hypnosis, relaxation training, and certain types of psychotherapy can improve health outcomes and positively alter the course of illnesses.

NIH-Sponsored Studies

Through studies in this new field of PNI, researchers are now examining changes in the immune and endocrine systems that correlate with psychological states, life events, health and disease. Furthermore, they are determining the mechanisms by which these effects are produced. At the NIH, for example, we are supporting a number of basic science and clinical studies to further our understanding of the bi-directional links between the brain and the immune system.

Several studies have been designed to examine the immune system's capacity to learn. It is well known that the central nervous system learns; it has 'memory' cells. But we also have determined that the immune system has 'memory' cells and these specialized lymphocytes are produced to fight an infection and remain in the blood, ready to multiply and destroy the same invader faster the next time the person is exposed to the disease-causing organism. The immune system also is susceptible, like the central nervous system, to a kind of learning called conditioning. This is the phenomenon whereby a particular stimulus can change the system in ways that make it respond differently the next time it is exposed to that same stimulus.

Consider this study supported by the National Institute of Mental Health. The results suggest that breast cancer patients who receive immunosuppressive chemotherapy will experience subsequent immune suppression just by being exposed to substances or objects that were paired with the immunosuppressive treatment, for example, pictures on the wall of the waiting room or the uniforms worn by the staff. They have been conditioned to a stimulus within the hospital environment in much the same way that Pavlov's dogs were induced to salivate in response to the ringing bell.

In other studies, a decline of activity of immune system cells has been demonstrated in several groups of people experiencing stress: medical students taking final exams, people caring for loved ones with Alzheimer's disease, and people who have recently lost their spouse. Studies are also underway to determine how these changes affect people's health. Other scientists are exploring the role of psychological factors on the course of autoimmune diseases such as rheumatoid arthritis, Grave's disease, lupus erythematosus and multiple sclerosis. We're also studying the effects of psychotropic drugs, such as anti-depressants, on immune function, and the mechanisms by which illnesses and the responses of the immune system to these illnesses affect our behavior, our thoughts and our emotions.

If stress can make you sick, as some of the studies I have described to you have suggested, will learning to cope with stressful events boost our immune systems? That is a central question in the mind-body field, and finding the answer to that question is a high priority for many investigators. Scientists are also curious about this issue and are currently investigating the effects of behavioral and psychosocial interventions on the progression and prevention of disease.

They are also studying the effects of these behavioral and psychosocial interventions on the utilization and cost of both out-patient and in-patient services. Some investigators have demonstrated that people who have more friends and more family support tend to live longer than those who lack adequate social support networks. For example, one year after a heart attack, people with more friends and family are twice as likely to survive as those who lack such support. Other studies, which you will also read about in this proceedings, have found that patients with metastatic breast cancer who participate in support groups live an average of 18 months longer than women who do not receive this intervention. You are going to learn about how the body turns states of mind like close relationships and relaxation into a biological advantage that improves health. In yet another study, psychotherapeutic consultation to elderly hip-fracture patients resulted in them leaving the hospital an average of two days sooner than patients who did not receive such consultation. Scientists want to understand the biological underpinnings of these improved health outcomes.

Benefits of Psychoneuroimmunology Research

In the past, our nation has focused on finding the drug or the surgical intervention to treat disease. I want to underscore that this is a critical part of our mission, and it is very important. But the evidence to be presented, combined with other studies published in the scientific literature, makes a compelling case for including these low-cost social and behavioral interventions in the treatment regimen of many patients. Not only are there important data that these treatments can improve the quality of patients' lives, but evidence exists that they can potentially increase survival rates, as well as decrease health care costs. The latter is critical in the climate of a nation where our health care costs are escalating tremendously, perhaps as much as 15 percent of the Gross National Product in the coming year.

Studies in PNI being supported by the NIH and other organizations are enhanced by the new collaborations made possible by the recent merger of the National Institute of Mental Health, the National Institute on Drug Abuse, and the National Institute on Alcoholism and Alcohol Abuse. This symposium is sponsored by the NIH Reunion Task Force, which is a group with representation from all of the NIH's Institutes, Centers and Divisions. It has helped to facilitate and celebrate the merger of these Institutes into the NIH community and its enhanced potential for improving the health of the nation.

The goal of the Task Force is to promote further scientific collaboration across institutes, to give the behavioral sciences and neurosciences prominent focus, and to place the mental and addictive disorders at the heart of our nation's research agenda, side by side with cancer, diabetes and heart disease. After 25 years of separation, the NIH has finally gotten its head back! We have rectified that dichotomy established long ago that separated mind and body.

This merger of the institutes, we believe, is a major step forward in increasing our ability to understand the causes, the treatment, and the prevention of all diseases. I think it is very encouraging for investigators to know that with this expanded research mission, the NIH is creating new opportunities for research in PNI and related fields. It is also wonderful news for the American public, who can expect more comprehensive approaches to the treatment and cure of all diseases like cancer, mental illness, and AIDS, in this decade and beyond into the 21st century. We hope to rectify the dichotomy established by the Greek rational philosophers that split mind from body, and to fully integrate behavioral treatments into the practice of medicine.

Today, you will learn that the mind, as one journalist has written, is neither a miracle cure nor is it a lethal weapon. We do not yet know with complete certainty whether emotional distress predisposes people to diseases such as cancer, or whether interventions such as psychotherapy, social support, or relaxation training will make a tumor disappear. But what we do know is that there is a growing body of scientific evidence published in prestigious journals such as *Lancet*, the *New England Journal of Medicine* and *Science*, that is underscoring the notion that thoughts, beliefs, emotions, and psychosocial interventions can have a major impact on our physical health and on disease progression.

Conclusion

In conclusion, throughout this century and into the next one, chronic illnesses such as cancer, heart, and lung disease have become the major health care burden in our country. Over 50 percent of the causation of these illnesses is due to behavioral and lifestyle factors. If Americans were to simply adopt healthy behaviors, this alone would have a far greater impact on preventing disease, improving the quality of life, and reducing the cost of health care than almost any other type of intervention.

According to an old Chinese proverb, "It is better to light a candle than curse the darkness". There has been considerable darkness surrounding our knowledge of how the mind and body interact in health and disease, but it is our hope here at the NIH that through the support of exciting new research, and through the exchange and sharing of knowledge such as will occur at this symposium, we can illuminate a pathway to a better understanding of the intimate, mysterious connections between the mind and the body. That pathway will lead ultimately to improved health for everyone.

PSYCHONEUROIMMUNOLOGY

George F. Solomon, M.D.

Introduction

A common misconception is that the area of study popularly referred to as Psychoneuroimmunology or PNI is the product of recent technology and a better understanding of how biological systems function. In fact, there is a rich tradition in both Eastern and Western philosophy linking what we now term emotions with somatic health. Currently, we are witnessing the application of the scientific method to document principles and phenomena that our ancestors practiced and often accepted through astute observation and/or intuition.

Dr. George Solomon provides a historical perspective beginning with the ancient Greek and Roman philosophers. He subsequently traces the historical milestones that have perpetuated a continued interest in this area of study as well as providing the basis for further advances.

Dr. Solomon is a pioneer in the field of mind-body research, having conducted some of the original studies in PNI. In 1965, after studying emotional factors associated with autoimmune diseases, he published his observations on traits and coping styles of the 'Rheumatoid Personality'. Dr. Solomon's current work focuses on the psychoneuro-immunologic aspects of Human Immunodeficiency Virus (HIV) infection, aging, and the relationship among stress and assertiveness, and the immune system. Dr. Solomon is Professor Emeritus of Psychiatry and Biobehavioral Sciences at the University of California, Los Angeles.

23

Definition of Psychoneuroimmunology

Continuing the theme begun by Dr. Blumenthal, I would note that throughout the ages and across cultures, wise physicians have linked psychic and bodily well being. For example, the Transylvanian physician Papai Periz Ferenc essentially reiterated Aristotle and anticipated PNI when he said in 1680, "When the parts of the body and its humors are not in harmony, then the mind is unbalanced, and melancholy ensues. But on the other hand, a quiet and happy mind makes the whole body healthy".

Mechanisms underlying this linkage are now becoming understood. PNI is the trans-disciplinary scientific field concerned with the interactions among behavior, the immune system and the nervous system. Its clinical aspects range from an understanding of the biological mechanisms underlying the influence of psychosocial factors on the onset and course of immunologically-resisted and -mediated diseases, to an understanding of immunologically-induced psychiatric symptoms. Its bioregulatory aspects include understanding of the complex interactions of neuroendocrine and immunologically-generated networks in maintaining health and in combating disease. PNI aims at clarifying the scientific basis for humanistic medicine and at developing new models of health and illness.

Common Features of the Immune and Central Nervous System

If one assumes an adaptive rationality to evolutionary processes, it makes sense, albeit perhaps at the cost of over analogizing, that the nervous system and the immune system communicate bi-directionally with each other, even that they monistically might be conceptualized as a single integrated adaptive-defensive system. Both have a sense of identity, of self and non-self. Both relate the organism to the outside world and assess its components and inhabitants as friendly, or harmless, or as dangerous. Both allow the organism to survive in an often hostile environment by adaptation and defense. In order to do so, they possess memory and learn by experience. Both also monitor the inner world and evaluate its makeup and institute defenses against noxious inner components. Both the brain (psyche) and the immune system sometimes make mistakes that can lead to illness, even death. Actually innocuous substances or organisms can be perceived as dangerous, and phobias on the one hand, or allergies on the other, ensue. True self may not be accepted and depression or autoimmunity may ensue. Both depression and autoimmunity are more common with aging. Recent but not remote memory tends to fail with age, and immunosenescence - or aging of the immune system - is characterized by poor primary response to novel antigens and relatively good secondary response to recall antigens.

Roger Booth and Kevin Ashbridge recently stated, "There is a need to reassess and perhaps redefine the concepts, symbols and languages of immunology and psychology in ways which allow the relationships between immunological and psychological processes to be expressed in terms of a coherent, teleological perspective. In order to make sense of psychoimmune relationships, we must be open to modifying some of our preconceptions about the immune system and of our psyche."

Pre-contemporary psychosomatic medicine, which dates to the late 1930's and early '40's, anticipated PNI, whereas pre-contemporary immunology did not. Immunological doctrine (as if science ever should be doctrinaire or dogmatic) held that the immune system was autonomous and self-regulatory, responding only to antigenic challenge. During a recent lecture, David Felten recalled criticism of an unapproved NIH grant proposal that stated, to wit, "(Neuronal) innervation of immune organs obviously can have nothing to do with immune responses since such reactions can occur in test tubes, which have no nerves." On the other hand, by the early 1940's Franz Alexander realized that psychosomatic pathology was the result of the physiological concomitants of conscious or repressed emotions.

Psychological Variables and Autoimmune Disease

In the 1940's, Hans Selye began to conceptualize stress as a non-specific perturbing influence on homeostasis, Cannon's conceptualization of inner physiological balance. A stressor, which is a demand that places an adaptational requirement on the organism, leads to a state of stress (strain or distress) that in turn, depending on external modulators such as social support and on internal modulators such as coping ability, leads to no change, to psychological growth (thus the stressor being "eustress" or good stress), or to an adverse health change. Selye emphasized the HPA axis as mediating stress effects on health. By 1960, the great internist/psychiatrist, George Engel, had formulated the bio-psychosocial model of all disease.

Depending on efficacy of coping, which comprises a variety of mechanisms that serve functions of maintenance of psychic homeostasis or equilibrium, stress may lead to distress. Mechanisms of coping tend to be relatively stable and characteristic of individuals, and range from mature problem solving to more primitive mechanisms of denial and repression or detachment and withdrawal. Classical psychosomatic medicine had been concerned with particular styles of coping or patterns of personality traits associated with particular diseases. A time-pressured, competitive, hostile pattern has been supported by some evidence as associated with coronary artery disease and is labeled a 'Type A' pattern. In a series of controlled studies of persons with the autoimmune disease rheumatoid arthritis, Rudolph Moos and I concluded that arthritics, in comparison with non-arthritic siblings, showed more compliance, difficulty in expression of anger, sensitivity to anger of others, conservatism and self sacrifice, as well as being more anxious and depressed. Patients with other autoimmune diseases, such as systemic lupus erythematosus and thyroiditis, seemed similar. Yet, which was cause and which effect (i.e., personality and distress vs. disease)?

We compared healthy (as assessed by medical history, physical examination, and joint X-rays) relatives of patients with rheumatoid arthritis. One healthy group (about 20 percent) possessed and the other lacked the characteristic autoantibody of rheumatoid arthritis, an anti-immunoglobulin-G (IgG) or antibody against one's own antibodies called rheumatoid factor. Those relatives lacking this factor were just "ordinary folks", a random population like blood bank donors ranging from psychologically healthy to psychiatrically disturbed in a normal distribution curve, with most somewhere near the middle. On the other hand, those with the autoantibody were all in excellent emotional shape, with no anxiety, depression or alienation, and reporting satisfaction in work and personal relationships. Thus, it seemed to us that psychological well being was serving a protective function in the face of a genetically determined predisposition to autoimmune disease, since asymptomatic persons with rheumatoid factor have a greater actuarial chance of subsequent development of arthritis, and since onset of autoimmune disease relatively frequently follows a stressful life event such as loss of a loved one.

On the other side of the coin, working in a clinic for rheumatoid and autoimmune diseases, the fact that one condition, systemic lupus erythematosus, can sometimes produce serious psychiatric disturbances, often schizophrenia-like, even as an initial symptom, impressed me and a colleague, Jeffrey Fessel. Because of this immunological-psychiatric association, we looked for abnormal levels of immunoglobulins and presence of various autoantibodies in patients suffering from schizophrenia, and found some of both.

Stress and Immunity

By the early 1960's, there was experimental evidence of stress effects of viral infections reported by Rasmussen. These lines of evidence, as well as awareness of little-noticed Russian work by Korneva and Khai on the suppression of immunity by placing lesions in specific hypothalamic regions of the brain in experimental animals, led Rudolph Moos and me to write the 1964 speculative theoretical integration, "Emotions, Immunity and Disease," that posited neuroendocrine regulation of immunity and the effects of experience on immunity. Obviously, animal experiments concerning such effects on measures of immunity, on central nervous system and immunity, on stress effects on immunologically-resisted and -mediated diseases were called for and were begun in my Psychoimmunology Laboratory at the Stanford-affiliated Palo Alto VA Hospital, at first under private foundation funding because of the initial impossibility of obtaining NIH or VA grants for such 'far-out' research that 'fell between the cracks' of medical and behavioral disciplines.

Experiments on early experience (neonatal handling) and immunity, several stressors on primary and secondary antibody response to a novel antigen (with varied results, depending on nature and timing of stress), stress effects on experimental adjuvant-induced arthritis, graft vs. host reaction, and virus-induced tumors ensued. In the latter group of experiments, Alfred Amkraut, the first immunologist to work full-time in PNI, and I observed in a then little-noted work that spontaneous behavioral differences within a single inbred (genetically identical) strain were accompanied by differences in tumor immunity. Mice that spontaneously developed fighting behavior developed smaller tumors that were more likely to regress completely. Thus, it is good for your health to express anger openly, even if you're a mouse! We found that stress effects on immunity were not entirely mediated by adrenal cortical hormones because stress could, to some degree, still lead to suppression of humoral (antibody) immunity in animals that had been adrenalectomized (had their adrenal glands removed) but maintained in good health by administering fixed doses of corticosterone. After visiting then-Leningrad, we were able to replicate Dr. Korneva's brain lesion work.

Historical Milestones

This talk is not nearly long enough to adequately outline the history of PNI, but I shall mention a few highlights. What put PNI on the map in the face of so much skepticism really was the 1975 report of Bob Ader's elegant taste aversion conditioned immunosuppression experiments. If saccharine alone, after having been paired with the immunosuppressant drug cyclophosphamide, produced immunosuppression, then the brain must be involved. (Remarkably, in an overlooked work, Metal'nikov and Chorine in 1926 at the Pasteur Institute had classically conditioned peritoneal inflammation using microbial extracts and warming or scratching the skin as the conditioned stimulus.) David and Suzanne Felten's studies of sympathetic innervation of lymphoid organs, particularly the thymus, clarified the hard wiring of the immune system and the role of neurotransmitters at synapse-like junctions between nerves and immunologic cells. They furthered the integration of PNI with neuroscience. Gerard Renoux and colleagues carried neuro-immunoregulation to the cortex with the discovery of cerebral laterally differential effects on T-cell maturation and function. The logically essential afferent, immune system to brain, limb of the brain-endocrine-immune axis, was shown by changes in corticosterone levels and in firing rates of hypothalamic neurons after antigenic challenge by Besedovsky and Sorkin. In then-doubted work, Blalock and Smith set the stage for the current flood of information about the effects of immune cytokines, or peptides produced by immunologic cells, on the brain, and of neurohormones, neurotransmitters and neuropeptides on immunologically competent cells by their discovery that lymphocytes synthesize adrenocorticotropin hormone (ACTH) and beta-endorphin, formerly felt to be synthesized only neuro-endocrinally.

Studies on human stress and immunity began with space flight and continued through naturalistic situations such as bereavement, marital discord, examinations, and the caretaking of patients with Alzheimer's disease, to experimental stressors such as mental arithmetic. Naturally occurring human distress and immunity have been evaluated, especially in depressive illness, as originally shown in T-cell function by Schleifer, Keller and Stein, and in natural killer cell function by Irwin. Valuable experiments were begun to understand the effects of social stress with primate models by Laudenslager and by Coe. That the outcome of a stressful encounter, rather than the encounter itself, is critical was shown by the immunosuppression of defeated fighting fish by Faisel and UCLA colleagues, supporting Freud's observation that illness is more common in the defeated than in the victorious army.

Effects of cytokines on brain functions and in neuropathology grows apace. In 1985, I listed 14 postulates concerning classes of evidence for brain-immune interactions of varying degrees of probable validity, as based on at least some evidence to date. In 1987, I published 35; now I have 117. Since time is running out, I'm only going to give a recent example. Psychogenic and stress factors may influence the development of cardiovascular disease by means of psychoneuroimmunologic mechanisms, not only because macrophages are the cells that take up cholesterol into the endothelium of blood vessels, but also because high cholesterol-containing liposomes can stimulate production of anti-cholesterol antibodies.

The first text in the field edited by Ader had 14 chapters. Ten years later, the 1991 edition had 43. There have been half a dozen books in 1992 and 1993 about this field, but these do not obviously include the plethora of exploitative, partially accurate, but overstated and often misleading "how to do it" pop books.

Two major developments for the field were the publication of the journal *Brain, Behavior and Immunity*, edited by Ader, Cohen and Felten, appearing first in March of 1987, and the establishment of the Psychoneuroimmunology Research Society, which was organized at the Fourth Research Perspectives in PNI meeting in Boulder, Colorado in 1993.

Conclusion

I wish to end with a tribute to Norman Cousins, who wrote several influential bestsellers on his own recoveries from illness and about the beginnings of PNI in a very effective way. Norman, who was not a physician but had an honorary M.D., saw the medical profession itself as his patient, and he had three ways to cure medicine. The first was education of the public to refuse to accept dehumanized, impersonal, insensitive care and prognostic death sentences promulgated by doctors; secondly, to humanize medical education; and finally, to establish the biological bases of the role of attitude and relief of distress in healing by furthering research funding and training in PNI.

DISCUSSION

Question: Would you please distinguish between the concepts of 'eustress' and 'distress' and comment on the potential beneficial effects of distress in countering the effects of boredom?

Dr. Solomon: That's a very good question. I like to sky dive, but other people might be freaked out by jumping out of an airplane. The issue in humans is not stress, it is distress or discomfort. With animals, we can only know what we do experimentally to them, but in humans, we can assess the response, which depends on coping. There are some people who are high arousal people and are distressed when not enough is going on, and consequently they are bored. Thus, boredom for them is a stressor.

SCIENTIFIC EVIDENCE

STRESS, GENETICS AND TUBERCULOSIS

Bruce Zwilling, Ph.D.

Introduction

Tuberculosis is an example of a latent infection capable of causing life-threatening symptoms in some, but not all individuals. While many people are infected with the microorganism, it remains encapsulated within the lung and never becomes active. It is only in a small percentage of individuals that the microorganism becomes reactivated resulting in the expression of the disease. The question is, why does the microorganism remain latent in some individuals but becomes reactivated in others?

The following presentation discusses the inter-relationship between a genetic predisposition to the disease and the effects of stress on activation. The data suggest that neither a genetic predisposition nor a stressful event by itself is responsible for reactivation. Using an experimental animal model and using a microorganism that is a cousin of tuberculosis, Dr. Zwilling describes how the interactions may occur to trigger reactivation of tuberculosis. The HPA axis is one of the main chemical cascades activated following a stress response. In many situations the cortisol that is produced in humans and corticosterone that is produced in rodents, along with catecholamines, contribute to stress-related changes in the immune system. Dr. Bruce Zwilling is a Professor of Microbiology at the Ohio State University. His research focuses on how immune system mechanisms can be triggered or suppressed by stress and other such events. Dr. Zwilling began his career at the NIH as a post-doctoral fellow at the National Cancer Institute.

Epidemiology of Tuberculosis

I will begin by mentioning a few names from the past, to show that tuberculosis is not necessarily a disease of the homeless or the indigent, but a disease that can affect all of our lives, no matter how wealthy or lavish our lifestyles. I'm sure that you all recognize such individuals as D.H. Lawrence, George Orwell, Edgar Allen Poe, Eugene O'Neill and Vivian Leigh; you may not be aware that they all died after contracting tuberculosis.

Forty years ago there were approximately 84,000 cases of active tuberculosis in the United States. Over the course of time, due largely to the advent of very effective antibiotics, the incidence of tuberculosis in this country declined to 22,000 cases per year, and it was projected that by the turn of this century, tuberculosis would be virtually non-existent in the United States. However, during the middle of the last decade, the declining curve for this disease changed to one of increasing incidence. To a large extent, the increase in tuberculosis can be attributed to the rise in infections with the human immunodeficiency virus (HIV), and to the immigration of individuals into this country from areas of the world that have a very high prevalence of tuberculosis. But these trends do not account for the total increase in tuberculosis. Tuberculosis is also disproportionately concentrated among Black and Hispanic populations in this country. That may be due to innate differences in susceptibility of those populations, compared to European populations, which were historically exposed to tuberculosis much earlier in the history of man, and have developed a resistance over the centuries.

Infection with *Mycobacterium tuberculosis* is being found in as many as 50 percent of homeless persons, and active disease is being diagnosed in 18 percent of individuals living in homeless shelters. These statistics indicate that tuberculosis is becoming, once again, a significant public health problem in the United States. The problem is compounded by the fact that through the years multi-drug resistant microorganisms have developed. This

36

has made treatment more difficult, and has resulted in greater dissemination of the disease. The problems that we experience with tuberculosis in this country are dwarfed by the problem of tuberculosis worldwide. Tuberculosis infects 1.8 billion individuals or one-third of the world population. That is not all mycobacterial diseases - just tuberculosis. Tuberculosis accounts for approximately three million deaths per year with eight million new cases being diagnosed annually. That is more deaths than caused by any other infectious disease.

Role of the Immune System

In order to fully understand the role of the mind and immune system in tuberculosis, one needs to understand the progression of the disease and the manner in which the immune system responds. Tuberculosis is spread by droplet aerosol; the microorganisms are inhaled into the deep lung and are picked up by alveolar macrophages. Eventually, a specific immune response will be induced, which will result in the activation of thymic-derived T-cells, and the production of chemotactic cytokines. These serve as chemical magnets causing more macrophages to infiltrate the site of infection. The production of macrophage-activating cytokines results in various degrees of activation of the lung macrophage population. These cellular responses represent an initial attempt to control the growth of the microorganism and to isolate it in the form of a granulomatous reaction. While some viable organisms will be present, the microenvironment is not favorable to their growth. For most individuals who are infected with tuberculosis, this steady state infection can last the rest of their lives without necessarily causing a significant health problem. However, there is a ten percent lifetime chance that the disease will reactivate. For reasons which we don't quite understand, the control mechanisms that keep the growth of the organism in check lose their effectiveness. The organisms start to grow and disseminate. This results in active disease and in the spread of the organisms in the form of droplet aerosols to other members of the population. The probability of an individual becoming infectious is about 1 in 32.

If tuberculosis is to be brought under control, we need to understand those events that culminate in reactivation and dissemination of the disease. What are the events that can alter the host-pathogen relationship in a way that leads to a diminution of normal control mechanisms? They include immunosenescence as a result of aging, protein malnutrition, chronic alcoholism and stress.

Stress and Tuberculosis

Following a stressful experience, a part of the brain (hypothalamus) stimulates the pituitary to signal the adrenal gland to produce glucocorticoids. This is called the HPA axis. Both the pituitary hormone, adrenocorticotropin hormone (ACTH), and the adrenal hormone, cortisol, normally inhibit their own production via a classic negative feedback loop. But tuberculosis is a chronic disease that results in the copious production of several macrophage-derived cytokines which are known to stimulate the HPA axis. This might serve to short circuit the negative feedback loop, giving rise to continued production of glucocorticoids.

Based upon a number of experimental models, it has always been assumed that, under the right circumstances, glucocorticoids are capable of mediating some of the adverse effects of stress upon immunity. Whether glucocorticoids play that role during the pathogenesis of tuberculosis, however, is not clear. If they do, it most likely occurs as a consequence of emotional distress that culminates in the production of corticosteroids. In addition, catecholamines would be released, not only in the blood, but also within immunologic tissues innervated by catecholaminergic nerve endings. The latter include the lymph nodes as well as the spleen.

Given the worldwide incidence of tuberculosis, it is really not surprising that one of the first reports indicating that stress may affect the outcome of tuberculosis was based upon studies conducted in 1919 by Ishigami, reported in the *American Review of Tuberculosis*. This study was designed to understand the increased incidence of tuberculosis in both Japanese school children and in their instructors. The conclusions Ishigami reached were that, "Psychic acts frequently influenced the course of pulmonary tuberculosis unfavorably, and rendered treatment difficult. Furthermore, over-taxation of their minds seemed to be the cause of the high mortality of young consumptives. The high mortality of our youths from tuberculosis is also partly due to the infection from teachers, who are also victims of excessive mental strain, and that prevention of excessive mental strain is one effective means of preventing the spread of consumption (tuberculosis)."

In a more modern context, Don Smith of the University of Wisconsin, stated in a review article that, "If individuals progressed to pulmonary tuberculosis, it was assumed that some antecedent event, either stress or steroids or cancer chemotherapy resulted in a suppression of cell-mediated immune response". Frank Collins also wrote in a review article that, "Under conditions of stress, a higher incidence of active disease may occur". Much more recently, Graham Rook is quoted as saying that, "Our understanding of the pathogenesis of tuberculosis requires more attention to the physiology of the disease, particularly to the macrophage and to the cytokine-pituitary-adrenal axis."

Against this historical background, we felt that three separate questions needed to be addressed. First, does activation of the HPA axis result in an increased susceptibility to mycobacterial disease? Secondly, does *Mycobacterium tuberculosis* grow differently in strains of mice that are innately resistant or susceptible to mycobacterial growth. Finally, does stress-induced activation of the HPA axis result in reactivation of the growth of *Mycobacterium tuberculosis* under conditions in which we can establish a steady state infection?

A Laboratory Model of Tuberculosis

The animal model that we used is one that was originally defined by Emil Skamene. Innate resistance in this animal model system is defined as the ability of the resistant mice to control the growth of the microorganism in the spleen and in the lungs following intravenous infection. Resistance is autosomally dominant and maps to a gene on chromosome 1. The gene not only controls the growth of mycobacterium, but it also controls the growth of *Salmonella typhimurium* and *Leishmania donovani*. It is alternately called Bcg, Ity or Lsh. There is also a syngenic group of genes on human chromosome 2q. The resistance gene in man is probably responsible for the documented differences in resistance and susceptibility among different populations of individuals. It has further been shown that Bcg acts at the level of the macrophage. Work in my laboratory more than ten years ago revealed that resistance correlates with the stable expression of macrophage class II antigens. These are proteins on the surface of the cell which are involved in interactions between macrophages and T-cells. The Bcg gene in mice has been cloned. Unfortunately, cloning hasn't led to any significant insight into the gene's function. However, none of the studies conducted over the past 15 years have been designed to determine whether this 'resistance' gene actually controls the growth of *Mycobacterium tuberculosis*. That is what prompted us to evaluate this as part of these studies.

Our initial studies did not use *Mycobacterium tuberculosis*, but *Mycobacterium avium*. This is an opportunistic pathogen with a relatively high incidence in immunosuppressed individuals, particularly those that are infected with HIV. Injected mice were stressed by restraint for ten 18 hour cycles interrupted after five cycles by two days of rest. Following each cycle, mice were returned to their regular cages. They were then sacrificed immediately after the last stressor at day 12. The number of microorganisms in the spleen and the lungs was then counted.

40

My intent is to summarize a large number of studies without delving in the specific details. First, it became readily apparent that increasing the amount of restraint stress resulted in an increase in the susceptibility of the experimental mice to mycobacterial growth. We observed many more mycobacterial colony-forming units in the spleens of those mice that were stressed for ten cycles as compared to those mice that were restrained for less than ten cycles.

Genetics, Stress and Infection

We then designed an experiment to determine whether there were any differences in the ability of this stressor to differentially influence mycobacterium growth in resistant and non-resistant mice. We found that many more colony-forming units could be isolated from the spleens of the susceptible mice after a 12-day period of restraint than from the resistant mice. Furthermore, activation of the HPA axis increased the susceptibility of the susceptible mice to infection, but did not affect the resistant mice. Both adrenalectomy and the administration of the glucocorticoid receptor antagonist RU-486 (also known as the abortion pill) were able to abrogate the effect of restraint stress on the increased susceptibility. Thus, our work demonstrates that the increased mycobacterium growth due to stress is mediated by the activation of the HPA axis. We have also shown that activation of the HPA axis results in an increased permissiveness of macrophages from the susceptible mice to mycobacterial growth, but does not affect the ability of the macrophages from the resistant mice to influence mycobacterial growth.

It is important to note that the differences that we observed between the resistant and susceptible mice with regard to the effect of restraint stress was not due to an unresponsiveness of resistant mice to stress. Both strains exhibited comparable increases in plasma glucocorticoids, and it was possible to suppress other macrophage functions using the restraint stress paradigm. These functions included the induction of MHC class II expression, the production of tumor necrosis factor, and the production of reactive nitrogen intermediates. It became apparent that in resistant mice we were affecting the function of some macrophage products, but not the mechanism conferring resistance to mycobacterial growth.

The second question we addressed was whether Bcg is able to control resistance to *Mycobacterium tuberculosis*. We took a different approach than most other individuals have in the past. We inoculated mice with very low numbers of organisms instead of the high numbers used by other investigators. We found that, after an initial delay, the organisms begin to appear in the spleen and lungs. The number of colony-forming units increased until about 34 days after inoculation in the susceptible mice. Eventually the immune system responds and the growth of the organism is controlled and reaches a steady state level. In the resistant mice, the resistance mechanisms are activated initially and appear to control the growth of the microorganisms throughout the course of the infection. In other words, there was a marked difference in the growth of *Mycobacterium tuberculosis* in the Bcg-resistant and Bcg-susceptible mice.

Once the steady state infection was established in the susceptible mice, activation of the HPA axis resulted in reactivation of the growth of the tuberculosis microorganism. Restraint resulted in an increase in the numbers of microorganisms isolated from the lungs of the experimental mice, while no such increase occurred in the non-stressed control mice.

Conclusion

In summary, we have established that restraint stress-induced activation of the HPA axis increases the susceptibility of mice to the growth of *Mycobacterium avium*. Stress increases the susceptibility of the susceptible strain, but does not increase the susceptibility of the resistant mice. Furthermore, stress can lead to a reactivation of the growth of mycobacterium, and perhaps is one of the reasons that accounts for reactivation of *Mycobacterium tuberculosis* in humans. The establishment of a steady state tuberculosis infection induces a very complex series of events involving macrophages and T-cells. Each cell type controls the growth of the organisms at different times during the course of infection. We are now exploring the specific changes that occur during reactivation which, in turn, allow the microorganism to grow.

STRESS AND SUSCEPTIBILITY TO
THE COMMON COLD

Sheldon Cohen, Ph.D.

Introduction

Dr. Sheldon Cohen is a Professor in the Department of Psychology at Carnegie Mellon University and an expert in the field of PNI. His research has provided the medical community with scientific evidence for something that many people have suspected for a very long time - that you are probably more likely to get a cold when you are under stress. Many investigators have shown specific correlations between changes in immune system measures and stressful events. This is especially the case in laboratory research using experimental animals. Dr. Cohen's studies are designed to assess whether the changes in specific immune cell functioning are sufficient to increase one's susceptibility to an infectious agent. Furthermore, these studies were designed to determine if a prediction could be made based upon a person's psychological state as to how likely he or she would be to manifest symptoms of clinical illness following exposure to a virus. These studies are important because they go beyond the test tube to address highly relevant questions that affect all of us.

Psychological State and Infection

"Just from waiting around for that plain little band of gold, a person can develop a cold." These lyrics from the musical, *Guys and Dolls*, written in the 1950's and popular again today, demonstrate how ingrained in our culture is the idea that stress is associated with susceptibility to illness, and particularly to colds. Unfortunately, there has been very little research in this area and little concrete evidence that this is indeed the case. Our own work has focused not only on whether stress may put people at higher risk for developing colds, but also on how that might occur. What is it that stress would do to people that would make them more susceptible?

We start with the premise that stress causes some change in the body that leads to greater susceptibility to infectious disease. Two issues then need to be addressed. The first issue is exposure. That is, one way stress could make you more likely to develop a cold is by increasing exposure to upper respiratory viruses. We know, for example, that stressed people often seek out social support. They have contact with more people and are therefore more likely to be exposed to a virus. In the work reviewed in this presentation, we eliminate exposure as a possible explanation for the relationship between stress and colds. The other issue is immunity. In some way stress influences the immune system in a manner that makes people more susceptible to developing a cold, given exposure to a virus. A discussion of the potential mechanisms whereby this might occur are reviewed elsewhere in this Proceedings.

As noted by other contributors to this volume, there is a tremendous literature that links stress with alterations in immune function - that is, that people under stress exhibit changes in their immunity. What is less clear is whether the changes we find in immune function among people under stress are relevant for susceptibility to infectious agents. Are those changes of the magnitude and the type that are important in predicting whether people will be more or less susceptible to infectious agents?

In our work we investigate whether people under stress are more likely to develop a cold following exposure to an upper respiratory virus. The study I will describe is a large trial with over 400 people. All subjects were healthy, between the ages of 18 and 55, and not pregnant. During the initial assessment, psychological measurements, including stress measurements, were performed. Additionally, the individual's health practices and immune system were assessed. We then exposed the subjects to an upper respiratory virus. The dose used in the study would be expected to induce clinical illness in roughly one-third of the participants.

The question posed when designing the study was, can we predict from psychological states assessed at the onset of the study who is going to develop clinical illness? Clinical illness was defined as a combination of two things: infection and symptomatology. First, the subjects had to be infected with the virus. Infection was indicated either by our detecting the virus in nasal secretions or by a significant increase in specific antibody to that virus in serum collected three weeks after the trial. Second, to meet the criteria of having a cold in these trials, a person had to have the usual symptoms people exhibit when they develop a cold, such as a runny nose, coughs and sneezes.

Before volunteers arrive at the unit for the trial, we collect demographics and medical histories. On the first two or three days of the trial, we draw blood and collect nasal secretions. The physician does an initial rating on a standard protocol of symptoms of upper respiratory infections. We also perform a physical exam since everybody has to be in perfect health to go through the trial. Finally, we measure health behaviors, such as smoking and dietary practices, and psychological variables, including those indicative of stress.

After we collected those data, we inoculated the participants either with one of five upper respiratory viruses or with saline. Three of the viruses were rhinoviruses, one was a respiratory syncytial virus, and the other a coronavirus. With their heads tilted back, subjects received viral particles in each nostril. None of the people who were given saline developed colds.

On days four through eight, everyone was in isolation. We performed daily nasal washings so that we could look for the virus and determine if the person was infected. This is accomplished by placing saline into the patient's nostrils and letting it drop into a petri dish. We also had them place used tissues into a plastic bag which we then counted and weighed. Each day of the trial, a physician assessed the severity of their symptoms taking precautions not to spread the infection. This individual was blind to the volunteers' psychological state and also blind to whether the volunteers received saline or virus. The assessment consisted of a standard upper respiratory symptom protocol.

At the end of the trial, both the physician and the patient used the same scale to determine whether a cold had occurred, and how severe that cold was. It turns out there was 94 percent agreement between the physician and the volunteers, confirming that people know when they have colds. Three weeks later, we collected the final blood sample to determine if there was a significant increase in specific antibody, one of our measures of infection.

Psychologists define stress as a situation in which demands exceed one's ability to cope. In this particular study, we used three measures of stress. One was a major stressful life event scale. The second a perceived stress scale. Perceived stress is the person's perception that the demands on them exceed their ability to cope at a particular time. The third scale was a negative mood scale, which documented a number of different negative moods, such as anxiety, depression and anger. These three scales are highly correlated so the data that is presented will be an index based upon the combined results of these three scales.

A number of different factors in this study were controlled for, including age, gender and education level, as well as serostatus - that is, whether the individual had antibodies to the virus that they're exposed to prior to exposure. Their allergic status, which virus they get, their body weight divided by their height, and the season of the year were also determined. Since data were collected over three years during different seasons, we were concerned about the possibility that 'stressed' people might be more likely to participate in the Winter or the Summer. Consequently, we controlled for this possibility as well. Thus, the data that are presented to address the question, "What is the relationship between stress and infection susceptibility?" reflect controlling for the possible contributions of any of these factors.

Stress and the Common Cold

One of the most important observations stemming from this study is that there is a dose response relationship between the stress index and the probability of developing a cold. With every increment in stress, there was an increased probability of developing a cold. One of the things we were interested in was whether the effect occurred similarly for each of the viruses, or whether it occurred in just certain of the viruses used. Further analyses of the data revealed that the effect was similar across the five different viruses, even the corona and respiratory syncytial viruses, which are very different from the rhinoviruses.

These data reveal that stress increases susceptibility to a cold-causing virus, but they do not reveal the underlying mechanism for this phenomenon. A number of possibilities were considered. The first one was health practices. We know that people under stress smoke more, drink more, exercise less, don't sleep as well, and don't eat as well. Could it be that stressed people, because of their poor health practices, exhibit a greater susceptibility to viral infection? When we controlled for these health practices, it became apparent that they were not responsible for the observed link between stress and infection susceptibility. It should be noted, however, that smoking and alcohol consumption were both predictors of increased susceptibility, but they did not account for the relationship between stress and susceptibility to colds in this study.

The immune system was assessed in two ways. One was the measurement of total antibody and the other was a white blood cell count which also included an assessment of the number of lymphocytes, monocytes and neutrophils. While not as meaningful as other methods available for assessing the immune system, these were cost effective and appropriate since this was an initial study.

Total antibody levels were evaluated just prior to viral exposure. We wanted to determine if this measure might be correlated with stress and, if so, whether it would account for the relationship between stress and susceptibility to colds. We asked the same question with respect to white blood cell count. In both cases, if you take out the possible associations between these measures and cold susceptibility, stress still predicts susceptibility to cold virus. None of the immune measures did, nor did they account for the relation between stress and colds.

Conclusion

In conclusion, we know that stress puts people at higher risk for upper respiratory infections. What we don't know so far is why. We know it isn't due to changes in health practices, we know it isn't total immunoglobulins, and we know it isn't white blood cell count. Our current studies are designed to assess the contributions of a number of additional factors that might be indicative of potential mechanisms. For example, a variety of stress-related hormones, including epinephrine, norepinephrine, and cortisol, are being studied to determine if they play a role. We know that changes in these hormones can alter immune function, so we want to know if they are in part responsible for mediating the effects of stress upon cold virus susceptibility. In this next phase of the research, we are also going to assess the function of immune system cells rather than just perform quantitative measures as we did in the previous study described in this paper. In particular, we are focusing on natural killer cell activity, the ability of lymphocytes to produce interferon, as well as other measures that we think may be associated with the development of increased susceptibility to colds. Finally, we are continuing to look at possible behavioral mediators in addition to the health practices we've already examined, for example, how people cope with their stress. One of the things we are interested in is the possibility that more active coping with stressful events may alter hormonal and immune function and therefore serve as a primary mediator. So, in future research we will carefully assess how people cope with each stressful event that they report.

DISCUSSION

Question: Would you comment about your observation that smoking and drinking were not factors during the course of your studies?

Dr. Cohen: In fact, of the health practices, both smoking and drinking relate to developing a cold. Smoking puts people at higher risk, and moderate drinking for people who don't smoke actually puts them at somewhat lower risk for developing a cold. But the question here is, can smoking and drinking explain the relationship between stress and a cold. For example, is it that stressed people smoke more and because they smoke they develop a cold? Even though smoking and drinking alcohol are related to susceptibility, neither explains the stress-susceptibility relationship. It is an independent effect.

Question: I was curious that no one in your control group developed colds. Did they know that this was a cold-related study?

Dr. Cohen: They all knew it was a cold-related study. However, only persons receiving viruses developed clinical colds. The saline group serves primarily to help keep investigators blind to whether or not any specific volunteer received a virus. As apparent from the results, neither volunteers nor investigators diagnosed colds in persons who were not infected.

Question: Can persons develop colds that are attributable to viruses other than the ones you exposed them to?

Dr. Cohen: Yes. Occasionally we get people with what we call 'wild colds'. They get colds that are not the one we gave them, and they get dropped from the study.

Question: You demonstrated a difference between illness in these two groups on the basis of their psychological rating. How about the incidence of infection? Was the infection similar in the groups independent of symptomatology?

Dr. Cohen: It becomes a little complicated, because it depends on how we look at stress. But in general, the stress index that I described is related to infection; it predicts infection. So if you split the notion of a clinical cold into two pieces, 1) are people infected, and if you only look at infected people, 2) do they develop a cold, the question then becomes does stress lead to the greater likelihood of infection, or does it lead to the development of symptoms among infected people? Each has different implications for mechanism. It turns out, at least using this particular index, that it actually predicts infection, but it does not predict the development of symptoms among infected people.

Question: Sorry, I didn't follow the last point. In other words, the occurrence of infection was the same?

Dr. Cohen: The answer is that stress does in fact increase the risk for developing an infection.

Question: The take-rate of the inoculum, if it were a vaccine, should also be affected by your stress factor. So if you had increased stress, the take-rate of a vaccine would be markedly affected by stress also?

Dr. Cohen: That's correct.

BEREAVEMENT AND THE THREAT OF MORTALITY INFLUENCE THE PROGRESSION OF HIV INFECTION

Margaret E. Kemeny, Ph.D.

Introduction

Dr. Margaret Kemeny conducts research that could very well help prolong the lives of many people who are suffering from AIDS. Dr. Kemeny is an Assistant Professor in the Department of Psychiatry at the University of California, Los Angeles. She is studying how emotional and psychological states may affect the progression of the AIDS virus. She has found that bereavement for a spouse or lover can accelerate immune system failure in HIV positive individuals. Her work also focuses on discovering interventions that could help AIDS patients cope with bereavement and other life stressors and potentially bolster the immune system.

The T-helper cell has been viewed as the conductor of the immune orchestra. Because of its ability to modulate so many other cells within the immune system, its ability to function properly is paramount if one is to successfully fight illness. Dr. Kemeny's studies are attempting to determine how psychological variables, especially the emotional changes that occur after losing a loved one, can influence the biological activity of this particular cell type. While not designed to demonstrate the mechanism whereby psychological variables can influence the immune system, these studies are, nonetheless, extremely important in that they show a relationship between how one reacts following stress and changes that can influence the progression of HIV.

HIV Follows a Highly Variable Course

As we all know, AIDS is a very serious and significant health problem in the United States. There have been more than 300,000 individuals in the United States who have developed AIDS, and there are believed to be between 650,000 and 1.5 million individuals in the United States who are infected with the AIDS virus, HIV. Few people in the United States are untouched by the AIDS epidemic and the impact of the disease is increasing. Given the large number of individuals who are infected with the AIDS virus and the continuing rate of new infections each year, an important question in AIDS research is what can be done to decrease the chances that an HIV positive person will go on to develop the life-threatening manifestations of AIDS.

Many of you may read *Dear Abby*. In a recent letter, a nurse admonished an 'uneducated' gay man who differentiated between HIV and AIDS. He said he was HIV positive, but he did not have AIDS. She responded to that by saying, "Doesn't he know that everyone who is HIV positive will go on to develop AIDS?" From what we know scientifically at this moment in time, she is not correct. We do not know that everyone who is HIV positive will go on to develop AIDS. In fact, the medical picture for individuals with HIV is remarkably diverse. Some people who become infected with HIV develop AIDS relatively rapidly, within a number of years, whereas other individuals who have been infected with HIV for ten years or more are healthy and completely symptom free. So there is a great deal of diversity in the medical course of this disease.

Let me just illustrate this on a biological level. One of the things that happens in the course of HIV infection is that individuals lose a certain cell in the immune system over time - the helper T-cell. On average, their number of helper T-cells diminish. If you assess these changes over a five year period, there are individuals who lose their helper T-cells relatively rapidly. However, there are other individuals who lose them more slowly, and there are some individuals who lose helper T-cells at the beginning, followed by a plateau period, in which they maintain an adequate number of helper T-cells over extended periods of time. We know from a number of research groups around the country that the individuals who lose their helper T-cells rapidly are the individuals who are much more likely to go on to develop AIDS. These are the people vulnerable to the microbial conditions that can give rise to the life-threatening illnesses that HIV positive people can develop. One reason for this is because the helper T-cell is a central cell in the immune system. It produces substances called cytokines that regulate the function of a variety of immunologic cells. Consequently, it is an extremely important cell for maintaining the integrity of the immune system. As these cells diminish over time, there is an increased risk that the HIV positive person will develop AIDS.

A very important question is, what are the differences between these groups of people? Who are those people who maintain their helper T-cells over time, and who are those people who lose their helper T-cells really rapidly? How can we understand the differences between these two groups? One of the differences may be the nature of the virus that they are exposed to, with some individuals having been exposed to a much more virulent form of HIV. On the other hand, over the last few years it has become clear that there are other factors in addition to HIV that contribute to the progression of this disease. HIV is the causative agent, but there are other factors that can accelerate disease course and potentially other factors that can even inhibit disease course.

Psychological Co-Factors and AIDS

A very important question in AIDS research is determining co-factors that may accelerate the progression of HIV infection. That is why we have been looking at psychological factors, and whether these variables could in any way function as co-factors contributing to the onset of AIDS and to its course - either to worsen or to improve prognosis. We have looked on a psychological level at two stressful experiences that many of the gay men that we are studying have been exposed to as a result of the AIDS epidemic. One of them is bereavement as friends and partners go on to develop AIDS and die. The other is the threat of mortality as individuals confront their own mortality, the risk of AIDS, and dying at a young age. Both of these, as we all know, are significantly stressful and traumatic experiences.

Bereavement

What we have found is that bereavement - the loss of a loved one to AIDS - is associated with immune changes consistent with HIV progression, particularly in those individuals who have lost an intimate partner to AIDS. Those individuals show patterns of immunologic change over time that indicate a worsening course of HIV. We studied a group of individuals who had had an intimate partner die of AIDS. We obtained blood samples before the bereavement event took place, and again within the year after the event took place. We also had a comparison group of individuals who had blood samples taken over an equivalent interval of time where no losses took place in the intervening time period. I'm going to focus on the HIV positive individuals that we studied. We looked for differences over time in the immune system between these two time points. We looked at a variety of immune parameters that we know from our research and research in other laboratories are very highly tied to the progression of HIV. For example, we tracked the loss of helper T-cells; individuals who lose their helper T-cells are more likely to go on to develop AIDS, as I mentioned. Also, we tracked certain immune functions such as the ability of the cell to proliferate or make copies of itself. These measures also decrease in many individuals with HIV and are related to the development of AIDS.

Another very central component of the immunology of AIDS is immune activation. In contrast to what might be expected given the nature of the syndrome, HIV positive individuals who have a more activated immune system are more likely to develop AIDS.

In the context of HIV infection, immune activation contributes to the loss of helper T-cells which then contributes to the onset of AIDS.

What we found was a significant increase in immune activation in the bereaved individuals from before to after the death of the intimate partner - a change we didn't see in the non-bereaved individuals over the same time frame. In other words, these individuals, after the loss of their partners, were showing immunologic changes that suggest a worsening course of HIV. There were also significant changes in the proliferative response, with individuals who had been bereaved showing a decrease in the proliferative response after the loss.

Chronic Depression and the Immune System

At a preliminary level, we have begun to investigate psychological responses to bereavement events, since it is our belief that it is not the stressful event by itself, but one's psychological reaction to that event that is key if we're going to be looking at biological correlates of stress. We have differentiated those individuals who respond to a loss with depressed mood from those individuals who respond to a loss with grief. We have found that those people who respond with a pure kind of grief reaction - sadness, missing the person, crying - show no negative immunologic changes following a loss in the context of HIV. However, individuals with a predominantly depressed mood, characterized by demoralization, hopelessness, and emptiness, do show negative immunologic changes over time, particularly if the depressed mood is chronic over a period of time. So we believe, even on the basis of these preliminary data, that it is important to begin to differentiate the emotional reactions that individuals have to particular events in studies linking stress with health.

Threat of Mortality and AIDS

The second stressor that we examined in our study is the threat of mortality. Individuals who confront the threat of their own death as a result of a life-threatening illness respond very differently on a lot of dimensions. One of the most interesting and important dimensions we have found is the expectation that these individuals hold about their future health. Just as you would find with other serious illnesses, we have found that some HIV positive individuals have very negative expectations about their future health. They are very pessimistic, in some cases fatalistic about their future health. You might also view it as acceptance. They have accepted the death sentence of AIDS; they are even resigned to it. Consequently, they have a negative set of expectations about the future. In contrast are some individuals with very positive expectations about their future. They are optimistic. They believe that they may not go on and develop AIDS and die from AIDS. They feel that they can survive. To some people this would be considered unrealistic optimism, particularly those who view HIV as a death sentence. I don't want to put a value judgment on it, but clearly there are those with an optimistic perspective about the course of the disease.

Pessimism vs. Optimism

We were interested in whether the pessimistic and optimistic groups of individuals would differ in terms of the actual course of their illness over time. In the first study, Dr. Geoffrey Reed in my research group found that those men with a diagnosis of AIDS who responded with negative expectations about their future - more fatalism or acceptance, depending upon your perspective - died more quickly than men who had a more optimistic outlook. The fatalistic or accepting individuals lived an average of nine months less, which is significant when a person has a diagnosis of AIDS.

I would caution that it is important to recognize that there are innumerable considerations that must be controlled for in this kind of study. You need to know, for example, whether the fatalistic men are already sicker at the time that we discovered they were fatalistic versus optimistic. Alternatively, did they neglect their health by not taking AZT or other medical treatments because they were fatalistic? Or perhaps they used drugs or engaged in risky behaviors that might have contributed to the disease course. We controlled for these and other factors that may have explained the relationship between fatalism and survival time, and the relationship remained independent of these variables. It is interesting to note that the men whose survival time was the shortest were those who were both fatalistic about their future health, and had lost someone close to them to AIDS during the previous year.

We then decided to look again at these very same characteristics in a group of men who were HIV positive but who had not developed AIDS. We wanted to determine if changes over time in the immune system could be correlated with these psychological states. Two groups were selected for this study; one group of individuals was very extreme in terms of their positive expectations, having very optimistic expectations about their future. The other group of men was just the opposite. They were very pessimistic about their future, and very negative in terms of what they expected in terms of their health. At the outset of the study, we made that assessment and also measured parameters of immune system functioning. We then followed them over time, re-assessing their immune system two or three years later. Significant differences were observed in the pattern of change in the immune system over time in these two contrasting groups of men. Individuals who were both fatalistic about their future and who had experienced a bereavement event showed a more rapid loss of helper T-cells over time, showed a more rapid reduction in the proliferative function of immunologic cells, and an increase in a variety of markers of immune activation. We looked at serum and cell surface markers, and found increased evidence of immune activation. All of these changes would be indicative of a worse prognosis in the context of AIDS. Consistent with the results of the study using men with AIDS, the group that showed the worst course was the one that was both fatalistic about the future and had experienced a bereavement event over the past year.

Once again, it was necessary to determine that the effects that we were observing were not due to differences in behavior or in health status at the time of the fatalism assessment. They were not. Furthermore, the observed differences could not be attributed to differences in depressed mood, hopelessness, loneliness, or a variety of other psychological states. Thus, these negative expectations did not appear to be related to changes in the immune system merely because the individuals with a more negative set of expectations were more depressed. There was something else occurring over and above the effects of depressed mood and other psychological states that have been the focus of other studies.

Conclusion

In summary, we have shown that certain psychological processes are related to disease progression and survival time in HIV positive individuals. Furthermore, those same psychological processes are related to immunologic markers of HIV, suggesting that the immune system may be responsible for the observed correlation. Thus, we can suggest that negative expectations about the future in the context of HIV may be related to immunologic processes that are key to the course of HIV. In addition, these same psychological processes are related to health outcomes in these individuals, suggesting that the immune system may function as the mediator between psychological state (or mind) and health in this case.

Fortunately, our results do not suggest that the effects are due to stress exposure. If they did, we would be in a difficult situation if we wanted to psychologically intervene, because it is very difficult to eliminate stressful events from the lives of HIV positive people. Instead, we found that it is the way people respond to a stressful experience that is important. This response might be 'affective' in terms of depressed mood or grief, or it might be in terms of expectations about the future and an individual's way of conceiving their future health. We are now conducting intervention studies to determine if we can substantiate our previous findings using a stronger non-correlational methodology, and if an intervention based on these responses to stress can have an impact on the immune system and health of HIV positive individuals. From an experimental and humanistic perspective, well controlled intervention studies designed to test different types of interventions and their impact on the immune system and health in HIV positive individuals, as an adjunct to good medical care, is what I believe is the next important step in mind-body research in AIDS, and a very important aspect of AIDS research in general.

DISCUSSION

Question: I just wondered two things; first, how you measured fatalism, and second, whether you thought about how that was related to pre-morbid personality.

Dr. Kemeny: We have been working on measuring fatalism for a long time using a statistic called factor analysis. We have come up with a set of items that represent attitudes and beliefs reflecting one's expectations about future health. For example, you can ask people very simple questions like, "How likely do you believe you are to develop AIDS?", or "How much control do you feel like you have over whether or not you will go on to develop AIDS?" It is a series of items like that. We don't know how that state is related to personality. So far, we haven't found a very strong relationship with the few personality measures we have looked at.

Question: It appeared from your discussion that negative expectancy and bereavement were associated. Would you comment on that? Also, would you comment on two recent articles that came to opposite conclusions about depression as a co-factor in the progression of AIDS?

Dr. Kemeny: Yes. We have found that the relationship between expectations about the future and HIV progression is seen basically only in the bereaved individuals. The group of individuals who were bereaved but optimistic about their future are the group that showed the best course of immunologic change, whereas the group of individuals who are bereaved but fatalistic showed the worst course. The other two groups don't significantly differ. In other words, in the non-bereaved individuals, this state of mind is not related to immunologic change, so that is why you see that pattern. In terms of depression and the immune system in HIV, it is a very controversial area, and we have not yet determined the relationship. I believe there may in fact be an association but, because of the high density of bereavement events in the gay community, you have to differentiate between bereaved individuals and non-bereaved individuals. Some of the high depression level is really grief in these people, and I think there are different immunologic correlates of grief and depression. That is one possible explanation for the inconsistencies in this area.

A BEHAVIORAL INTERVENTION STRATEGY THAT IMPROVES THE PROGNOSIS OF MALIGNANT MELANOMA

Fawzy I. Fawzy, M.D.

Introduction

Dr. Fawzy I. Fawzy is a Professor in the Department of Psychiatry at the University of California, Los Angeles, and Deputy Chairman of its Neuropsychiatric Institute. Dr. Fawzy is an expert on behavioral medicine research, having conducted some important studies with cancer patients. Dr. Fawzy has data indicating that psychological interventions can significantly improve the quality of life, retard disease progression, and prolong the lives of patients suffering from a very virulent form of skin cancer called malignant melanoma. Specifically, he has found that such intervention enhances the capacity of patients to cope with their disease, reduces their psychological distress, and modulates natural killer cells within the immune system. His research holds tremendous promise for improving and prolonging the lives of thousands of people suffering from melanoma as well as from other forms of cancer. Other studies presented in this symposium have revealed that psychological variables, especially emotions associated with stress, can have a deleterious impact on our ability to fight disease. Dr. Fawzy's research is designed to obtain additional evidence that behavioral interventions are capable of countering some of these negative effects.

Experimental Approach

My research has been influenced by several groups and individual investigators in the United States. One such group, directed by Dr. David Spiegel, showed that a behavioral intervention can reduce the effects of stress on cancer patients. Another, led by Dr. Marvin

Stein, demonstrated that depression can be correlated with suppression of certain immune system measures. A third investigator, Dr. Avery Weisman, is studying how coping skills can be enhanced to better manage disease. Finally, Norman Cousins, who drew upon his own personal experiences to conclude that individuals should view cancer not as a threat but as a challenge, was an important catalyst in promoting this type of research. Our research program has been an assimilation of these approaches and philosophies. It has culminated in an intervention model that can serve as an integral part of comprehensive medical care. It is based upon a strategy of reducing stress and enhancing coping skills. Our studies indicate that this approach can improve functioning of the immune system thereby reducing the recurrence of disease and promoting survival.

Research of this type has to be conducted by a multi-disciplinary group. Ours included psychiatrists, psychologists, research assistants, nurses, immunologists and surgeons. The working hypothesis was that individuals go through life on a forward trajectory. When they are confronted with a life-threatening disease such as cancer, that diagnosis in and of itself causes a disruption of this trajectory. According to the hypothesis, physicians should be able to use medical means, including psychiatry, in order to reduce that disruption and to help the patient resume a more normal life trajectory.

We studied malignant melanoma to determine if a psychological intervention can affect the immune system. By studying a disease where the initial treatment of choice was surgery, we were able to measure changes in the immune system without the complicating factors of chemotherapy or radiation therapy.

Eighty patients who met the criteria were randomly divided into one of two groups. For those in the experimental group, seven to ten participants met in weekly sessions over a six week period. Follow-up meetings were conducted at three months, six months and one year. The control group received all the appropriate medical treatments, but received no psychotherapeutic intervention. However, they were assessed in exactly the same manner as were the experimental subjects. The details of a six year follow-up will also be described.

Reducing Anxiety and Improving Coping Skills

The intervention took place every Saturday for six successive weeks. Each of the sessions was divided into four segments: 1) education; 2) problem solving in the group; 3) relaxation training; and 4) social support through the disclosure and sharing of experiences.

We set about to reduce the patients' anxiety by providing information about their condition. This approach was used because we suspected that when individuals are confronted with a diagnosis of cancer, a lot of their distress results from a lack of knowledge about their disease. With adequate information, we felt that they would be better able to master some of the things that they were confronted with, thereby reducing their distress. The next step was to teach them problem solving skills. We went through the course of the disease from the diagnosis to treatment phase, emphasizing those areas that individuals had told us were distressing to them. We then helped them develop a method of problem solving to better manage their problems. We also taught them a variety of relaxation techniques. In addition, patients were provided with psychological support that is inherent in the overall design of support groups.

Visual Images

Coping skills were enhanced using the model developed by Avery Weisman in Project Omega. Patients were asked to respond to pictures by describing what they thought the picture was telling them or what the person depicted was feeling. For example, the person might be described as feeling concerned, isolated, or worried about the diagnosis of cancer. We would then contrast this response by describing what can be done about the diagnosis. We would tell them that the best response would be to actively cope with the situation. Go to a hospital, establish the diagnosis, and then establish a positive alliance with a physician. Do not remain worried and passively resigned. That is not going to help. In fact, it would be detrimental to the prognosis. We then went through the whole trajectory of the treatment.

Another image shown to the patient focused upon the family. Should family be involved? Should the family even be informed? This was followed by a discussion centering upon the importance of family-based social support, and the significance of that social support during the management of their melanoma. The role of children was also discussed in this context.

The doctor-patient alliance was discussed after showing a picture depicting a very distant doctor, separated by a desk, talking down to the patient. The patient depicted in the picture was shown to be concerned, but getting no support. Helping the patient to see that they do not have to settle for that type of unsatisfactory relationship, that they can establish a working alliance and feel part of the working team, was one of the objectives of this phase of the intervention.

The next image depicted a patient coming home worried about the surgical scar. What should they do about it? Should they share it with family members? We would then ask each person in the group to reflect upon the same experiences suggested by the picture. Then we would talk about the appropriateness of discussing scars with family members, including children.

We used a number of other images, but those that I have described convey the general approach that was used. In general, the discussions about the pictures served as the basis of the problem solving techniques that we employed in this study.

Reducing Stress

Our first objective was to determine if this intervention would reduce distress. To do this, we used the six factor Profile of Mood States to measure distress over time. The factors measured included tension, anxiety, depression, anger, hostility, fatigue, inertia, and confusion. Based on these factors, a Total Mood Disturbance score was calculated.

Based on the anxiety measure, the patients in the intervention group, perhaps because they were in a group setting, showed more distress at the beginning of the study. But the measure of distress decreased significantly over time. That decrease was observed not only immediately after the intervention, but was still present five years later, i.e., based upon this measure of anxiety, we can still differentiate between the intervention and control groups five years after the onset of the study.

The same significant findings were observed regarding depression. Confusion, bewilderment, concern, and worry declined as early as six weeks and persisted up to five years. The measure of lack of vigor was also significant. We interpret lack of vigor as a psychobehavioral indication of distress. Starting at six weeks and lasting through to five years, there were significant differences between the two groups. Finally, persistent significant differences between the two groups for Total Mood Disturbance were observed starting at six months.

Enhancing Coping Skills

Our next goal was to enhance coping and adjustment skills. We used an approach based upon a model developed by Lazarus and Folkman. Coping was viewed as being comprised of three methods: 1) active-behavioral coping; 2) active-cognitive coping; and 3) avoidance coping. Active-behavioral coping refers to all the positive behaviors (i.e., the things that a person actually does) deal with an illness. These are ways in which one tr[i] positively change some aspects of the illness by such active means as exercising, improving diet, using relaxation techniques, forming a collaborative partnership with a physician, going out more socially, or doing something nice for one's self. Active-cognitive coping refers to all the positive thoughts and mental processes that a person uses to deal with an illness. These are ways in which one tries to understand the illness and accept its effect on life. This includes focusing on positive rather than negative changes that have occurred since the onset of illness, thinking about the illness one day at a time, trying to understand how other people in this situation are feeling or thinking, learning more about the illness and its consequences, having trust in a doctor's medical knowledge and technical skills, and forming a mental plan of action.

Avoidance coping refers to all the behaviors and mental activities that make one feel better in the short-term but usually don't solve problems and don't make one feel better in the long-term. These are ways in which one tries to avoid actually dealing with the problem. This includes simply refusing to think about the situation, avoiding being with people, and eating, sleeping, drinking (alcohol), smoking, or taking drugs more than usual.

Our intervention was designed to enhance active-behavioral coping and active-cognitive coping. The results indicate that we were successful with both for up to at least the five year follow-up time point. In particular, active reliance and depending upon emotional and physical support from family and friends also were found to be improved.

Behavioral Intervention and Quality of Life Measures

It is always important to inquire as to what is the significance of a given intervention. For example, did reducing distress and enhancing coping actually influence the quality of the subject's lives? We differentiated quality of life into physical, psychological, and social factors. The results of our study did indeed reveal a negative correlation between psychological distress and quality of life. Those individuals who were able to reduce their distress had reduced depression and demonstrated an enhancement in their quality of life.

We also examined a number of immunologic parameters to determine if they were influenced by the intervention. These measures were assessed only through year one because of the prohibitive expense. However, some significant differences between the intervention and control groups were seen in that first year.

The intervention group had a significantly greater percentage of CD57-large granular lymphocytes and of the natural killer cell subset CD56 at six months. We also examined whether the function of these cells was affected by the intervention. Function was measured by a chromium-51 release assay. A significant difference between groups was observed at six months, although it leveled off at one year.

Behavioral Intervention and Survival

Because of David Spiegel's studies demonstrating an increase in survival time following a behavioral intervention, we examined survival and tumor recurrence six years later. At six years, there were 13 people in the control group with recurring tumors, compared with seven in the intervention group. Further, ten of the control subjects had died, compared with only three in the intervention group. This difference was significant.

We then used a Cox regression model to identify the main factors accounting for recurrence and survival. One of the main factors revealed by this analysis was Breslow Depth. This is a measure of the tumor depth which correlates with prognosis. Thus, the deeper the tumor, the worse the prognosis. As expected, the Cox regression model revealed that the physical state of the tumor was the most significant factor correlated with survival. But participating in the group intervention was also significantly related to tumor recurrence and to survival time. The data also revealed a difference in the time of recurrence to death between the two groups. But what about the time from surgery to death, which is even more important? People in the control condition that had recurring tumors started to die at 14 months. However, the first death of an individual in the experimental condition didn't occur until 56 months. In addition, there were nine control group patients who had already died by the time the first experimental patient died.

Conclusion

In summary, these results support the following conclusions:

1. A structured intervention like the one described is feasible.

2. Early diagnosed cancer patients, told that the tumor was taken out and they should not worry, remain very distressed.

3. The diagnosis of melanoma, and possibly other cancers, warrants seeking an intervention program similar to the one described.

4. An intervention like this can be instituted in a clinical setting as part of an active, comprehensive medical care program because it is time-limited and because it is structured in a way that can be readily duplicated.

5. An intervention like ours can reduce distress for at least five years following treatment.

6. The reduction in distress and enhancement of coping is correlated with enhanced quality of life.

7. An intervention like this can affect some aspects of the immune system.

8. Finally, a psychiatric intervention designed to enhance coping and reduce distress might have a beneficial effect with respect to tumor recurrence and survival.

DISCUSSION

Question: Is this type of social intervention paid for by third-party payers at the present time?

Dr. Fawzy: This was an experimental project. It was free for patients. But since then, we have established in our surgical oncology program an intervention module for every patient coming into the clinic. We give them the module and tapes at no cost.

Question: Do you know any of the neuroendocrine correlates? Did you look at the glucocorticoid axis?

Dr. Fawzy: Unfortunately not. We are hoping to replicate it. We have done it in AIDS patients and we have done it in breast cancer patients. We are also hoping to replicate it in prostate cancer patients since in prostate cancer surgery is the first treatment, and there is no initial chemotherapy. We want to look at endocrine parameters at the same time.

Question: This is very exciting. I'm wondering if anybody is paying any attention to this in hospital settings in any place in the United States.

Dr. Fawzy: I hope NIH is paying attention to this research.

Question: Your program included several educational components which are not specifically psychological.

Dr. Fawzy: Correct.

Question: For example, nutrition education and use of sun block. Were there differences between the control and intervention groups with respect to these factors?

Dr. Fawzy: I think that is a very important question. We did question the patients in follow-up about sun block use and the way they sit in the sun, because that is a very direct factor in the occurrence of melanoma. There was a difference between the two groups. The intervention group subjects learned more about sun block and when and how to sit in the sun. So there was a direct behavioral change in the experimental group compared to the control group.

The reason we included nutrition is, patients come in with the knowledge that good nutrition is beneficial for patients with cancer. What we were interested in doing was giving them up-to-date information that we could get from the National Cancer Institute about the role of nutrition. So in the group setting, we were able to either support what they came in with, or give them a method that they could learn more about.

SOCIAL SUPPORT AND CANCER

David Spiegel, M.D.

Introduction

Dr. David Spiegel is a Professor in the Department of Psychiatry and Behavioral Science at the Stanford University School of Medicine. He is an expert in behavioral medicine research and is widely recognized for his studies of breast cancer patients. Dr. Spiegel has discovered that patients with advanced breast cancer who participate in weekly group therapy and social support sessions have significantly greater survival times compared with patients who do not participate in such groups. Scientists have suspected that social support is a very important factor enabling the effects of stressors to be buffered. Dr. Spiegel's work demonstrates in a well controlled research study how social support and group therapy can serve as an effective intervention in women diagnosed with breast cancer. Dr. Spiegel's latest work focuses on determining whether the differences in survival can be attributed to immunologic or hormonal changes that occur as a result of this psychological intervention.

Extreme Views of the Mind-Body Model

I am very pleased that the NIH has sponsored this symposium, and to observe the interest being expressed today. It is an area that until very recently was the domain of either disbelief or exaggerated beliefs. It is a tribute to many investigators, many of whom are contributing to this volume, that it has become an area of solid and exciting scientific investigation.

The problem in what has been called mind-body medicine is that we have been caught between two extremes. Either we have treated the body as if it were a machine like an automobile, in which parts could be replaced and removed. Doctors in this conception are 'body mechanics' who simply replace parts. In this scheme, the elegance and complexity with which the body and the brain interact is basically ignored; yet the whole is greater than the sum of its parts. However, the other extreme has been a problem as well. That is the belief that if you simply have the right mental attitude, you can wish away problems like cancer. If you sit in a circle and picture white cells killing cancer cells, somehow that will be magically transformed into such activity going on in the body.

There is a *Peanuts* cartoon drawn by Schultz which summarizes the current state of knowledge in mind/body medicine. Lucy states, "My body just doesn't seem to want to do what my brain tells it to." Charlie Brown replies, "I can understand that; my body and my brain haven't spoken to each other in years." I would submit that this is the state that we have been in. What I would like to do in this talk is review with you research that we and colleagues have been doing over the past 15 years, looking at the relationship between clinical intervention in the form of providing psychological and social support, and the rate of disease progression.

Social Support and Mortality

Part of the problem is that we have been so focused on the characteristics of the tumor itself that we have paid relatively little attention to the functioning of the body that is resisting the growth of that tumor. There is a middle ground that we and others are exploring and which I plan to review. Is it indeed plausible that providing social support could have an influence on the progression of a lethal illness such as cancer? A study published in *Science* magazine by Jim House in the late '80's, examined the relationship between social isolation and mortality. About 10,000 women were studied in five excellent studies, all of which showed the same thing. With one exception, the lesson of these studies is that social isolation increases your risk of dying from all causes. In the Alameda County study for example, the relative risk was 2.8 times higher.

I am not describing a complex measure of social interaction. It is simply a matter of asking if you see other people every day. Are there people whom you can call on to talk over problems, to receive help, to get a ride to the hospital or to the airport? People who lack such social support are at far higher risk of dying prematurely. Indeed, the strength of this relationship is as great as that between high serum cholesterol and mortality, or between smoking and mortality. Yet very few people are aware that social isolation is a risk factor for death. We do very little to help counter the social isolation that often accompanies illness. It might interest you to know, by the way, that the kind of social support that confers protection against mortality for women is a relationship with other women, with sisters, mothers and friends. For men, it's being married. This leads me to the conclusion that having a relationship with a woman does your health a great deal of good regardless of your own gender.

I will first describe some of the interventions that have been used to help provide social support, and then look at the health outcomes and discuss possible mechanisms for them. Rather than going into the mechanisms in great detail - which is something that we're actively investigating now - I will instead focus my comments upon the clinical link between an intervention and health outcome. Some of the factors that are important in helping people cope successfully with serious illness, such as advancing cancer, include building emotional bonds. People who have a serious illness often feel removed from the flow of life; "Everybody else out there is happy and having a wonderful life, and here I am with my death sentence." Their friends and family, even very well meaning, don't know what to say. They tend to avoid talking about important issues, they are afraid to bring up the dreaded 'C' word, and it creates social isolation. However, the very thing that removes you from the flow of life is your ticket of admission to a support group. These people tend to feel much more included. It is important to be able to express strong emotion, deal with fears of dying, re-orient life priorities, deal with social relationships and control symptoms. I will briefly review these, beginning with the building of emotional bonds.

Building Emotional Bonds

It is very important for people to feel that their reaction to the illness is not an abnormality, but rather a normal reaction to an extreme situation. The message of joining a group is that you are important. The fact that you have an illness does not remove you from connection with humanity. Just at the time when people need social support more in terms of health support, they often get it less. Secondly, people can use their experience of dealing with cancer or other serious illness as an asset to help other people who are coping with the same problems. So what seems to be a meaningless tragedy can have meaning if you can use it to help someone else in the same situation, the kind of thing described by Dr. Fawzy in his presentation. Expressing emotion is also very important. I often think that doctors are trained to treat crying as if it were bleeding. We all know what you do about bleeding; you apply pressure until it stops. At Stanford University, I tell my medical students that if they see a patient crying, don't just do something, stand there. Yet very often, people who have good reason to be upset find that they are not allowed to express those feelings, and this further reinforces their sense of isolation. One woman who had been a frustrated poet all of her life described her experience in our group in this poem:

"Most of us don't know
and those of us who do, won't tell.
So we build you a reason,
a barrier to shut out any probing of our scars,
self-inflicted or not.
If you will love us a little
and let us weep when we must,
we may find out who we are."

76

Disclosing Emotions

This ability to talk about feelings is a very important part, I believe, of good medical care, and it is something that is being encroached upon by restrictions on the amount of time that doctors, nurses and others can spend with patients. In addition, in our groups we deal with fears of dying. Ironically, people deal better with even the most serious and difficult subjects when they face them head on. The fear of dying becomes a series of problems and fears. It includes the process of dying, being in control of care, being in pain, being isolated from loved ones. When you face these problems directly, you recognize that there are things you can do about them.

We were quite worried when we began the study in the late '70's that we would discover that we were hurting these cancer patients rather than helping them. It would seem that putting someone in a room with someone else who was likely to die of the same illness would scare them to death. But what we found was that death is not a novel concept to a cancer patient; it is the first thing they think of, and if you deprive them of seeing other people with the disease, they can't observe how other people cope with it. They can't learn to admire how people face the death and the disability of the illness and still conduct their lives. That is what we found in one of our intervention groups. When one woman died, our poet circulated some cards that she had made;

"Dear Eva
whenever the wind is from the sea
salty and strong
you are here.
Remembering your zest for hilltops
and the sturdy surf of your laughter
gentles my grief at your going
and
tempers the thought of my own".

The women in our group actually came to feel better about themselves. They knew they too would be grieved, because they could look death in the eye. One woman said that death in the group is, "a bit like that fear you have standing at the top of a tall building or at the edge of the Grand Canyon. At first, you're afraid to look down, but gradually you learn to do it and you can see that falling down would be a disaster. Nonetheless, you feel better about yourself because you were able to look". That is how I interpret the patients' feelings about death in the group. They are able to look at it. They draw a sense of strength and courage from being able to face even the worst that the illness represents.

Role of the Family

It is also important to recognize that cancer and other serious illnesses affect families. We are well aware from the studies of Kiecolt-Glaser and Glaser at Ohio State University that caring for a patient can have a profound effect upon their well being as well as their immune systems. This deleterious impact of disease upon families is being increased as we restrict the amount of care patients can get from health care institutions. Yet we have done comparatively little to help families cope with the illness. It is for that reason that we run groups for family members as well as patients. One man described the group as a place where "I go to feel better about feeling bad". Many of the stressors that family members experience need attention in ways that are quite distinct from those required by the patients. We also help patients improve their communications with physicians. Very often, patients are afraid to talk about serious issues with their doctors, or hide information. Consequently, we spend a good deal of time helping them improve their ability to communicate with physicians.

What we found at the end of the initial year was that patients and their families who had been through this program had a substantial reduction in anxiety and depression on a standard measure called the Profile of Mood States, compared to an increase in the randomized control sample. Emotionally they were doing much better. I should mention that there are other approaches to treating anxiety and depression. You have all heard about Prozac by now, I'm sure. Its effects are depicted in a cartoon suggesting what well known figures would have said had Prozac been available in the nineteenth century. Karl Marx is saying, "Gee, maybe capitalism can work after all." Nietzsche is saying, "Gee, mom, that priest's sermon was pretty good, wasn't it?" And Edgar Allen Poe is saying to the raven, "Hello, birdie."

Hypnosis and Pain

We also have been studying the effects of inducing altered mental states using hypnosis, for controlling symptoms like pain. Hypnosis is simply a state of attentive, focused concentration with a suspension of peripheral awareness. All of the time, we are making perceptual attention allocation decisions about what to pay attention to and what to ignore. Pain tends to commandeer your attention, but it doesn't have to. What we are able to do is teach patients with cancer and other serious illnesses how to re-direct their attention to other sensations. One way of summarizing our intervention strategy is that we divert patients' attention to something else. That is in part true, but it is also more than that.

What we actually do is teach patients a simple exercise that has two components. One is inducing physical relaxation and having patients imagine that their body is floating. This is because muscle tension exaggerates pain. We then teach the patients to alter perception, to filter the hurt out of the pain, making the painful area warmer or cooler. What we found after a simple instruction once a week is that the patients in our support groups, by the end of the year, had half the pain that the women in the control group did on the same low regimen of pain medication. So it is possible for us to mobilize attentional resources and to reduce the amount of discomfort that even severe physical pain causes people. Briefly, I would like to describe some research that we're doing on one mechanism that we think accounts for this. In our laboratory we record electrical activity over the scalp in response to a series of shocks administered to the wrist. After we hypnotize subjects and instruct them to concentrate on a competing but imaginary sensation, there is less electrical activity in the same region in response to the same stimulus.

In another experiment, we told subjects to pay maximum attention to these electrical signals. They were told that they were very important and interesting. It resulted in an elaboration of the electrical response to the stimulus. This may account for the fact that anxiety about what pain means can amplify pain. Thus, you can think of the cortex as being an amplifier. It can either turn up the signal of pain or can reduce it. This is something that we can teach people to control with simple techniques like self-hypnosis.

We had published the data I just described in the early '80's and pretty much forgot about them, as did everyone else. But I became so irritated with the wish-away-your-cancer school of thought that it occurred to me I had a potentially interesting, negative experiment. If we could show that we helped these women so much emotionally, but it had no effect on the course of their cancer, that would be the end of it.

Social Support and Cancer Survival

We collected follow-up data ten years later on all of the women who had been in the original study. Eighty-three of the original 86 had died, all but two of them of causes related to breast cancer. Then we plotted out what is called a Kaplan-Meyer survival curve which plots the odds of being alive at a given number of months after the study began. I was nervous in the first year, because more of the treatment patients than the control patients had died. But by the end of 48 months, all of the control patients had died, and a third of the patients receiving the intervention were still alive. Much to my surprise, it turned out that there was a significant difference in survival time favoring the women who had been given this weekly group therapy. In terms of average numbers, the control group lived 19 months after the study began and the intervention group 36.6 months. The difference in survival time obviously favored the intervention group. We are currently conducting an NIH-supported study using a new sample of women with metastatic breast cancer. In addition to determining whether we can once again influence survival time with the help of psychosocial treatment, we are also assessing a number of potential mechanisms which might account for the anticipated differences.

Reasons Why Social Support May Be Beneficial

There are four possible mechanisms that could account for this effect. The first may be simply the 'grandmother effect' - diet, exercise and sleep. Perhaps women who are feeling less anxious and depressed take care of their bodies in the way their grandmothers told them to. This may in turn help their bodies better cope with the illness. This is unlikely because interventions that have tried to influence those variables, especially diet, have not shown much effect on the progression of illnesses like cancer. The second explanation has to do with better compliance with medical interventions. Perhaps the patients in our groups interacted more effectively with their doctors, or elicited more effective treatment from their doctors. But we have just completed a re-analysis of the subsequent medical care the patients received, and we did not find any significant differences in the amount of treatment the intervention versus the control patients got after they were in our support groups. In a study by Jean Richardson at the University of Southern California, a group of lymphoma and leukemia patients was given home visiting interventions. She compared those who received it to those in a control condition and found, as you might expect, that the ones who received the intervention were more compliant with their medical care, which is what she had intended to find. However, independent of that, she found that those in the intervention group lived longer than those in the control group. This is the same result we observed in our studies. Consequently, there are now two independent studies focusing upon different kinds of cancer. Both these studies reveal that a psychosocial intervention has a medical effect.

A third mechanism that may account for the differences that we observed involves the endocrine system. You have heard a great deal of fascinating information about the reciprocal activity of the endocrine and the immune system, and how components of the endocrine system, especially ACTH and cortisol, are a kind of damper on excessive activity of the immune system. If you look at it the other way around, though, hypersecretion of cortisol - as occurs during depression - may create an internal environment that suppresses immune function or has other effects directly upon the tumor. For example, breast cancer is a hormone-sensitive tumor. That is why Tamoxifen, which is an estrogen receptor blocker, is so effective in treating the disease. It is possible that other steroids, such as corticosteroids, stimulate the progression of the tumor. Consequently, if you can alter the internal environment by reducing the general level of corticosteroids, it is possible that you could influence the rate of tumor progression.

Research conducted by Dr. Seymour Levine at Stanford University suggests that such a mechanism may be viable. He took a squirrel monkey and paired a light flash with a shock. Subsequently he recorded cortisol levels in the plasma after light flash alone. It resulted in a significant increase. If you do the same thing, but now the squirrel monkey has one of his friends with him, you will observe only half of the increase. If he has five of his friends with him, you will observe no increase at all.

Think about walking around a dangerous neighborhood after dark, either alone, with one friend, or with five friends. You feel safer when you are with a group of people. Especially when they are friends. I ask you to consider that social support may be a means by which to buffer the effects of stress. Social support may dampen the emotional and physiological consequences of a stressful environment. So it may be that what we're doing during the course of our intervention is altering the endocrine system through social support. That is why our current focus is upon measures of endocrine functioning.

Dr. Fawzy's excellent studies of group therapy are highly relevant to this discussion. His work with malignant melanoma patients revealed that during and following the intervention there was an improvement in mood as well as in natural killer cell activity. There was also a reduction in disease recurrence and an increase in survival in the cognitive therapy intervention group such that the intervention subjects were less likely to die at six year follow-up, and they had lower rates of recurrence.

Conclusion

I want to briefly mention one other issue as we consider the proposal for a new health plan. We need to take the mind-body interaction seriously in designing any kind of health care program, because poorly adjusted patients may do worse medically; they also cost the health care system more. A study conducted in Canada showed that patients with medical illnesses who are less well adjusted cost 75 percent more to care for than well adjusted patients. They have more emergency room visits, more tests, and spend more days in the hospital. So it is not only humane and effective, but also cost effective to consider applying these so called 'alternative' interventions. Finally, I will leave you with the thought that while we should have the deepest respect for reality, we should not let it control our lives.

DISCUSSION

Question: Have you conducted research using brain tumor patients and, if so, do you obtain similar findings?

Dr. Spiegel: You are correct in making the statement that in essence, I am assuming a fully functioning brain, although there are peripheral variables that can influence the brain even in people who don't have primary brain pathology. It is a problem. Tumors in certain parts of the brain, tumors for example that damage the left cerebral hemisphere near the frontal pole, tend to produce substantial amounts of depression. So that can be a complicating factor. Brain problems resulting in impaired communication or comprehension will make doing this kind of work much more difficult. I haven't done systematic studies, although I have had a fair amount of clinical experience with it. If a brain tumor is present, you need to shift the intervention more in the direction of the family and the support system. If the patient can't respond fully, then I think you would shift your attention to the caregivers.

Question: You mentioned that you were going to offer four possible explanations of the effects of the psychosocial intervention, but the fourth one somehow wasn't clear to me.

Dr. Spiegel: One was diet, exercise and sleep. The second was adherence to medical care. The third, effects on the endocrine system, and fourth, the immune system. You have heard some excellent talks about that earlier. Dr. Fawzy's study is one example in which the intervention influenced one aspect of immune system function.

Question: What I want to know is if there have ever been any studies on the effect of relationships, either the family or in a social support group, directly on the endocrine system, in terms of the endorphins, the secretion of serotonin, and the way that relates to the survival rate of cancer. I guess the way I hear you describe this is that your thought is that you are less susceptible to the stress of cancer if you feel you're surrounded by people. But I am also asking you the way the connection with others affects directly the neurotransmitters and how they are secreted, and the interrelationship of that to the immune system and the way the body copes with something like cancer.

Dr. Spiegel: Well, there are studies. For example, Goodwin and colleagues did a large study of marital status and cancer progression, and showed that people who were married, all other things being equal, are likely to have slower rates of cancer progression and lower mortality. Reynolds and Kaplan did a study in Alameda County showing that social support is related to lower occurrence and mortality from cancer. So there are these broad-based studies that show that. We are now looking at the relationship between marital stress and immunosuppression in our new sample, but it is too early to know what the results are. I know Dr. Kiecolt-Glaser has done some research in that area as well.

Question: I guess the thought I had is that it could go toward making someone less healthy, but the connection could also go toward triggering endorphins or other kinds of chemistry in the body that would make someone more capable of surviving. It could go either way, and that it would be important to try to tease that out as to what direction - when you just study marital issues, I don't know that we know how to quantify that.

Dr. Spiegel: I think you're making a very good summary point, although the mechanisms aren't clear. By and large, social support is a good thing, that on many dimensions of health and mortality, you do better if you have social support than if you don't. Nonetheless, involvement with people can be stressful, and there can be certain adverse effects of stressful interactions as well. But it is a bi-directional relationship. There are things about social relationships that can have adverse consequences, but many that can have positive ones.

DRUG ADDICTION AND HEALTH

Mary Jeanne Kreek, M.D.

Introduction

Drug abuse in the United States is a well recognized national health problem. With the continued rise in new cases of HIV as well as of tuberculosis it is very important to understand the impact that drug addiction has on the hormonal and immunologic functions that are needed to combat these illnesses. Dr. Kreek's research has clearly demonstrated that specific changes in certain cell types that are essential during the course of fighting disease occur in heroin addiction. Dr. Mary Jeanne Kreek is Professor and Head of the Laboratory of the Biology of Addictive Diseases at Rockefeller University, Senior Physician at the Rockefeller University Hospital, and an internationally recognized expert in the field of addictive disorders.

Dr. Kreek, with Professor Vincent P. Dole and the late Dr. Marie Nyswander, conducted the first clinical studies that demonstrated the phenomenon of what we call "narcotic blockade", that is, the tolerance and cross-tolerance that prevents patients in chronic treatment with a long-acting opioid agonist such as methadone or 1-alpha-acetylmethadol from experiencing any narcotic effect from superimposition on another short-acting opioid such as heroin. Her earlier studies on short-acting opiates and most recent studies concerning cocaine dependency and alcoholism suggest that the normal HPA responses to stress may be significantly altered by long-term use of these substances. Her work is profoundly important for understanding drug dependence and for developing new therapeutic approaches to combat this widespread public health problem.

Epidemiology

The addictive diseases comprise one of the most important health care problems confronting our country today. Over 54 million persons in the United States use tobacco. Approximately 10 to 15 million are heavy ethanol drinkers, or alcoholics. Over 23 million in the United States have used cocaine at some time, and over 600,000 to one million are addicted to cocaine. Approximately 2.7 million have used heroin at some time, and over one million are heroin addicts, operationally defined for entry criteria into long-term pharmacotherapy with an opioid agonist such as methadone. Each of these licit or illicit drugs of abuse has been found to have some negative impact on normal immune function. In this paper I am going to focus on the opioid drugs. Also in my laboratory we have found that an atypical response to stressors may be one important component of the neurobiology of addictions and may contribute to the vulnerability and possibly even be an aspect of the genetic basis of addictions.

The Immune System

Among the early observations of the effect of heroin on immune function is that of the late Dr. Milton Helpern, the medical examiner in New York City. He found diffuse lymphadenopathy in most persons with deaths from narcotism. Clinical investigators at the United States Public Health Service facility for treatment of opiate addicts at Lexington, Kentucky, the predecessor of the intramural program of the National Institute on Drug Abuse, described elevated levels of immunoglobulins in heroin addicts. In our earliest prospective studies begun in 1964 - at the time of the development of our first research at the Rockefeller University Hospital which led to a methadone maintenance treatment modality - we found that over 30 percent of patients had abnormally elevated levels of circulating lymphocytes when they came in from the streets as heroin addicts. Up to 70 percent had elevated serum levels of immunoglobulin (Ig) G and IgM. Early work by other investigators found abnormal T-cell rosette formation in this population. These findings were attributed primarily to mixing foreign substances with heroin by drug dealers, and also to the multiple diseases that are common in the addict population, particularly those who share contaminated needles.

Infectious Disease

Addicts - especially the intravenous drug users - are susceptible to many diseases including hepatitis B, C and delta and tuberculosis. Of particular note, however, is AIDS. In 1983, we unbanked bloods which we had collected in our laboratory from 1969 onward. We removed identifiers, and analyzed these specimens for HIV markers of virus infection. What we found was that the HIV virus entered the drug abusing population in New York City in 1978 and prevalence of infection with the virus rapidly rose over the next several years, plateauing around 1983-84, with 50 percent or more of all street, untreated heroin addicts infected with the HIV virus by that time. Recently, parenteral (i.e., intravenous) drug abusers have become the highest risk group for infection with the AIDS virus in the United States. Now, of course, AIDS itself is one of the most serious confounders of clinical research examining immune function in addictions, as well as one of the most incredibly serious diseases confronting mankind.

Numerous studies were done in both animals and humans to demonstrate that the effects on immune function seen in addicts are not primarily direct effects of opioid drugs. In our laboratory we have done extensive work demonstrating that opioid drugs do not have direct effects on natural killer cell activity except at concentrations far exceeding those reached in settings of opiate (heroin) addiction or in treatment with methadone. However, questions remained about the indirect drug effects and about the impact on immune function of the diverse stressors heroin addicts confront every day. Before addressing these questions, I must briefly discuss the endogenous opioid system, i.e., I must describe the opioids which naturally occur in organisms and how they work.

Brain Opioids

The endogenous opioid system is now well defined. There are three classes of endogenous opioids: 1) the endorphins, which is now a popular name used to refer to all of these peptides, 2) the enkephalins, and 3) the dynorphins. Each of these has been defined biochemically, and by using molecular biological techniques. A gene for each class has been cloned in many species, including man. In addition, there are at least three types of opioid receptors, mu, delta and kappa, well defined by competitive binding studies using increasingly selective agonist and antagonist ligands. These specific opioid receptors were first discovered in 1973, but eluded cloning until late 1992, when Chris Evans and Brigitte Kieffer, working independently at UCLA in Los Angeles and in Strasbourg, France, almost simultaneously reported the cloning of the delta opioid receptor. This was rapidly followed by the cloning of the mu opioid receptor, and later, the kappa receptor, by George Uhl of the intramural program of NIDA, by Lei Yu of Indiana University, and by Robert Thompson and Huda Akil of the University of Michigan.

The endogenous opioid system is involved in many normal body functions, ranging from pain modulation, control of reproductive biology and, also pertinent to today's discussion, the stress response and immune function. One of these endogenous opioid peptide precursors, proopiomelanocortin (POMC), yields adrenocorticotropin hormone (ACTH), the important stress responsive peptide in man. POMC is produced and initially processed primarily in the anterior pituitary gland, and released to affect sites outside the central nervous system. It is also produced and released in the hypothalamus, presumably having central nervous system effects. POMC also gives rise to beta-endorphin - one of the important long-acting endogenous opioids which is similarly released into the peripheral circulation, from the anterior pituitary, as well as from the hypothalamus for central action.

Stress-Induced Endocrine Profile

Other presenters have discussed the classic 'stress' response circuit, the HPA axis, in animal models and in man. Briefly, corticotropin releasing factor (CRF) produced and released in the hypothalamus drives the anterior pituitary in man to process and release POMC peptides, beta-endorphin and adrenocorticotropin hormone (ACTH), the latter of which acts on the adrenal cortex. In man, cortisol, a glucocorticoid, is released from the adrenal cortex, which acts in a negative feedback mode both at sites of CRF production in the hypothalamus and at the sites of POMC production at the anterior pituitary level. We know that this negative feedback circuit modulation yields the normal circadian pattern of release of ACTH and beta-endorphin, as well as the cortisol response to ACTH. Under stress, increased amounts of CRF and POMC peptide are released and, in turn, increased amounts of glucocorticoid are released. We know from our own studies as well as those of others, that in man, but not in rodents, opiates such as morphine acutely suppress the release of both ACTH and beta-endorphin. (In rats, administration of an opiate increases the release of these peptides.) In man, chronic self-administration of a short-acting opiate such as heroin continues to suppress the hormones of the HPA axis. However, although the heroin addicts self-administer heroin two to six times a day, an even larger part of each day is spent in opiate withdrawal. Since the addict has developed tolerance and physical dependence, physiological signs and symptoms result when blood levels of opiates fall. In that setting of opiate withdrawal, the opposite neuroendocrine findings pertain, that is, there is activation of the HPA axis.

Heroin and Stress Hormones

We have studied prospectively heroin addicts entering and during long-term methadone treatment, and we have found that there is a normalization of plasma levels of hormones from POMC peptide release - beta-endorphin and ACTH - and in response to ACTH, of

91

cortisol levels. Normal circadian rhythm and normal feedback control of these hormones is also observed in steady-dose methadone-maintained patients. Whereas heroin has a half-life of only one to two hours in man, and its major morphine metabolite four to six hours, methadone is very long-acting in humans with a half-life of around 24 hours. A normal response to a chemically-induced stressor has also been observed in our studies of former heroin addicts well stabilized in methadone maintenance treatment. The latter is an extremely important observation since it is well established that glucocorticoids are potent immunomodulators (usually for suppression or inhibition of activity), and ACTH and beta-endorphin may also have effects on immune function. Whereas the heroin addict has hypo-responsivity to an induced stress, we have made preliminary findings that the drug-free and medication-free former opiate-dependent person may be hyper-responsive to such an induced stress. In methadone maintained former addicts, the response to an induced stressor becomes normal.

Drug Withdrawal and Natural Killer Cell Function

We have proposed that the observed natural killer cell abnormalities, and possibly other immune system changes in heroin addicts, may be due to an indirect effect of the withdrawal experienced by individuals addicted to short-acting opiates such as heroin. The opioid withdrawal causes activation of the HPA axis, with excessive release of POMC peptides and cortisol, which may then lead to natural killer cell activity suppression. In studies of normal volunteers with no history of addictive diseases, we have found that there is a pronounced circadian rhythm of natural killer cell activity. This rhythm is inversely related to the circadian rhythm of cortisol levels, which in turn are responsive to ACTH fluctuations. As cortisol levels drop from early morning, even over one hour from 9 AM to 10 AM, a time where there is a brisk fall in cortisol levels in a controlled setting, one observes an increase in natural killer cell activity. But if one uses that same normal volunteer and administers very low doses of dexamethasone (a glucocorticoid), just enough to blunt the CRF and POMC release, one sees no change in natural killer cell activity due to the long-acting properties of dexamethasone itself and the absence of a circadian rhythm of cortisol after dexamethasone suppression.

Conclusion

In summary, in heroin addicts, we find disruption of the HPA axis (suppression when opiate is present, activation when the opiate is withdrawn) and abnormal stress responsivity. We also find suppression of the hypothalamic-pituitary-gonadal axis, and profound effects of heroin on increasing prolactin levels. We also find immune disruption in heroin addicts including reduction in natural killer cell activity, abnormal absolute numbers of T-cells and of T-cell subsets, B-cells, and significantly reduced natural killer cell activity, along with elevated levels of IgG and IgM, reflecting abnormal B-cell function. In the long-term methadone-maintained patient who has stopped all drug abuse and excessive alcohol use, and probably has also experienced a significant reduction in exposure to other kinds of stressors due to normal socialization and rehabilitation, we find normalization of these indices of immune function and normalization of neuroendocrine function. In this population we also found a significant reduction of conversion to HIV positivity, that is, a significant reduction in infection with the AIDS virus, due to reduction or elimination of use of unsterile needles. In those who were fortunate enough to enter treatment prior to the AIDS epidemic in 1978, only a nine percent prevalence of HIV infection was found when they were studied in 1984, a time when over 50 percent of untreated heroin addicts were HIV positive.

It is going to be a complicated research task to tease out all the factors: neuroendocrine effects, drug effects, and personal stressor effects, all of which may impact upon the immune system of the addict. Those factors just mentioned are in addition to the presence of multiple infections and chronic injections of diverse foreign substances. However, work undertaken using an interdisciplinary approach has taught us a great deal about the molecular biology, neurobiology, and human biology of both the addictions and the immune system as they intersect with neuroendocrine function and, in turn, the potential impact of the drugs of abuse upon the natural history of other diseases.

CHRONIC FATIGUE SYNDROME

Stephen Straus, M.D.

Introduction

Chronic fatigue syndrome is a disorder that afflicts many individuals and which appears to involve many of the systems that are of interest to researchers in the area of PNI. Recent research reveals a subtle deficiency in the stress-related HPA axis as well as changes in psychological well being and the immune system. It is a complex and poorly understood syndrome which has the potential of serving as a model to study many of the interactions that are of interest to scientists working in the field of PNI. Dr. Stephen Straus is Chief of the Laboratory of Clinical Investigation in the National Institute of Allergy and Infectious Diseases, and one of the NIH's most talented scientists. Dr. Straus' research over the past 15 years has examined a wide range of issues related to herpesvirus infection. Dr. Straus has clarified how the viruses that cause herpes and chicken pox persist in the body. Recently Dr. Straus conducted the first human studies of recombinant vaccines for genital herpes. While pursuing his research, Dr. Straus has maintained an interest in post-infectious medical problems, including fatigue, which often persist in the wake of some infections. He has made major contributions to defining and characterizing chronic fatigue syndrome.

Historical Perspective

Chronic fatigue syndrome is a disorder that I can describe, but not fully explain. I don't know precisely how to treat it or what causes it, but it is an excellent model of those illnesses that are characterized by problems in the mind-body interaction. This presentation will illustrate some of these points, as well as discuss certain avenues of research that are underway in chronic fatigue syndrome.

By way of a simple introduction, chronic fatigue syndrome is a disorder that has had many names over the years. It is characterized by a state of constant fatigue and further exhaustion from slight tasks, and a large number of recurring chronic symptoms as well: dull headaches, joint and muscle aches, a sense of feverishness and chills, depressive symptoms, difficulty with concentration and sleep, and tender lymph glands. It is a syndrome whose manifestations affect adversely the physiological as well as the intellectual and emotional aspects of an individual's makeup.

By whatever name it has been known, chronic fatigue syndrome occurs mostly in women. Various studies suggest that between 65 and 80 percent of affected individuals are women. The formal studies verify that most of these individuals were very active at the onset of their fatigue, and that the fatigue often began rather suddenly. Most of the patients described in the formal studies are of the middle class, and most are Caucasian. There is a debate as to whether this accurately reflects the population of those who suffer from it, or the distribution of individuals who were brought to the attention of research institutions. Consequently, it is not clear yet, as to how widely distributed this disease truly is.

In 1750, Richard Manningham published a textbook about a disorder that he called febricula. An excerpt from page 57 of that book says, "The symptoms of the febricula, or little low continued fever, are little transient chilliness, a listlessness with great lassitude and weariness all over the body, little flying pains, and sometimes the patient is a little delirious and forgetful."

That describes chronic fatigue syndrome today. It has gone under many names: neurasthenia, effort syndrome, chronic brucellosis, and many others that I will mention. One of the historically most important names for this syndrome is epidemic neuromyasthenia, or what is still termed in England today, myalgic encephalomyelitis. This has been called Icelandic disease, Akureyri disease, epidemic vegetative neuritis, and atypical poliomyelitis, based upon outbreaks of this type of disorder. The syndrome was also described in 1934 in Los Angeles, with multiple outbreaks or epidemics seen in the Western world between the 1930's and 1980's.

Onset of Chronic Fatigue Syndrome

Individuals affected in these outbreaks appear to begin with an acute infectious-type illness. They have fever, aches and pains, sore throats, and sometimes, neurologic symptoms. In the wake of the acute illness, they are left with exhaustion and other symptoms that are now lumped together as chronic fatigue syndrome. This form of chronic fatigue syndrome arising in case clusters is relatively uncommon. The more prevalent appearance of chronic fatigue syndrome is sporadic. But, even in these cases many recall an episode of bronchitis, diarrhea, sore throat, cough or infectious mononucleosis, that is followed by debilitating fatigue.

My own involvement with this syndrome dates back about 15 years, and came as a result of my studies of individuals who had infectious mononucleosis. This is a viral infection caused by a herpes virus known as the Epstein-Barr virus. There were individuals who were referred to me for evaluation who had infectious mononucleosis, but who remained awfully fatigued and continued to suffer tender lymph nodes. As part of the evaluation, we performed studies of blood antibody levels to this virus, and were surprised to find that a number of these individuals had higher levels of antibodies to Epstein-Barr virus than did the average man or woman of the same age. We collected many such individuals, as did researchers in other institutions, and discovered that those higher antibodies could occasionally be seen in individuals with severe fatigue, even if it didn't clearly begin with acute mononucleosis.

About a decade ago, we set out to determine whether the viral cause of mononucleosis is a major factor in this syndrome. The end result of our studies and those from many other institutions is that it is not. But these same studies led us down some very interesting paths. A colleague of mine drew a cartoon suggesting that Epstein-Barr virus was a red herring in this syndrome; that it was diverting our attention from other processes, which I, as a virologist, was naturally drawn to. But it required us to think far more broadly.

Definition of Chronic Fatigue Syndrome

As part of that reappraisal of the illness, a number of people in the United States were brought together in 1987 at the Centers for Disease Control to attend a workshop from which the name 'chronic fatigue syndrome' emanated, as well as a research case definition for the illness. This definition included some major criteria as well as a menu of minor criteria. The major criteria required individuals to have persisting or relapsing fatigue that was sufficiently severe to reduce their activity by at least half for six months or longer. This is not what one would expect as part of recovery from a typical viral infection. This is now more prolonged than that. The impossible was requested as well by these criteria, namely, that we exclude all other identifiable psychiatric and medical disorders that could lead to fatigue. Additionally, minor criteria were described involving a menu of symptoms or physical findings including feverishness, sore throat, tender lymph nodes, muscle weakness and discomfort, exacerbated fatigue with activity, headaches, sleep disturbance, as well as some other signs that certain patients could manifest.

We have had now five, almost six years of experience using this case definition. It is currently being reconsidered. Those of us who have been studying patients find that there are some aspects of this case definition that are useful and some that are not. Soon this definition will be changed, to simplify it and to make it more practical, manageable and realistic. But it is still going to be a descriptive diagnosis of exclusion.

When we see patients who fit the diagnosis - whatever set of criteria we choose - we recognize that many of them became fatigued in the wake of an acute infection such as influenza, diarrheal illnesses, mononucleosis, or various forms of infectious hepatitis. There are other infections as well, some which are of historical importance. Brucellosis is a bacterial infection acquired from domestic farm animals that can cause a very serious infection in people, and some individuals in their recovery are left fatigued. From the 1930's, up until 1962, brucellosis was considered to be a major precipitant of fatigue outbreaks.

Link Between Emotions and Chronic Fatigue Syndrome

Studies of the relationship of brucellosis to chronic fatigue syndrome culminated finally in the '50's and '60's with brilliant studies from Johns Hopkins University by Dr. Leighton Cluff and his colleagues. They showed that there were some brucellosis victims who experienced either delayed recovery, or in some cases failed to recover. They found that the delay or failure in symptomatic recovery from brucellosis is critically dependent upon the emotional state or attitude of the person at the time of onset of their illness. This kind of work was extended to studies of epidemics of influenza sweeping through the United States in the late 1950's. Those same investigators showed that individuals who recovered quickly from classic influenza differed from those who remained symptomatic for three weeks or longer on the basis of psychological vulnerability as assessed by the MMPI and Cornell Medical Index Health Questionnaire administered before the illness. It seemed that the patients who remained ill were more neurotic and had secondary reasons to accept the continuation of their symptoms. Today's meeting verifies that the story is far more complicated than simply concluding that one could imagine a state of fatigue.

To turn to another point that relates to chronic fatigue syndrome, about 40 to 60 percent of the patients who meet the Centers for Disease Control criteria also have local aches and pains and tenderness. Many of them meet the criteria that rheumatologists use to define a disorder known as fibromyalgia. This illness is characterized by the accumulation of a set of focal areas of tenderness around the body. But rheumatologists recognize that fibromyalgia not only has these focal tender points, but that most patients are fatigued and have many of the same features that are characteristic of chronic fatigue syndrome. In fact, one-third to one-half of patients with chronic fatigue syndrome also meet the criteria for fibromyalgia. So we're now drawing together a series of syndromic entities, all of which seem to be related.

Immune System and Neuroendocrine Abnormalities

In our studies of patients with chronic fatigue syndrome, we find that as many as 80 percent of them have allergies to various foods, molds, dust, spores, mites and the like, as defined by skin testing. Their rate of allergies is greater than that of the public in general, suggesting that their immune system has heightened sensitivity to environmental irritants. There have been over a dozen publications within the last few years showing that some patients with chronic fatigue syndrome differ immunologically from the general population. Depending upon one's immunologic focus, different parameters are often examined. My colleagues, along with scientists at other institutions, have found that patients with chronic fatigue syndrome tend to have higher antibody titers to many things - Epstein-Barr virus, brucellosis, candida. They also found abnormalities in the number and distribution of certain classes of lymphocytes, particularly T-lymphocytes. Furthermore, patient cells respond less readily to irritants and produce reduced amounts of interferon and other cytokines that contribute to the inflammatory process. The differences from normal are quite subtle and they are not consistent, so none of them constitutes a diagnostic test. Nonetheless, these changes strongly suggest that this syndrome has some resonance with the immune system.

Ongoing studies as well as some conducted several years ago in collaboration with Dr. Phil Gold and Dr. Mark Demitrack at the National Institute of Mental Health reveal that in addition to abnormalities in the immune system and allergic responses, there also are some subtle abnormalities in the neuroendocrine system in chronic fatigue syndrome, perhaps at the level of the hypothalamus. For example, chronic fatigue syndrome patients, on the average, excrete about 30 percent less cortisol over 24 hours than age- and sex-matched healthy controls. We showed as part of these studies that the levels of free cortisol - the cortisol that is not bound to protein in the blood - were reduced in chronic fatigue syndrome patients compared with normal control subjects. A series of studies suggested a cycle of abnormalities in the regulation of this stress hormone. Because cortisol exerts well documented effects upon the immune system, we think it may be playing a critical role in mediating abnormal interactions that are observed between the endocrine system, the brain, and the immune system in chronic fatigue syndrome.

Additional insights are forthcoming from an evaluation of the behavioral symptoms of these patients. It is common for patients who are suffering from chronic illnesses that are not well understood to become dejected, anxious and frankly depressed. But the rates of depression in chronic fatigue syndrome are remarkably high even when compared to the rates of depressive symptoms in individuals with other types of physical illnesses such as recent myocardial infarctions, multiple sclerosis and other diseases. In a study we did with scientists at NIMH a few years ago, we showed that about 46 percent of patients have had episodes of major depression, sometimes pre-dating the onset of their fatigue. About 30 percent have histories of phobias, and anxiety disorders are seen in 30 to 40 percent as well. In fact, about 80 percent of the patients fit one of the existing DSM-IIIR categories for psychiatric diagnoses. This has been verified in five of the six major studies of chronic fatigue syndrome conducted worldwide.

Conclusion

So to bring a very complex web of studies together, we have an entity that leaves people with debilitating fatigue and a variety of other symptoms. There seem to be allergic and other immune system abnormalities as well. Infections somehow play a role in precipitating this response and it has some resonance in terms of the neuropsychological function of the patients. This is a puzzle that is still missing a few pieces. We don't understand the relationship between this syndrome and some of the others that are being discussed today in the context of mind-body interactions. But if I were to project, I would argue that in the coming years, we will learn more about such interactions in chronic fatigue syndrome. My sense is that the mind and body are driving each other. A meeting like this one underscores that point. Our present understanding of chronic fatigue syndrome strongly suggests that it is an excellent model for gaining a better understanding of the mind-body connection.

DISCUSSION

Question: What types of therapies are available to treat chronic fatigue syndrome?

Dr. Straus: There have been many informal studies, and a few relatively small, more formal studies. The more formal studies from Toronto and from the United Kingdom particularly have looked at cognitive behavioral therapies in these patients, trying to restructure patients' beliefs about their illness. There is a sense that the preoccupation with the concept that some infection is causing damage to the immune system results in excessive consternation, and misdirects some people's energies.

Those studies need to be done better. Most centers today recommend the use of anti-depressant medications, particularly tricyclic anti-depressants, as part of a multi-disciplinary therapeutic approach. There have been only a couple of small prospective studies suggesting that these are beneficial. There have been no completed controlled trials yet. Many of us who participated in a recent workshop on how to manage this syndrome believe that the therapeutic approach requires behavioral interventions, anti-depressants, graded exercise to sustain one's conditioning and to improve it, and the use of anti-inflammatory medications to provide symptomatic relief for the aches and pains and feverishness. There is a very complex series of educational and coping strategies that people recommend as well. However, I don't propose to know how best to treat chronic fatigue syndrome.

Question: What would you say about the use of psychosocial interventions such as group support described in Dr. Fawzy's talk with malignant melanoma patients? Is that being done? It seems that such interventions might be helpful.

Dr. Straus: Group support is a big part of chronic fatigue syndrome management nationwide. In fact, there are major national support organizations, some of which have branches in every state. There are support mechanisms set up now in most of the Western European nations as well as in Canada. They serve very important purposes in terms of patient education. When you have a syndrome that is so poorly understood and about which there are so many claims, sometimes correct, support groups can channel that information and articulate it very well for the patients. The information office at the National Institute of Allergy and Infectious Diseases serves as one of the focal points at NIH for information. They have distributed tens of thousands of pieces of literature following inquiries from the public. The Centers for Disease Control has a similar mechanism for providing information to the public and to practitioners in the community, to help guide and update their thinking.

Question: Have you checked the mental history of those patients prior to the diagnosis?

Dr. Straus: This would be very valuable. One of the problems that we have with chronic fatigue syndrome is, although there are several thousand or maybe even tens of thousands of people in the United States who have this entity, it is relatively rare as a consequence of infections. So there aren't really good studies yet of observing and studying people before they develop the chronic fatigue. Thus, we have only the retrospective analysis of their medical records. By and large, the medical records of these patients indicate them to have been healthy prior to the diagnosis of chronic fatigue syndrome. Some findings are emerging from these retrospective analyses which suggest that there is an increased rate of depressive and anxiety disorders in some of the patients. There are family histories of abuse and alcoholism in some studies, and other research suggests higher rates of certain types of stress. None of these studies are as of yet compelling or conclusive.

INFLAMMATORY DISEASE AND RHEUMATOID ARTHRITIS

Esther Sternberg, M.D.

Introduction

In the papers presented thus far, the HPA axis has been mentioned in the context of the stress response. Dr. Esther Sternberg's research reveals that this hormonal circuit, which clearly plays a critical role during the stress response, may play an important role in regulating the immune system, even when the individual is not stressed. It became readily apparent during the presentation by Dr. Zwilling that excessive activation of this axis can impair the immune system, resulting in opportunistic diseases such as tuberculosis. However, it is important to recognize that the immune system is a double-edged sword. If the immune system works to excess, autoimmune disease may occur. The experimental model that will be described by Dr. Sternberg is of just such a disease. Rheumatoid arthritis and the symptoms associated with various other inflammatory diseases occur in large part because of prolonged activation of the immune system. This prolonged activation may go unchecked because of a deficiency in the chemical within the brain that normally triggers the domino-like cascade that gives rise to the anti-inflammatory hormone, cortisol.

Dr. Sternberg is Chief of the Unit of Neuroendocrine Immunology of the Clinical Neuroendocrinology Branch of the National Institute of Mental Health. She is internationally recognized for her work in the area of central nervous system-immune system interactions. Her work has focused specifically on defining the role of the brain's stress response and susceptibility to rheumatoid arthritis as well as to other inflammatory diseases. Her research also has shed light on the biological mechanisms underlying the connections among stress, depression, and autoimmune disease. Dr. Sternberg has received many honors for her work in rheumatology as well as for her studies of L-tryptophan.

Susceptibility to Inflammatory Disease

During this presentation, I'm going to discuss susceptibility to inflammatory diseases in general - rheumatoid arthritis being one of them - and particularly the role of the brain-regulated stress response in susceptibility to inflammatory disease.

Because we are all walking through a very dirty soup filled with a myriad of potential inflammatory triggers, a pertinent question is, why is it that some of us are highly susceptible to developing inflammatory disease in response to those triggers, and others of us are relatively resistant? Other presenters have summarized the large amount of data indicating that although at least some of the susceptibility to inflammatory disease resides in the immune system, a very important part resides in the brain and particularly in the part of the brain that controls the stress response. While there are many connections that link the immune system with the brain, my presentation will focus on the HPA axis.

I first pondered this question one snowy Christmas Eve in Montreal in 1977, when I was called to see a patient. He didn't have rheumatoid arthritis; he had developed another autoimmune inflammatory scarring disease that resembled a disease called scleroderma. He was effectively bound down in a body cast of his own skin. The question that I was asked by the physicians taking care of him at that time was, "Was the experimental drug that he had received for his epilepsy responsible for causing that autoimmune inflammatory disease?" At that time, I didn't have the answer. It was like a Turkish puzzle ring or a jigsaw puzzle, where I just didn't have all the pieces to answer that question. I have spent the rest of my career, along with many other scientists, trying to characterize that connection. For me, that patient was a powerful example of an individual who developed an autoimmune disease after his brain chemistry had been intentionally changed by a drug treatment. I felt there had to be a connection.

Characteristics of Inflammation

In order to understand these connections, one has to understand something about how the body's immune system responds to potential foreign invaders or inflammatory triggers, something about the brain's stress response, and something about how the two systems communicate. Pretend you're at Disney World, sitting in the Body Wars pavilion, and imagine that Darth Vader has arrived amidst the immune system. Think of the cells of the immune system as soldiers. They are specialized soldiers. Each one has a different form of weaponry to attack the foreign invader. There is chemical warfare with toxic chemicals released from granules in different kinds of white blood cells, such as mast cells. Some white blood cells, for example, lymphocytes, can actually clone themselves, giving rise to a multitude of killer cells. Other cells are scavengers that engage in hand-to-hand combat. They actually engulf the foreign invaders and digest them. In addition, plasma cells make antibodies that attack foreign invaders.

You can imagine with such a complex army of so many specialized soldiers, if there were no means of communicating between the white blood cells, chaos would result. There has to be some coordination between these various soldiers of the immune system. Such a communication system does exist, and it is in the form of chemicals called interleukins. These are proteins and peptides, made by the cells of the immune system, which activate and signal specific cellular functions. Now imagine several sites of inflammation in the body. There would still be chaos if there weren't some means of coordinating the cellular activity; of bringing it to an end once the foreign invader has been vanquished.

There has to be a general to coordinate this very complex battle. It turns out that the general resides in the hypothalamus which is a part of the brain that regulates the stress response. But if the general doesn't know there is a battle going on - if there are no signals to communicate between the immune system and the brain - the general falls asleep.

Conveniently, the soldiers of the immune system use the same chemical signals to communicate with the general in the brain as they do to communicate with each other. Thus, the interleukins can signal the brain and alert the general that there is a foreign invader present. The general then transmits his signal in the form of corticotropin releasing factor (CRF). That stimulates the pituitary gland to release adrenocorticotropin hormone (ACTH) which stimulates the adrenal glands adjacent to the kidneys to release corticosteroids. It happens that the corticosteroids are amongst the most potent anti-inflammatory agents that our bodies make. They are the chemicals that signal the immune system to shut off inflammation as soon as it is necessary. But what happens if the general is lazy? If he doesn't receive the signals from the immune system? Or if there is a breakdown in his walkie-talkie, so he can't signal the immune system to shut off? Ultimately, the immune system will continue being active, even after the invader has been vanquished. The immune cells will then turn on the body's healthy cells, and the result is autoimmune disease.

Role of Stress-Related Hormones

How do we know that this scenario is true? The evidence comes from many types of experiments, but the best evidence comes from animal studies. Arthritis can be produced in Lewis rats by exposing the animals in a particular manner to the streptococcal cell wall. Lewis rats are a strain of rats which, if they are kept in a sterile, almost operating room-like environment, will live long, happy and healthy lives. But the moment they come into contact with any one of a variety of inflammatory triggers in the environment, they will develop an immune or inflammatory disease, the pattern of which depends on the trigger to which they were exposed. But their overall susceptibility to inflammatory disease, we have found, resides in their brain. Fischer rats, on the other hand, are histocompatible with Lewis rats, so that in one respect at least, they are like immunologic twins. Yet, in response to these same triggers, Fischer rats develop little if any inflammatory disease. So Lewis rats are an example of an animal in which the general is asleep in the hypothalamus and the immune system goes on unchecked even after the foreign invader is vanquished. I will briefly describe some experimental findings that illustrate that this indeed is what happens.

When we measure plasma ACTH and corticosterone as indices of HPA activation, we find that in every case, the Fischer rats secrete large amounts of ACTH or corticosterone, whereas Lewis rats secrete much less of these hormones in response to any inflammatory stimulus, for example, interleukin-1 (IL-1) alpha, or streptococcal cell walls. Similarly, if you directly measure the general's activity, by putting hypothalami from each rat strain into tissue culture and exposing them to IL-1 in the tissue culture dish, the Fischer rat hypothalami secrete greater amounts of CRF than do the hypothalami of Lewis rats. When we examine gene expression of CRF in the hypothalamus in the rats treated with a single injection of streptococcal cell walls, Fischer rats are found to express large quantities of CRF message in their hypothalamus, while Lewis rats remain at baseline.

But just because there is a sluggish general in the hypothalamus in Lewis rats doesn't mean that that is the cause of their susceptibility to inflammatory disease. There are several kinds of experiments that one can do to prove that a sluggish HPA axis response can increase susceptibility to inflammation. One such approach is to treat the animal with drugs that block at various regulatory points along the axis. For example, the release of CRF and ACTH could be blocked at the level of the brain or pituitary. It is also possible to block the corticosterone receptor using the pregnancy blocking drug, RU-486, which also blocks the effects of corticosteroids on immune system cells. Treating the inflammatory disease-resistant Fischer rats with RU-486 at the same time they receive streptococcal cell walls fundamentally changed them from an inflammatory disease-resistant rat into an inflammatory disease-susceptible rat. Many of them died from severe inflammation, and those that lived developed arthritis.

The Endocrine Brain and Inflammation

Can we do the reverse? Can we replace the general in the hypothalamus? Can we wake up the general in the hypothalamus in the susceptible Lewis rats? We have done this by transplanting the hypothalamic brain tissue from Fischer rats into the Lewis rat brain. The transplanted tissue grows well with no evidence of scar tissue or signs of rejection. The surrounding brain tissue is also healthy, with no scar tissue. The transplanted animals were then exposed to subcutaneous carrageenan which triggers an inflammatory response. The severity of inflammation can then be quantified by assessing the number of white cells and the volume of fluid that comes out of the inflammatory pocket. When the hypothalamus from an inflammatory-resistant Fischer rat is implanted into a susceptible Lewis rat, the symptoms of inflammation are greatly reduced. If a Lewis rat hypothalamus is implanted into a Lewis rat, there is some decrease in the inflammatory response, but not as much as in rats transplanted with a Fischer rat hypothalamus. Fischer rat spinal cord, or sham surgery, does not result in suppression of inflammation.

Environmental Toxins

We can view this HPA axis communication with the immune system in another way. So far, the focus has been upon genetic predisposition to inflammatory disease and to the specific chemicals produced by the brain. But could environmental toxins also act within the same hormonal circuit, and thus contribute to the onset of inflammatory disease? Ten years after the first patient I described to you, we examined another patient, a lady who had developed the same scarring inflammatory disease. Her muscles, skin and joints were bound down in scar tissue. However, she had developed the symptoms after taking the amino acid, L-tryptophan, which was sold over the counter and in health food stores. It resulted in an epidemic in the Summer and Fall of 1989 that spread across the country, involving patients in every single state in the United States. Between 1,500 and 6,000 people became ill with this disease. Close to 40 have died to date. The incidence or the rate of cases in each state, coincided almost precisely with the distribution of marketing and consumption of L-tryptophan. In order to solve this medical epidemiological mystery, scientists at the NIH, Centers for Disease Control, Food and Drug Administration, and at other laboratories in the country tracked this epidemic to impure L-tryptophan that was produced by a single company in Japan, Showa Denko KK. It contained over 60 different impurities, many of which were structurally related to neurotransmitters like serotonin or beta-carbolines.

To make a very long story short, we fed either impure L-tryptophan, pure L-tryptophan, one of the synthetic impurities, or vehicle control material to Lewis rats. The rationale was that Lewis rats develop the pattern of inflammatory disease related to the environmental trigger to which they are exposed. They in fact did develop many of the hallmarks of the human disease, exhibiting great thickening of the fascia, or the tissue that surrounds the muscle. The purpose of this presentation is not to talk about the very complex etiological and pathogenetic studies we have conducted during the course of studying this syndrome. It is to show you the effect of this environmental inflammatory trigger on the brain. But for those of you who may have been following the health food wars in the media, I will make some comments on the role of pure L-tryptophan itself in this illness. Our studies showed that pure L-tryptophan in doses patients were taking does contribute to the scarring in this illness. It does not cause the same degree of scarring that we observed in the studies with impure material, but it does cause severe scarring in the pancreas. When we assessed the effect that this environmental toxin has upon the hypothalamus, we also found an effect. Rats that received the impure L-tryptophan or the synthetic impurity exhibited a significant suppression of CRF in the hypothalamus whereas rats that received either the vehicle or the pure L-tryptophan expressed significant amounts of CRF in the hypothalamus. CRF, as I described earlier, is the first signal that is required in the cascade of hormones necessary to block the symptoms of inflammation.

A Multi-Factorial Model of Inflammation

So this leads us to at least one hypothetical construct. It is speculation, but it is something that we can begin to use to direct our research studies. Could it be that there are some toxins in the environment that simultaneously activate the immune system, and turn off the general in the hypothalamus, thereby removing the body's most potent way of fighting inflammation as soon as it begins?

Much has been stated about stress and the role of psychological stress in modulating this system, so I am not going to describe it in great detail. But suffice it to say that this general up in the hypothalamus is very easily perturbed. Not only can chemical signals such as drugs and toxins alter the responsiveness of the HPA axis, but so can certain stressors.

CRF also has important behavioral effects. You may have heard of the fight or flight response: a characteristic behavioral pattern induced by CRF. Do these genetically different strains of rats - the CRF hypo-responsive Lewis rats and the CRF hyper-responsive Fischer rats - behave differently in a situation of mild stress? Placing a rat in a new environment is relatively stressful for a rat. In this situation, Lewis rats tend to explore a lot around the periphery. On the other hand, Fischer rats tend to stay more in the middle, while Sprague Dawley rats, which are outbred, are about halfway between. We like to call Lewis rats the laid-back California rats and the Fischer rats the Type A New York rats. Behavior is a very complex phenomenon. I am certainly not implying that CRF is the cause of all of your stress feelings and actions. But certainly it contributes to some of the different behavioral responses to stress in these animals.

What does that tell us about diseases like rheumatoid arthritis, that are very highly associated with syndromes such as depression? For many years, as Dr. Solomon alluded to this morning, this relationship was well recognized by patients, well recognized by their treating physicians, but dismissed as perhaps secondary to the chronic pain of arthritis, or simply coincidental because these are two very common syndromes in the population. But we can begin to think about this association from a different point of view, based on the studies that I have shown you. For example, if one has a genetically low CRF response or a low CRF response for whatever reason, and one happens to encounter an inflammatory trigger in the environment, one might then go on to develop rheumatoid arthritis. We also know from studies conducted by my colleagues, such as Dr. Philip Gold, relating CRF to different forms of depression, that too little or too much CRF plays a role in different forms of depression. If one happens to encounter a major life stress such as grieving or loss of a loved one, one might go on to develop depression. You can then begin to understand that there might be a biological reason for a tendency to both rheumatoid arthritis and depression - that is, too little CRF.

Conclusion

In summary, one can think of this brain-immune system interaction as being very dynamic. It is an interaction that is changing from moment to moment, from second to second, from day to day. It is also changing during the course of the reproductive cycle in a woman's reproductive life, because sex hormones play a very important role in regulating the brain's stress response. It can change over a lifetime, since there are alterations in the stress response with aging. And it certainly can change in response to major psychological stressors in the environment. Stress in this context is not what happens to you, but how you respond to it.

DISCUSSION

Question: Dr. Straus reported that patients with chronic fatigue syndrome have low levels of cortisol. Now you have just given us some information as to how the brains of certain people might be less responsive to interleukin stimulation of CRF. If I remember correctly, Dr. Straus might also have said that the patients with chronic fatigue syndrome have low levels of interleukin-2 as well. Anyway, can you connect your findings with his results related to low cortisol?

Dr. Sternberg: The susceptibility to inflammatory disease in this system is probably related to a low HPA axis response. That is consistent with the findings of Dr. Straus in chronic fatigue syndrome, and findings of others in related states such as fibromyalgia. More and more studies are coming out now in the context of rheumatoid arthritis and other inflammatory diseases suggesting that some individuals have reduced levels not only of cortisol, but also of CRF and ACTH. There are many different points in which the brain-immune communication can be interrupted, but a low response tends to be associated with inflammatory disease.

The difficulty in studying patients is, once we see them they are already inflamed, and inflammation itself is a stressor that can send a signal to turn up the activity of the general in the hypothalamus - turn on the stress response a little bit. So it is hard to tell how much stress response activity is too little and how much is enough in any individual patient. The advantage of studying the rats is that we can study them before they are inflamed, and we know that their response is very low. Once they develop chronic inflammation, there is a little bit of an increase in their CRF, ACTH and corticosterone response, which obscures the level of activity of the stress response in the resting state.

LINKS BETWEEN STRESS AND MULTIPLE SCLEROSIS

Barry Arnason, M.D.

Introduction

Another disease which is related to over activity of the immune system is multiple sclerosis. In this disease the target of the immune system's misguided attack is the myelin which encases the processes of neurons that course throughout the brain. Dr. Arnason's research clearly shows a link between this disease and the immune system, and suggests a potential role for stress in modulating the course of this disease. Dr. Barry Arnason is the James Nelson and Anna Louise Raymond Professor of Neurology in the Brain Research Institute at the University of Chicago, and is one of the leading authorities on multiple sclerosis. Although he was trained as a neurologist, Dr. Arnason, early in his career, recognized the potential role of immunological abnormalities in certain neurologic disease. Dr. Arnason's pioneering studies of the role of T-cells in multiple sclerosis has led to new approaches in the treatment of people suffering from this disease.

Viruses and Multiple Sclerosis

Multiple sclerosis is a disease in which lymphocytes and macrophages attack and destroy myelin, the insulation around the nerves. Multiple sclerosis is characterized by attacks during which the lymphocytes and macrophages destroy the myelin, and by remissions, during which time the disease is quiescent. It follows, therefore, that something provokes attacks of multiple sclerosis, and something causes them to end.

It is well documented that viral infections can provoke attacks of multiple sclerosis. In the month following a viral infection, multiple sclerosis patients have five times as many recurrences of their symptoms as would otherwise occur. We also know that interferons are anti-viral agents. This was one of the reasons that led to the study of interferon-beta as a treatment for multiple sclerosis. What emerged from those studies was that this drug reduces the frequency of major multiple sclerosis attacks in half. This observation underscores the point that multiple sclerosis is potentially reversible and that attacks can be prevented by manipulation of the immune system. One abnormality that can be detected in the blood when patients with multiple sclerosis are having an attack is an abnormality of a subpopulation of lymphocytes called CD8 cells. The CD8 population is responsible for what is known as suppressor function, i.e., they turn off the immune response. If suppressor cells are turned off, there will be an augmentation of the immune response. Suppressor cell function is abnormally low in patients with multiple sclerosis and is restored by interferon-beta, both in the test tube and in patients receiving the drug. Thus, drugs that alter immune system function can affect both the course of the disease and the immune system abnormalities that characterize the disease.

Stress and Psychological Well Being

There appears to be a link between multiple sclerosis and psychological well being. Patients with multiple sclerosis believe that stress has something to do with provoking attacks of their disease. Having heard this story perhaps 2,000 times, I finally thought that I should pay a little attention to it. Unlike psychiatrists and psychologists, I really don't know how to measure stress. Yet, multiple sclerosis patients keep telling me that stress has something to do with their attacks, and I believe them, as do most neurologists. Furthermore, a number of studies have documented a link between exposure to a stressor and altered immune function. A depression of immune responsiveness during final examinations, for example, has been clearly documented. An intriguing observation was that four to six weeks after the examination period there was a big rebound, an overshoot, in the immune response. Patients with multiple sclerosis when questioned seldom say, "I'm under a lot of stress." Rather, they state that "I have been under a lot of stress." In my opinion, it is on the rebound from stress that they are most likely to have a recurrence of their symptoms which I ascribe to over-activity of the immune system. Reduced activity of the immune system may cause certain symptoms associated with opportunistic infection; over-activity of the immune system can cause symptoms associated with autoimmunity.

The first point I want to make is that you can't consider stress as just an 'on-off' phenomenon; the 'off' phase can have consequences as much as the 'on', and in fact, maybe a little stress is good for people with multiple sclerosis. To address this question experimentally, Dr. Ewa Schorr in our group designed some studies using stress-free mice. The serene mouse is generated by treating newborn mice with 6-hydroxydopamine, a drug which destroys the sympathetic nerve endings. During a critical period of development, the postnatal period in rodents, sympathetic nerve endings must make contact with their targets or they die. If the animals' nerve endings are destroyed during this window of time they can't make contact with their targets, and the neurons die. The consequence is an animal whose sympathetic nervous system has been destroyed. It is the relationship between the peripheral nerves and the immune system that I will address.

An Animal Model of Brain-Autoimmune Disease

The serene mouse is a little smaller than the ordinary mouse. It also has bilateral droopy eyelids because one of the muscles that elevates the eyelid is innervated by the sympathetic nervous system. Otherwise, the serene mouse appears normal. One can employ the serene mouse to examine the consequences for the immune response of precluding information flow from the sympathetic nervous system to the immune system. These consequences are considerable. Antibody production against certain kinds of antigens is increased by three- to five-fold. Lymphocytes from sympathectomized mice proliferate far more vigorously than would normally be the case. Production of certain cytokines by macrophages is increased, and the lymphocytes have increased numbers of norepinephrine receptors.

Using this model, it became evident that certain autoimmune diseases are made worse, although other autoimmune diseases are made better by sympathectomy. The autoimmune disease that we have studied most extensively is allergic encephalomyelitis (EAE). We found that sympathectomized animals have more severe EAE than controls. EAE is an autoimmune demyelinating disease that has many of the features of multiple sclerosis. When we treated normal animals with a drug that mimics epinephrine, we were able to prevent experimental allergic encephalomyelitis in animals. That is, we can, by providing one of the chemical stimuli that mild stress would also provide, actually protect against a disease in which the immune system is overactive. Other medications with similar actions accomplish the same thing.

Patients with multiple sclerosis have attacks, get over them, and then have other attacks. Ultimately, they tend to develop disabilities such as spasticity as their disease becomes progressive. At this stage of the disease the descending fibers to the sympathetic nerves themselves start to get picked off so that the patient in a sense partially sympathectomizes him or herself. One might predict, therefore, that they would show the same kind of immunologic aberrancies as the serene mouse. It is easy to show that people with multiple sclerosis have abnormal sympathetic function. The sweating response in the feet, which is mediated by the sympathetic branch of the autonomic nervous system, is clearly different in patients with progressive multiple sclerosis than in healthy subjects. While one might question the relevance of this observation to events occurring within the spleen, the lymph nodes, or other immune system organs, this is, nonetheless, an easy response to measure and one that presumably serves as a barometer of altered sympathetic activity elsewhere in the body.

Role of the Autonomic Nervous System

We looked for immunologic similarities between the sympathectomized mouse and patients with progressive multiple sclerosis. Earlier, I mentioned that animals with sympathetic denervation have up-regulated adrenergic receptors. So we looked at this in patients with progressive multiple sclerosis and found that the number of receptors on a particular subpopulation of lymphocytes, the CD8 cells, was substantially increased. The CD8 cells are the suppressor cells that don't work during attacks of multiple sclerosis. The adrenergic receptors turn out to be functional, perhaps even hyper-functional. This finding prompted us to assess the effect of a beta-adrenergic agonist, a drug that mimics one of the functions of the sympathetic nervous system, in multiple sclerosis. Such drugs reduce the number of receptors back to normal levels in multiple sclerosis patients. When the drug is stopped, the number of receptors once again increases. Most importantly, suppressor cell function also increases while the patients are on the drug. Whether this will translate into a benefit for multiple sclerosis patients is not known because the clinical trial is still in progress.

While the sympathetic nervous system releases norepinephrine, its nerves release many other neurotransmitters as well, and these other neurotransmitters may contribute to the effect that the sympathetic nervous system exerts on the immune response. This possibility has not been studied systematically. Second, cytokines may also contribute to the process I have described. Cytokines are proteins released by cells of the immune system that act on other cells of the immune system. They also act on the hypothalamus and neuroendocrine circuits. A common event when studying chemical substances in the body is that when an investigator finds a substance in a particular organ, it becomes identified with that organ. For example, cholecystokinin was originally found in the gall bladder, but it was later detected in the brain as well. Somatostatin was found in muscle, but it ended up in the brain as well. Cytokines made by the immune system are also produced in the brain. They are intrinsic to the nervous system and are used as a signaling system. These observations underscore the fact that we sometimes need to study a variety of physiological systems in order to fully understand the biological function of certain chemicals produced within the body. If the nervous system uses cytokines, then it is conceivable that the signaling system between the peripheral nerves and the immune system may rely not only on neurotransmitters, but also on cytokines. Dr. Schorr in our group has evidence that sympathetic nerves do contain a protein that exerts a profound inhibitory effect on the immune system. That is to say, the control that the sympathetic nervous system is exerting over the immune system is not solely due to neurotransmitters but also to the influence of cytokines.

The sympathetic nervous system is designed for fight or flight, as we all know. But there is a counterpart, the parasympathetic nervous system, which is involved in tranquillity and which is activated by, among other things, yoga. Lymphocytes have parasympathetic receptors, too. The parasympathetic nervous system uses acetylcholine as its transmitter, and lymphocytes have one type of receptor for acetylcholine. Interestingly, these receptors are also up-regulated in multiple sclerosis but on a different T-cell population than the adrenergic receptors. It has not been possible to demonstrate any parasympathetic innervation of the lymphoid organs. Nonetheless, the receptors are there for a reason, and they are functional. It follows that not only is there an interplay between stress, activation of the sympathetic nerves, and the immune system, but there could well be a role for the parasympathetic nervous system in the control of immune responses as well.

Conclusion

The focus of this conference has been the link between the central nervous system and the immune system. We have heard how the hypothalamus responds to cytokines. We have heard how the hypothalamus and the pituitary release hormones that act in the periphery. We have also heard how the peripheral nerves may influence the immune system. What is missing? Evidence that the immune system acts upon the peripheral nerves. Does the immune system exert an effect on the peripheral nerve endings as well? Of course. It is easy to show, in fact, that the norepinephrine content of the spleen changes with an immune response. Betty Soliven in our group has been able to show that if she exposes sympathetic neurons to tumor necrosis factor - one of the products of activated macrophages - the ability of those neurons to release norepinephrine is substantially reduced. Consequently, the control that the peripheral nerves are exerting upon the cells of the immune system locally within the lymph nodes and the spleen is reciprocated by the lymphocytes and the macrophages.

It is important to realize that in a disease such as multiple sclerosis there are large numbers of inflammatory cells - lymphocytes and macrophages - that have already crossed the blood-brain barrier. They are sitting in the brain parenchyma pumping out high concentrations of cytokines. I have already mentioned that the nervous system uses cytokines as a signaling system. The work of Drs. Breder and Saper at the University of Chicago reveals that interleukin-1 (IL-1) is contained within hypothalamic neurons, the axons of which project into brainstem regions involved in regulating sleep and other physiological processes. If one places IL-1 or tumor necrosis factor - two products of activated macrophages - into the lateral ventricle of an animal, the animal goes into slow wave sleep. In addition, there are receptors for these and other cytokines in the hippocampus, a region of the brain critical for memory. It is noteworthy that multiple sclerosis patients are always complaining of fatigue or increased sleepiness. These complaints may be secondary to the actions of locally released cytokines on neurons. Thus, the symptoms of multiple sclerosis may not depend simply on the loss of myelin; they may also depend on effects of cytokines on neuronal function. It seems likely that cytokines affect the most fundamental aspects of behavior - eating (tumor necrosis factor used to be called cachectin because it interferes with eating), sleeping, drinking, mood, and memory.

DISCUSSION

Question: I am very interested in what you said about the parasympathetic receptors and your last remarks about ignoring the mood. You mentioned something about yoga. You didn't say anything about meditation. Herbert Benson has done a lot of studies on the relaxation response. Have you or do you know of any studies examining the effects of meditation and yoga on the disease course?

Dr. Arnason: Have I? No. A point I was trying to make, though, is exactly the one that you make. There are two sides to every coin. When we focus upon 'stress', we perhaps ignore relaxation, and that has to be taken into consideration in these matters, but has been less studied. I don't doubt that there are some papers in the literature that describe the effects of yoga and relaxation therapy on natural killer cells.

IMMUNOLOGIC CHANGES IN ALZHEIMER CAREGIVERS

Janice Kiecolt-Glaser, Ph.D.

Introduction

Thus far, the presentations have focused on individuals with specific diseases in revealing a link between psychological variables, stress, and changes in the immune system. But changes associated with emotional distress can also impact upon the immune system of individuals without serious disease. Dr. Janice Kiecolt-Glaser has conducted research demonstrating that those who care for parents or for spouses suffering from long-term illnesses such as Alzheimer's disease manifest changes not only in specific cell types within their immune system, but also in their ability to produce antibodies after vaccination. She is a Professor of Psychiatry at Ohio State University and a scientist who is nationally recognized for her contributions to the field of PNI. During the course of her research with Alzheimer caregivers she has also found that the immune system responses that are affected can persist as long as three years after the death of a spouse. Thus, in gaining an understanding of how psychological variables may influence the course of disease susceptibility, it is necessary to examine not only those events immediately preceding the changes in susceptibility, but to examine events that might have occurred several years earlier.

Examination Stress and Immunity

Before I begin, I would like to acknowledge my collaborator and husband, Dr. Ronald Glaser of the Department of Medical Microbiology and Immunology at Ohio State University, who has worked with me on these studies since 1982. I am also indebted to Dr. John Sheridan from Ohio State University, who is responsible for performing the flu assays that are an important part of our newest study, which I will be describing.

In 1982, Ron and I began collaborating on a series of studies with medical students that spanned a ten year period, and those studies provide important background information for the work I will be describing. Every year for ten years, we studied our medical students at Ohio State University, which has an absolutely marvelous paradigm for studying stress. It is based upon the fact that exams are grouped into three-day periods. Consequently, we can follow students in their pre-clinical years during periods of low stress and then during exams. We can watch across the academic year as we follow them through low and high stress periods, and assess changes in a very large number of different immunological components.

One of our most recent studies was designed to determine if the stress of examinations might alter the students' immunologic response to a vaccine. It was felt that these studies would provide very important data for us in the context of a 'real world' situation. When you meet a new antigen, does stress alter your ability to respond to that new antigen? Hepatitis-B vaccine was administered in the standard way, except that we made sure that inoculations coincided with the student's examination blocks. Thus, they were subjected to a stressor simultaneously with exposure to the vaccine.

We found that between the first and second inoculation, 12 of the 48 students sero-converted, i.e., developed measurable antibody to hepatitis-B. Interestingly, those 12 students were significantly less stressed and less anxious than their fellow students (the remaining 36 who did not respond to the vaccine challenge). When we followed them out at six months, we found that in addition to reduced stress, students who had an improved response to the vaccine also reported more satisfying personal relationships. This was correlated with higher antibody titers as well as enhanced T-cell immunity.

Stress Associated With Caregiving

Those were very interesting data, but we wondered what would happen with very long term, enduring, and chronic stress. Alzheimer's disease, as you may well know, provides such a model: the family members who are taking care of an Alzheimer's patient experience chronic stress. The etiology of Alzheimer's disease is unknown, and the course is quite unpredictable. It may range from a few to as long as 20 years until the patient eventually dies. The disease is uncontrollable with no effective treatment. The following anecdote underscores the difficulties that Alzheimer caregivers face. Mr. M is a retired engineer who had been caring for his wife at the point we saw him for about five years. He told us how in the past, he and his wife had spent summers at a cabin they owned on an island in a lake. That year, his wife had had a sharp decline in cognitive function, and she was really confused when they started to go to the island by boat. When she reached the island, she became very confused, she didn't recognize her husband, and she ran screaming from him, yelling that he was trying to mug her. Mr. M was fortunate in that the people on the island knew him well, and knew his wife well, so they were able to calm her down and bring her back. But he was very distressed by the incident because, as he phrased it, "It seems I can never take her out again in public, because I can't risk something similar happening in a circumstance where they don't know me and they don't know her. I don't know what would happen to either of us in those circumstances." So his life became increasingly circumscribed and increasingly stressful after that time.

We first asked our caregivers how long they had been providing care. The average time was between five and six years, but the range was anywhere from a year or less to 20 years. So these are not new caregivers at the inception of the study that I am talking about.

Immunologic Changes in Caregivers

Another goal of this study was to follow the caregivers beyond the death of the Alzheimer's patient. We thought that this model could provide a good way to examine the effects of a naturally occurring chronic stressor. After the person adjusted to bereavement, perhaps a year, studies reveal that you generally don't observe the same intensity of anxiety and depressive symptoms. By that time, we thought that we might begin to see some return in immune function. When a woman wrote to us saying, "Do you want to keep me in the study? My husband died two months ago and I'm not sure if you still want me in the study, because I am no longer a caregiver?", we assured her that we did want her in the study.

When we started looking at some data in year five of the study - and this is from Brian Esterling, who is a post-doctoral fellow in Ron's laboratory - we first looked at natural killer cell activity in the first 61 subjects who happened to be evaluated within a several month period. There were no differences in natural killer cell activity as a result of being a 'continuing caregiver' or what we're going to be calling 'bereaved caregiver', though an average of two years has elapsed since the death of their patient. That is not surprising. Two other laboratories, including Mike Irwin's in San Diego, and Peter Vitaliano in Washington, have also failed to find differences between caregivers and control subjects in natural killer cell activity. But Ron decided to look at the augmentation of natural killer cell activity by two cytokines, first using interferon-gamma. When we looked at the natural killer cell response to augmentation by this cytokine, we found that there was very clearly a difference between caregivers and control subjects. The controls were responding better, and the continuing caregivers did not improve. It is important to note that the two groups here did not differ at all in terms of age, in terms of education, or proportion of women. We found much the same pattern when we assessed the effects of augmentation with interleukin-2 (IL-2). However, there were no differences between continuing and bereaved caregivers, but both were clearly doing more poorly than our control subjects in terms of natural killer cell responsiveness to augmentation.

Vaccine Responsiveness of Caregivers

One of the obvious questions is whether there were any differences in health behaviors. That is something we always assess every time we see people and draw blood. For example, caregivers sleep less and eat less well than controls. If you know anything about caregiving and the stresses of caregiving, you wouldn't be surprised to hear that. We did not find any other reliable differences in health behaviors between the groups. We also failed to find significant or reliable correlations between sleep and our immunological data. Next, we wanted to try a vaccine study using our caregivers as well, and examine the possibility that caregivers and controls might differ in their responsiveness to an antigen, in this case, to the influenza vaccine. We were in a transition period with grants, so we looked at people we already had in the sample, which in this case were spouses as opposed to children. The study included 75 controls and 49 caregivers. Controls and caregivers didn't differ at all in terms of age or proportion of women.

But the caregiving sample wasn't all we might have wanted in terms of having a really stressed caregiving sample. They actually rated themselves as somewhat less depressed in the prior year, and our controls, for unknown reasons, were rating themselves as somewhat more depressed, although the groups still did differ significantly. Moreover, 26 of those caregivers were former caregivers and had not been caregiving for an average of two years. Of the 23 continuing caregivers, only 11 still had their patient at home. Another 12 patients were now in a nursing home. Even worse for us was learning that the caregivers had been much better about getting flu shots. So we weren't optimistic about what we might find in this trial balloon. In fact, we were quite surprised by what we did find.

We first looked at antibody to the vaccine as measured by an enzyme linked immunoassay (ELISA). What we found was that even though our caregivers had a better vaccination history, they had lower antibody titers, even at the point before vaccination. When we vaccinated them and then followed them for 10 to 14 days, we found that caregivers were still lagging behind controls in terms of their antibody response. This was a surprising finding. We had been talking with someone about this at a site visit, and one of the people at the site visit said, "That doesn't really count. What you really need to know is the T-cell response. That is the real gold standard." We disagreed, but John Sheridan had already made plans to do some follow-up examining the T-cell response so we carried out those assays. Was it only an anomaly in terms of the antibody response, or were there going to be T-cell differences there as well? At time zero, the groups didn't differ. Ten to 14 days out, everybody was responding very well and there were no significant differences. But when we followed the subjects for three months, when you hope to see the IL-2 response to a component to the vaccine *in vitro* maintained at as high a level as possible, we found that our caregivers were not doing as well as our control subjects. Again, we found no difference at all between our former and our continuing caregivers.

These data are very important in terms of public health. Pneumonia and influenza together are the fourth leading cause of death in people over 75 years of age. The immune response declines with age. It is one of the reasons why older adults are told to get flu vaccinations. Yet we find in terms of immune responsiveness at least to this antigen, that chronic and long term stress appears to decrease the effectiveness of the vaccine.

Psychological Variables

There is one other thing that we don't know and hope to be able to tease out over the next few years. That is the issue of what exactly is happening in our former caregivers. We have high rates of syndromal depression and anxiety disorders in our caregivers. We know in following people out through five years of the study that approximately 55 to 60 percent of our caregivers will meet syndromal criteria for an anxiety or depressive disorder during the years that they are caregiving. We also know from lifetime assessments that we carry out when we first see the caregivers and controls that the two groups do not differ prior to the point of caregiving. What that reveals in terms of the stress of caregiving is that caregiving is sufficient to induce anxiety and depressive disorders in older adults with no prior history. Furthermore, at the outset of the study, we predicted that our former caregivers would be less symptomatic after they stopped caregiving. To the contrary, we found that after an average of two years following caregiving, there were no differences in rates of syndromal depression between the two groups. There is no diminution two years after caregiving has ended.

Conclusion

One possible explanation for our data is that we were simply observing a group that continues to be depressed and anxious, but we don't think that that is the entire story. When examining the standard errors between our continuing and our former caregivers, there was no great difference; we weren't seeing an inordinate amount of variability among our former caregivers which might suggest that this interpretation is correct. However, there is another alternative hypothesis, not inconsistent with these data, which we think may be very important. Studies by David and Suzanne Felten from the University of Rochester have examined the plasticity and recovery from stress in young and old animals. They have found that young and old animals are quite different in terms of their recovery. The older animals don't seem to have the same plasticity in terms of recovery. Thus, it is possible that chronic stress, especially in an older adult population, may serve to age the immune response, to accelerate the process of aging in ways that may or may not be recoverable.

DISCUSSION

Question: You mentioned the aging process as being enhanced. Did you do any studies comparing young versus older caregivers?

Dr. Kiecolt-Glaser: Originally, when we first started this series of studies, we had both spousal and offspring caregivers. Our offspring caregivers were on the average about 50 years old and the spouses were on the average 70 years old. The offspring do somewhat better, but it is also hard to say, because in terms of family life they are also different. The offspring caregivers were generally married, they had their own families, and they were enormously stressed by the experience. The spouses on the other hand had lost their major source of support and it had become their major source of strain. So it is hard to untangle what effects age may actually have on the process. We're hoping as we follow people over time to determine whether the age of the caregiver impacts on immune function.

Question: I'm wondering if any studies have been done on long term caregiving of parents with disabled children. I'm talking 15, 20, 25 years.

Dr. Kiecolt-Glaser: I know certainly that there have been a number of studies examining stresses on the families of parents who have disabled children and also of families who have children or other family members with severe mental disorders. My knowledge of that literature, which is certainly limited, is that no immunological studies have been done in those situations.

Question: In terms of your study, have you thought about including in the future, cultural aspects that may perhaps play a role? For example, certain groups in which the caregiving of elderly family members is incorporated in a particular culture that may have an influence in terms of the level of stress?

Dr. Kiecolt-Glaser: I think that is an excellent question. We have been trying to recruit in Columbus a sample of African-Americans to help answer that question. What I do know, however, from Bill Haley at the University of Alabama, who has a sizable sample of African-American caregivers, is that there does appear to be a very different response. In a brief discussion with him, he said, if I understood it correctly, you do not see the same high levels of stress among African-Americans, because the family unit is much tighter knit and care of the elderly is more of a family responsibility. Consequently, the stress is less.

ANATOMICAL LINKS BETWEEN
THE BRAIN AND IMMUNE SYSTEM

David Felten, M.D., Ph.D.

Introduction

Hormones, especially those that are released during the course of stressful events, clearly play a role in modulating the immune system, as suggested by a number of presentations that have been discussed to this point. But it is important to recognize that in addition to chemical messages that link the brain with the immune system, there are also anatomical pathways that transmit information from the brain to the white cells that fight disease. The subject matter of this chapter is more technical than that presented by other speakers participating in the symposium, but it is included for those readers who are interested in learning more about the anatomical links between the brain and immune system.

Dr. David Felten is Professor of Neurobiology and Anatomy, as well as Psychiatry at the University of Rochester, where his pioneering work has demonstrated the close association between nerve endings and lymphocytes. His studies revealing the anatomical basis of mind-body links have earned him a MacArthur Prize Fellowship in 1983 and other national awards and recognition.

Pathways Between the Brain and Immune System

A question that always arises when we talk about mind-body interactions, particularly when we talk about psychological and psychosocial factors having an impact on the immune system, is how do you get there from here. How can a stimulus that comes into the nervous system and exerts an influence manage to get messages out to the immune system, which resides in many sites such as the bone marrow, the thymus, the spleen, the lymph nodes, mucosal-associated structures such as the gut and the lung, and distant structures such as the skin? How does the communication network actually transmit information and provide the appropriate signals? That is the subject I would like to discuss. Evidence shows that there is abundant communication between the brain and the immune system, so much so that many of us look back on some of the earlier days of eight or ten years ago and wonder how we missed it in the first place. The evidence for direct connections between the brain and the immune system is to be found in the results of studies showing that stressors, a variety of sensory stimuli, or other signals that have an impact on the nervous system somehow manage to influence cells and organs of the immune system.

There are two routes that serve as major conduits between the brain and immune system. The first route is endocrine and utilizes a part of the brain called the hypothalamus, which controls the pituitary. This endocrine gland, in turn, sends pituitary hormones out to target organs such as the thyroid gland, the adrenal gland, and a wide variety of other glands, which in turn secrete hormones that also circulate through the entire body. It has recently been demonstrated that cells of the immune system are highly responsive to virtually all of the hormones from the target organs and from the pituitary. In fact, these hormones have a profound influence on immunity. Of course, physicians have known this for decades. Steroids have been used to reduce inflammation and to try to dampen unwanted immune responses, even before the field of PNI was appreciated. If we are going to hypothesize a hormonally-mediated influence between the brain on the one hand, and the immune system on the other, we have to identify the players, that is, the hormones.

The second potential route is the hard-wired system - the autonomic nervous system. We did not previously anticipate that there would be autonomic nervous system or sensory nervous system connections that would directly influence cells of the immune system, but that turns out to be the case. So we have hormones and neurotransmitters as the major signals that can interact with cells of the immune system.

Functional Links Between the Brain and Immune System

I think it is very important, especially from a mechanistic point of view, which I have been asked to discuss, to ask the question, "So what?" "Who cares?" Just because there are hormones and transmitters that hypothetically could act on cells of the immune system doesn't mean they control the cells of the immune system. Scientists in the field have been active over the past decade documenting the actions of various players - the different hormones and the neurotransmitters. They have been looking at cells of the immune system, and identifying receptors and identifying mechanisms by which these neurologically-derived signals might have a chance to act upon cells of the immune system and actually change their function.

Then the next question is, if we can demonstrate that there actually is an influence of these neurologically-derived signals on cells of the immune system, what consequence does this have for disease when an individual is confronted with pathogens? Obviously, if there is no consequence, then it isn't really an integral part of medicine that has to be worried about. However, not only is the link very real between the nervous system and the immune system in both directions, but it really does make a difference with regard to reactions to pathogens and the outcome of disease. Immunologists made an important early contribution to this field of study several decades ago, and didn't even realize it. They demonstrated back in the '70's in some very good laboratories that there were receptors for neurotransmitters such as norepinephrine, one of the major transmitters of the sympathetic nervous system, that sat on T-cells, B-cells and macrophages. In fact, some of these investigators even showed some of the intracellular chemical messengers, the second messengers, that were activated, and began to explore this. But then, for some reason, things quieted down for a decade or so, and this no longer seemed to attract the kind of interest that had initially been stimulated.

Neuroendocrine Circuits

When we consider the signal molecules from the nervous system, we have to turn our attention to the two major routes of communication, as I mentioned. One route comes from the brain through the pituitary hormones, which in turn can then affect a wide variety of organs in the periphery that can secrete hormones. Perhaps, as you have heard a number of times today, the best characterized of these is the HPA axis, that releases adrenal corticosteroids. This turns out to be an extremely important axis with regard to the immune response. In fact, we are now realizing more and more that glucocorticoids can have an influence on cellular immunity and on humoral immunity, and can greatly influence the status and outcome of autoimmune diseases, as was described by Dr. Sternberg.

We should also not neglect some of the other hormones, such as growth hormone and prolactin, without which we probably wouldn't have a functionally intact immune system. In fact, some of the pioneering studies of Keith Kelly have suggested that growth hormone can restore cellularity to a thymus that is not working very well, and can actually restore some T-cell functions to old mice that have poor thymus function and poor T-cell function. Consequently, there is an opportunity to explore a variety of hormones which then get secreted into the blood and can act either directly or through their target organs on cells of the immune system.

Autonomic Nervous System

The second route is via the autonomic nervous system, or the so-called hard wiring which traverses the brain stem and spinal cord. It is a two-neuron chain, with one neuron in the central nervous system and the second neuron in an autonomic ganglion. What is conspicuous in most of the neuroscience and pharmacology textbooks is that the immune system tissues are seldom mentioned as targets of the autonomic nervous system. The immune system, we were taught, is completely self-regulatory and autonomous. It turns out, however, that the autonomic nervous system, with both noradrenergic fibers and also with some fibers that we think utilize many neuropeptides, appears to go directly into organs of the immune system, including the bone marrow, the thymus, the spleen, the lymph nodes, and virtually all other sites where you find immune tissue.

Some of the sympathetic fibers which use norepinephrine as a neurotransmitter travel along blood vessels into the bone marrow. But other fibers seem to send branches out among the stem cells in the bone marrow. This is a very common pattern of nerve distribution in lymphoid organs. It had previously been thought that the nerve fibers going into lymphoid organs just talked to smooth muscles of the blood vessels, or just talked to contractile smooth muscles. But it appears that many of the nerve fibers innervating the thymus, spleen and lymph nodes actually go directly into the parenchyma, ending adjacent to cells of the immune system. The relationship is present in the spleen, where noradrenergic fibers penetrate into areas that are heavily populated with T-lymphocytes, both of the helper subset and also of the suppressor or cytotoxic subset. So what was initially hypothesized as just a vascular control system turns out to have the potential of regulating the immune system as well. Suzanne Felten has examined this network of neuronal projections in the spleen at the electron microscopic level and has identified nerve terminals that sit right along the blood vessels. But some of these nerve terminals form direct contacts with T-lymphocytes along the adventitia, and other nerve terminals end up wandering out among lymphocytes in the parenchyma, and forming some of the closest physical contacts ever found in the peripheral nervous system, especially between sympathetic nerve terminals and T-lymphocytes and macrophages. In fact, we have done a tremendous number of tracing studies to show that these are indeed sympathetic nerve terminals, and that they do utilize norepinephrine as their neurotransmitter.

Assessment of the Immune System

When we focus our attention upon the immune system to test what these nerve fibers do, we have a couple of choices. We can use drugs that act to change these neurotransmitters, or we can actually remove or stimulate the nerves. The next step is to assess the immune system for changes in function. We have begun at the fundamental level of immune responses to look at individual cellular responses. How can cells proliferate, how do they differentiate, how do they express novel products such as immunoglobulins for B-cells or cytokines for macrophages and T-cells, what kind of cell adhesion molecules do they express, and how do they migrate? These are individual cell functions. But that does not tell you what happens in an organism. That only tells you a specific cell's function.

The second step is to move beyond individual cell functions to collective cellular interactions that require cooperation among many different cell types, for example, responsiveness to a viral challenge, a primary antibody response to a brand-new antigen that the organism has never seen before, a secondary memory response, a cytotoxic killing of a cell that has been labeled as foreign, or perhaps an attack on a tumor cell. These collective cellular interactions become very important to study. We can then take them apart and examine the individual cellular responses utilizing the tremendous power of cellular and molecular biology to go after the underlying mechanisms.

The third level with respect to the patient's response to a challenge is the most revealing. The response of an individual to a virus depends on many things. It may depend upon the social support that an individual has. It may depend on the age of the patient. It may depend on his/her nutritional status, or a wide variety of factors that do not have so much of an influence that we can test them so easily at this level. But the host can mobilize an extensive array of responses. The person also has tremendous plasticity, both with respect to the nervous system and to the immune system. I'd like to provide three simple examples of where this might lead. If we take nerves away from the lymph nodes of a mouse, then challenge the mouse and ask its lymph node cells to respond to a foreign antigen, we find a rather striking loss of cytotoxic T-lymphocyte activity (cellular immunity), and we find a concomitant decrease in interleukin-2 (IL-2) production. So cellular immunity is impaired when the nerves are taken away, whether assessed per lymph node or per cell. These data are potentially clinically relevant in HIV patients.

T-Cell Subsets and HIV

An important recent observation in immunology is that T-cells can be directed towards a T-helper 1 (Th-1) or a T-helper 2 (Th-2) pathway. The Th-1 pathway produces cytokines that favor cellular immunity that can either hold the progression of HIV in check, or certainly diminish its progression. On the other hand, the Th-2 pathway favors humoral immunity through interleukin-4, -5, -6 and -10 production, which may lead to the more rapid progression of HIV. Glucocorticoids from the HPA axis can influence this shift, and possibly favor a switch towards the Th-2 route more than the Th-1 route. Norepinephrine from nerves in lymphoid organs appears to favor the Th-1 route. But what happens if the patient has a noradrenergic sympathetic neuropathy, as so often happens in HIV patients? They lose the boost they might get to cellular immunity. They also can be influenced by glucocorticoid secretion which could shift their cells towards the Th-2 response. Consequently, these neurally-derived compounds may turn out to be major switching molecules in this Th-1/Th-2 ratio and thus the progression of HIV.

Another disease state that might be influenced by this network of autonomic projections is autoimmunity. It appears that glucocorticoids and catecholamines can make a profound difference in how autoimmune disease progresses. We have found in rheumatoid arthritis that if we selectively chemically sympathectomize the nerves from draining lymph nodes, we can actually provoke much more severe arthritic responses in adjuvant-induced arthritis in the Lewis rat model. Using another approach, Esther Sternberg has demonstrated very clearly that deficiencies in the HPA axis through the corticotropin releasing factor (CRF) system can profoundly alter an animal's susceptibility to autoimmunity. Consequently, both the autonomic nervous system and neuroendocrine circuits appear to be very important in modulating the progression of autoimmune disease. It is noteworthy that genetically autoimmune animals, in virtually every model we have looked at, show a very poor sympathetic innervation of the affected lymphoid organs as they develop autoimmunity.

Aging

Another example I would like to mention is that of aging. We were very surprised to stumble upon the finding that in old animals, the normally abundant innervation of the spleen and lymph nodes is severely diminished. You might again ask, so what? If we take the nerve fibers out of the spleen and lymph nodes in a young comparable rodent and then ask the system to perform for us, we find severe deficiencies in cellular immunity. Interestingly, the deficiencies reported in immunosenescence are deficiencies particularly in the T-cell arm of the immune response, and cellular immunity. We have hypothesized that perhaps the loss of sympathetic nerve fibers to these lymphoid organs in old age is actually contributing to some of the decline in immune responsiveness that has been documented. We have identified a host of changes in aged animals. Not only are nerve terminals lost, but the content of the neurotransmitters changes, the cells of the immune system actually change in their responsiveness, and their ability to regulate beta receptors is altered. These changes shift the metabolism of the sympathetic nervous system to a state that appears to encourage self-destruction.

Catecholamine fibers have the interesting capacity to self-destruct. These neurotransmitters are highly beneficial, but if the fibers produce too much of it, or are asked to turn it over too quickly, they then can produce metabolites that are extremely toxic. In fact, we use one of those metabolites as a toxic tool to deliberately kill off sympathetic nerve fibers in experimental models. The organism can actually produce this on its own if it is asked to turn over catecholamines very quickly. So if we have a system that is starting to lose fibers and subsequently accelerates catecholamine metabolism faster and faster, it really is leading into a self-destructive cycle. We believe that this goes on in the periphery with the innervation of lymphoid organs. It also goes on in the brain in the system affected by Parkinson's disease (and probably elsewhere in the brain). The next question we would want to ask is, can we restore some of these nerve fibers and, in turn, restore competent functioning? We are now working on that, and we have found that the drug Deprenyl can lead to a more rapid restoration of nerve fibers back into a denervated spleen than in a spleen where nerve fibers recover spontaneously or naturally. So we do have hopes that we can manipulate this system.

Conclusion

One of the ultimate goals of this kind of research is not only to identify the mechanisms by which stressors and psychosocial factors can have an impact on immunity, but to identify the key players - the hormones and the transmitters - and perhaps intervene with some pharmacologic agents to help mimic or block some of those compounds. In other words, we will treat the immune system using neurologically active drugs. I would like to finish with one philosophical comment. If you're talking about immune cells with receptors for neurotransmitters and hormones, I don't think it matters how you manipulate the system; if you give a drug or if you do something behaviorally, the bottom line is, you can affect the cell in a fashion that employs these agents. So I think we should look at behavior in the same way that we look at pharmacology, in that it is ultimately targeting these lymphoid cells.

DISCUSSION

Question: What is known about the relationship between prolactin and the immune system?

Dr. Felten: Actually, there is an extensive body of literature on that. Perhaps rather than try to explain it just in a brief question and answer period, I can give you some references. It is very clear that prolactin acts on certain cells of the immune system and may act in concert with growth hormone to assist some of the functions of the immune system. It is an extremely complex topic.

EDITORS' SUMMARY

The research findings presented at the *Mind-Body Interactions and Disease* symposium clearly established the multifactorial nature of disease. Exposure to a virus or bacteria is not enough to give rise to illness. The research focusing upon tuberculosis clearly demonstrated under well controlled laboratory conditions the critical role of one's genetic blueprint as well as the significant contribution of stressors. But even exposure to a stressor is not enough to predict the clinical outcome of exposure to a pathogen. A person's psychological responses clearly shape the physiological responses. This has been demonstrated using HIV and cancer. It stands to reason that if psychological responses can contribute to the progression of disease, that behavioral interventions designed to attenuate those responses may have efficacy in slowing that progression. Evidence of such effects was also presented during the course of this symposium.

Many questions still need to be answered. And different experimental approaches are needed to address those questions. Attention needs to be directed towards environmental triggers of specific symptoms. The body does need to be reduced into its component parts to address mechanistic issues. But at some point, the cells of the immune system will need to be plucked from the test tubes and petri dishes and put back into the body where they can be studied in their natural environment - one comprised of both mind and body.

PSYCHONEUROIMMUNOLOGICAL ASPECTS OF HEALTH AND DISEASE

Proceedings of a Conference Sponsored
by the Reunion Task Force of the
NATIONAL INSTITUTES OF HEALTH

Health Dateline Press

147

INTRODUCTION

Committee Report

Research in the field of Psychoneuroimmunology has profound implications for the development of new models of the body, of health, and of disease. Indeed, it is very difficult to draw a line between the body of nature and the body of experience. The history of medicine has presented many different, often conflicting, representations of the human body. The advancement of medicine it seems now depends more than ever on breaking free of schemata that are incomplete and that no longer work. Understanding the endocrine system has set the stage for the blurring of the distinction between the inner (homeostasis) and the outer (adaptation) self. Now we have reached a time of systemic integration as exemplified by Psychoneuroimmunology, with its neural, endocrine, and immune components.

Design Issues

There is a tendency to describe experiments conducted in the field of Psychoneuroimmunology as either being mechanistically-based or as phenomenology. Our level of understanding of the complex interrelationships between the brain and the immune system is such, however, that there is a need to further identify and characterize the individual components of the system. Therefore, those experiments designed to address these issues should not be labeled as simply descriptive or phenomenology, since they are necessary first steps to get an understanding of how systems work. This is especially important since many of the interactions are very complex. There may, for example, be multiple steps involved in the transduction of a signal generated through conditioning, and changes in the dependent variables. A manipulation implicating a particular neurotransmitter or neuropeptide system is an extremely important first step in ultimately gaining a firm understanding of how the system works. It is important to realize that the 'mechanism' question can be applied at virtually all levels within the system, and just because the focus is upon characterizing an individual component, does not mean that this type of approach should be viewed any differently from a more reductionistic approach.

Once an experimental question has been formulated, the question then remains, "what is the appropriate way to manipulate the system?" In the past, manipulation of the brain through lesions or stimulation has been the focus of experimental designs. More recently, a wide variety of agents, including neuropeptides and transmitters involved in modulating behavior, as well as those produced by the immune system, have been infused into the central nervous system. Rigorous studies have been conducted in the context of pharmacology, where very specific neurotransmitter pathways have been manipulated with different categories of drugs.

Measurement Issues

Selecting an appropriate dependent variable is another important step. Because of limitations of methodologies, one is often restricted to looking in the periphery for evidence that changes occurred within the central nervous system. Such changes might include various releasing or inhibitory factors, as well as pituitary hormones, especially those that are capable of modulating the immune system. In the past, the approach has been to focus on a single transmitter or peptide. However, approaching the problem from a systems standpoint should be considered. In the case of influenza infection, one would certainly want to characterize changes within the glucocorticoid axis as well as the sympathetic nervous system axis. On the other hand, if the experimental model is inflammation within the gut, then peptides such as vasointestinal peptide might need to be the focus. Examining systems that appear to play multiple roles would also be useful. There is evidence that corticotropin releasing factor (CRF) may be involved in the progression of behavioral depression as well as modulation of the immune system. Due to the evidence that under some circumstances there is a link between negative affect and changes in immunity, expanding systems to examine multiple functions would clearly have some utility.

It is important to select the appropriate measure of the immune system. In the past, the dependent variables that have been chosen have ranged from extremely detailed observations at an intracellular mechanistic level, all the way to observing whether an animal dies following an infection. Even though there is a need to adopt different approaches depending upon the experimental question that has been formulated, more information will be gleaned by designing studies assessing the host response to an antigenic challenge. The latter might include bacterial, viral, tumor cell, autoimmune processes, as well as immunologic responses to parasites. This does not mean that there is no utility in examining individual cells and how they function, but it is important to not lose sight of the fact that the immune system does function within the intact body and not in isolation within test tubes and petri dishes.

Even at the molecular level it is necessary when dealing with the immune system to take into account interactions between cells. All aspects of immune responsiveness, whether the primary or secondary antibody response, cell-mediated immunity, or hypersensitivity reactions, take place only after a complex interplay between the various cells that comprise the immune system. The same is true of any inflammatory response. All of these responses involve the cooperation of many cell types all at once. This adds to the difficulties when formulating experimental protocols designed to address mechanistic questions. Psychosocial variables, for example, could impact at virtually any level of the immune system or any particular cell type, and leave a biological mark. One possible solution would be to direct experimental attention to a disease process that can then be dissected into its component parts with various observations being made across different levels of the immune system. The observations could extend from how the organism interacts within its environment, all the way to how individual cells might function.

The immune system also can influence the central nervous system. There is no question that certain types of infectious agents are capable of entering the central nervous system producing a variety of symptoms through the inflammatory process. In other instances, the antigen itself, by virtue of the fact that it is recognized by the host as being foreign, is capable of triggering changes within the central nervous system. Many of these changes are mediated by cytokines which are known to act upon specific neurotransmitter systems. In addition, a host of cytokines produced by activated immune system cells can alter the ratio of a variety of neurotransmitters.

Mechanistic Issues

A question which is relevant to studies of both the immune and nervous system is the mechanism whereby various molecules are able to traverse the blood-brain-barrier and transmit their signal. In some instances, immunologic products such as cytokines may be able to pass through the circumventricular organs but to a limited extent and with a restricted range within the brain. There is also evidence that certain molecules may release a mediator compound from the circumventricular organs which in turn can get deeper into the central nervous system, activating other neurotransmitters or even cytokine producing systems within the brain. Measuring parameters within the brain is more problematic, however, behavior can often be used as a dependent variable to indicate what the brain is doing. For example, one could examine the specific effects of cytokines upon spatial memory as a reflection of hippocampal function if this structure were the target of interest. In other instances, learning and memory paradigms might be evaluated in the context of studying those cytokines known to impact on neurotransmitter systems that are also implicated in memory consolidation. There are other physiological events mediated by the brain which can be measured quite readily. Fever, eating or drinking behavior, and reproductive behavior are dependent variables that could be used. The induction of sleep would be another. It would then be possible to assess through pharmacologic manipulation the very specific intermediary chemicals that might be responsible for bringing about the effect.

Many chemical changes can be measured within the body as barometers of changes within the brain. For example, assessing the production of CRF, adrenocorticotropin hormone (ACTH), and glucocorticoids, is a well documented measure of events that originate within the brain. Likewise, products of the sympathetic nervous system could be assessed to measure activation of that particular pathway. Ultimately, all of these issues need to be addressed in the context of early development because during critical periods of development, events can literally impact upon brain morphology, functions and reactions to stimuli for the rest of the animal's life. Within the brain itself, electrical activity can be assessed. Although important, it is easy to become preoccupied with measures of chemical changes and ignore other events that may be equally important.

Interpretation Issues

It is clear that both animal and human models are needed. Human models provide opportunities to address clinical issues directly, while animal models enable one to address mechanistic issues. For example, the use of genetically inbred animals provides for the assessment of very precise components of the immune and nervous system in ways that simply cannot be done in humans. Certain animals such as the Fischer rat are deficient in their ability to produce CRF. Others include the C57/Bl$_6$ mouse, which is a T-helper 1 (Th-1) predominant animal, as opposed to the BALB/c mouse which is a T-helper 2 (Th-2) predominant animal. The use of such strains provides an opportunity to assess the impact of manipulations in ways that will shed considerable light upon underlying mechanisms. In other instances, one can study spontaneously hypertensive rats which have very high sympathetic activity. By using such models, one can then return to human subjects to characterize the range of diversity that humans clearly have. A number of other factors are notably important. Age of the individual can have profound effects on functioning of the brain and the immune system. Gender is an extremely important issue, as are current health status and nutrition. Even past learning and early experiences, especially those that have a strong psychological component, can influence physiological systems within the body and the individual's response to stimuli.

Finally, we must not lose sight of the fact that even though glucocorticoids can have profound direct effects upon the immune system, they can exert indirect effects as well. They can alter the way that catecholamines function, and alter the biological activity of other hormones. They can also influence the manner by which cytokines are able to act and they do this in different ways within very specific micro-environments within the body. Typically, in the laboratory setting each is dissected into its component parts and assessed separately. But that is not the way they function in the body and eventually they have to be put back together and assessed within the body. Given the nature of the way that most people respond to illness, especially those that trigger stress-related changes, it is imperative to conduct studies that examine the interrelationships between the sympathetic and glucocorticoid systems.

There is valuable information to be gleaned from the associations that are not found. Sometimes it is possible to learn more about disease from things that cannot be observed, and infectious processes that people do not experience frequently. It is not possible to measure every domain in every single study, and sometimes we need to reflect upon what the negative findings are telling us because these can be just as important as the positive ones. The following sections will review some of the varied experimental approaches that are being employed to characterize the role of the brain and behavior in modulating the course of immunologically-mediated diseases. Some provide unequivocal evidence that the brain and behavior can have a profound impact upon the progression of certain diseases. Other approaches are preliminary in nature, but offer provocative findings which may well prove to have a great amount of clinical relevance.

CHANGES IN THE NEURAL INNERVATION OF LYMPHOID TISSUES WITH AGE

Presented by

David L. Felten, M.D., Ph.D.

There is extensive sympathetic innervation of lymphoid organs, with some of these being co-localized with various peptides (Felten et al., 1987; 1992b). They innervate bone marrow, thymus, spleen, lymph nodes, as well as mucosal-associated lymphoid organs. What is not clear is the functional role of this innervation. There are two ways by which the sympathetic input to the immune system can be studied. One is by administering drugs such as 6-hydroxydopamine (6-OHDA) to neonatal mice which will reduce catecholamines in the brain. One can also surgically sever the nerves going into the lymphoid tissues, although this would clearly impact upon other neuropeptides as well. Even though the use of neurotoxins such as 6-OHDA can be effective, because of the abundant source of nerve growth factor, damaged fibers do eventually grow back and usually within one month there is restored function (Lorton et al., 1988). Consequently, acute denervation has to be combined with reinforcing denervation at various intervals afterwards.

Catecholamines and Immunity

A number of functional changes in the immune system can be correlated with denervation of the sympathetic nervous system (Livnat et al., 1985; Madden et al., 1994a; 1994b). The cellular immune response in lymph nodes and spleen is reduced, particularly with respect to the T-helper 1 (Th-1) response, delayed-type hypersensitivity response, cytotoxic T-cell response, and interleukin-2 (IL-2) production. Antibody responses, however, show a more complex pattern of change. Both decreases and no changes in some primary antibody responses have been

157

detected. To summarize a large body of data, it would appear that if catecholamines are present before antigen is presented to cells, they are capable of enhancing the overall response, but if the effector cells are already generated, then the introduction of catecholamines is suppressive (Madden et al., 1995a). Thus, if there are effector cells in the target organ, catecholamines, especially from the circulation, will be suppressive. If, on the other hand, catecholamines are present in a lymph node or spleen at the beginning or the initiation of the response, they will enhance the generation of that response.

Age-Related Changes

The worst possible scenario from the standpoint of immune responsiveness would be large amounts of norepinephrine in the circulation, and no norepinephrine in the secondary lymphoid organs. This is precisely what happens in aging, and may also occur in individuals with HIV, particularly those patients with neuropathy (Bellinger et al., 1993). With respect to aging, there are a number of changes that occur in immune function, especially involving the T-cell arm of the immune system and, more specifically, the Th-1 responsive cells (Ackerman et al., 1991). There is also a decline in cytotoxic T-cell activity, and actually increased suppressor cell activity in some circumstances. In aging there is decreased lymphokine production, especially IL-2, lower resistance to some tumor cell and viral challenges, decreased responsiveness of T-cells to thymic hormones, and decreased proliferative responsiveness of T-cells. This also happens when the sympathetic nervous system is denervated in a young animal. However, in the young animal, when the nerves are allowed to grow back, these functional changes are reversed (Madden et al., 1995b). This strongly suggests that they are induced by removal of the source of the catecholamines. Relevant to this observation is the fact that during aging there is a loss of noradrenergic nerves in the secondary lymphoid organs but not in the thymus or bone marrow (Bellinger et al., 1993). Most of the evidence would suggest that in a 27 month old rat there is virtually an absence of nerve fibers in the spleen, except around the largest blood vessels (Bellinger et al., 1992). While it might be due to a metabolic down-regulation, most of the evidence suggests that it is actual nerve loss. This loss of nerves in the white pulp of the spleen but also in lymph nodes has been documented in several strains of mice as well as in Fischer rats. It occurs in all compartments of the secondary lymphoid tissues as well (Madden et al., 1996a; 1996b).

Antigen Exposure and 'Aging' of the Immune System

Interestingly, the nerve loss associated with increased age appears to depend upon how much antigen exposure the animal has previously had. In animals raised in a vivarium the loss is very rapid and by 17 or 18 months of age one sees very significant declines (Bellinger et al., 1986). If the animals are raised in a barrier facility, it is not until 24 months of age that a significant decline can be detected, although it begins at 18 months (Bellinger et al., 1992). It would appear that the more immune challenge the animal has had over its life span, the more rapid the demise of the nerves. In addition to the nerve loss, there is also a decline in norepinephrine content within the lymphoid organs. As is true of Parkinson's Disease where dopamine is lost, the loss of content is not quite as great as the loss of the number of nerve terminals, and that is probably because the remaining nerves are able to partially compensate for the diminished concentration. There is the possibility that the changes in target cells might, in turn, lead to a loss of nerves. However, in studies conducted in severe combined immunodeficiency (SCID) mice that are born without T-cells or B-cells, the catecholamine innervation is quite robust (unpublished). Therefore, the absence of lymphocytes does not seem to have any impact. This does not rule out a role for macrophages, however, since they are capable of stimulating nerve growth factor production, which does attract and maintain the innervation.

At 12 months of age there is robust innervation and a respectable number of T-cells, including both CD4- and CD8-positive cells, but by 27 months of age there is a very significant loss of both subgroups in the spleen (Bellinger et al., 1992). There also is a reduction in the marginal zone and marginal sinus macrophages that occurs with aging, although it is not clear whether one induces the other. There is, however, a correlation between a reduction in the content of neurotransmitter and number of nerve fibers and up-regulation of beta receptors on the target cells, if those cells are responsive to the catecholamine (Bellinger et al., 1992). Not only is there an up-regulation of the number of receptors on T- and B-cells, but there is a decrease in the apparent turnover of total splenic neurotransmitter which is correlated with this change in receptor. It is important to recognize, however, that an increase in the number of receptors does not necessarily mean that the cell is going to be more responsive to a particular ligand.

Cytokines and Catecholamines

An important question is why do the nerves decline with age within the lymph tissues? And why would this apparent self-destruction of nerves only apply to those going into the spleen and lymph nodes and not into other organs? It may be linked with cytokines, which are known to increase the turnover of catecholamines (Carlson et al., 1987). It is also clear that the faster one pushes turnover, the more oxidative metabolites will be produced. These give rise to free radicals which in turn can destroy the very terminals that produce them. In other words, the faster you use it, the faster you lose it. In fact, a single dose of metamphetamine given to a rat can produce measurable oxidative metabolites in the caudate nucleus, such as 6-hydroxydopamine. In summary, it would appear that the more the spleen or lymph node cells are bombarded with antigenic challenge, the more turnover there will be of catecholamine metabolism which in turn will help to self-destroy the terminals. Furthermore, whenever macrophages are challenged, these cells will produce inducible nitric oxide synthetase and the subsequent production of nitric oxide can not only suppress certain enzymatic reactions in adjacent cells, but in turn can generate free radicals which can contribute to the demise of these nerve terminals (see review in Felten et al., 1992a).

It is very interesting that sympathectomy-related changes in young animals closely mirror age-related changes, especially with respect to the cellular immune response (Bellinger et al., 1992). Thus, by reducing the number of nerve fibers, one creates diminished cellular immune responses which can be restored when the nerves grow back. In the old animals, the nerves do not recover and the immune response remains suppressed, especially the cellular branch of immunity.

Restoration of Functional Connections

A large number of experimental approaches are being used to restore functional connections between the nerves and lymph cells. One approach has been to use the drug Deprenyl, which is an MAO-B inhibitor (although it may act on other targets as well). There is controversial evidence that it may have some protective effect in Parkinson's Disease, although very low doses of Deprenyl will cause robust recovery from 6-hydroxydopamine denervated spleens. In fact, it actually hyper-innervates the spleens (unpublished). This approach is now being evaluated in aged animals, although because these animals lose a great deal of plasticity during the aging process, it is questionable whether the approaches will be analogous.

An exception to the general rule is the thymus gland, which is a primary lymphoid organ. As the thymus involutes, there is a huge reduction in thymocytes, but the noradrenergic fibers compact tremendously (Bellinger et al., 1989). Interestingly, norepinephrine in the thymus inhibits proliferation of thymocytes. This is because the surrounding thymic tissue involutes and shrinks, but one has the same number of fibers present, resulting in one of the most dense patterns of innervation that can be observed in any peripheral target organ. They are not being driven by interleukin-1 (IL-1), but simply compacting in much the same manner that drawing dots on an expanded balloon and then letting the air out would result in those dots getting closer and closer together. In turn, any remaining thymocytes that are present within this density of fibers would probably be exposed to an extremely high local concentration of norepinephrine, which would be inhibitory over proliferative responses. This, in turn, may contribute to the reduced number of naive T-cells that has been shown in some studies to occur during the aging process. The fewer naive T-cells that are being produced by the thymus, the greater the probability that there will be illness from immunologic-related causes.

References

Ackerman, K.D., Bellinger, D.L., Felten, S.Y. and Felten, D.L. (1991). Ontogeny and senescence of noradrenergic innervation of the rodent thymus and spleen. In: Psychoneuroimmunology, 2nd Edition. Felten, D.L., Cohen, N. and Ader, R. (Eds.) New York: Academic Press, (pp. 71-125).

Bellinger, D.L., Ackerman, K.D., Felten, S.Y. and Felten, D.L. (1992). A longitudinal study of age-related loss of noradrenergic nerves and lymphoid cells in the aged rat spleen. Exp. Neurol. 116:295-311.

Bellinger, D.L., Ackerman, K.D., Felten, S.Y., Lorton, D. and Felten, D.L. (1989). Noradrenergic sympathetic innervation of thymus, spleen and lymph nodes: Aspects of development, aging and plasticity in neural-immune interactions. In: Proceedings of a Symposium on Interactions Between the Neuroendocrine and Immune Systems. Nistico, G. (Ed.) Rome: Pythogora Press, (pp. 35-66).

Bellinger, D.L., Felten, S.Y., Ackerman, K.D., Lorton, D., Madden, K.S. and Felten, D.L. (1993). Noradrenergic sympathetic innervation of lymphoid organs during development, aging, and in autoimmune disease. In: Aging of the Autonomic Nervous System. Amenta, F. (Ed.) Boca Raton: CRC Press, (pp. 243-284).

Carlson, S.L., Felten, D.L., Livnat, S. and Felten, S.Y. (1987). Noradrenergic sympathetic innervation of the spleen: V. Acute drug-induced depletion of lymphocytes in the target fields of innervation results in redistribution of noradrenergic fibers but maintenance of compartmentation. J. Neurosci. Res. 18:64-69.

Felten, D.L., Felten, S.Y., Bellinger, D.L., Carlson, S.L., Ackerman, K.D., Madden, K.S., Olschowka, J.A. and Livnat, S. (1987). Noradrenergic sympathetic neural interactions with the immune system: structure and function. Immunol. Rev. 100:225-260.

Felten, D.L., Felten, S.Y., Steece-Collier, K. and Clemens, J.A. (1992a). Age-related decline in the dopaminergic nigrostriatal system: The oxidative hypothesis and protective strategies. Ann. Neurol. 32(Suppl):S133-S136.

Felten, S.Y., Felten, D.L., Bellinger, D.L. and Olschoska, J.A. (1992b). Noradrenergic and peptidergic innervation of lymphoid organs. In: Neuroimmunoendocrinology, 2nd Rev. Ed. Chemical Immunology. Blalock, J.E. (Ed.) Basel: S. Karger, (pp. 25-48).

Livnat, S., Felten, S.Y., Carlson, S.L., Bellinger, D.L. and Felten, D.L. (1985). Involvement of peripheral and central catecholamine systems in neural-immune interactions. J. Neuroimmunol. 10:5-30.

Lorton, D., Bellinger, D.L., Hewitt, D., Felten, S.Y. and Felten, D.L. (1988). Pattern and time course of re-innervation of noradrenergic fibers into the spleen following denervation with 6-hydroxydopamine. Soc. Neurosci. Abstr. 14:225.

Madden, K.S., Felten, S.Y., Felten, D.L., Hardy, C.A. and Livnat, S. (1994a). Sympathetic nervous system modulation of the immune system. II. Induction of lymphocyte proliferation and migration *in vivo* by chemical sympathectomy. J. Neuroimmunol. 49:67-75.

Madden, K.S., Moynihan, J.A., Brenner, G.J., Felten, S.Y., Felten, D.L. and Livnat, S. (1994b). Sympathetic nervous system modulation of the immune system. III. Alterations in T and B cell proliferation and differentiation *in vitro* following chemical sympathectomy. J. Neuroimmunol. 49:77-87.

Madden, K.S., Sanders, V.M. and Felten, D.L. (1995a). Catecholamine influences and sympathetic neural modulation of immune responsiveness. Ann. Rev. Pharmacol. Toxicol. 35:417-448.

Madden, K.S., Felten, S.Y., Felten, D.L. and Bellinger, D.L. (1995b). Sympathetic nervous system - immune system interactions in young and old Fischer 344 rats. Ann. N.Y. Acad. Sci. 771:523-534.

Madden, K.S., Bellinger, D.L., Snyder, E., Maida, M. and Felten, D.L. (1996a). Alterations in sympathetic innervation of thymus and spleen in aged mice. 1st Intl. Conf. Immunol. & Aging, June 16-19 (Abstract).

Madden, K.S., Maida, M. and Felten, D.L. (1996b). Sympathetic innervation of aging mouse thymus. PNIRS, April 17-21 (Abstract).

UNDERNUTRITION AND IMMUNITY

Presented by

Robert A. Good, M.D., Ph.D.

Malnutrition and Disease

There is no question that nutrition can have profound immunomodulatory effects. Children deprived of protein and calories - protein-calorie malnutrition - from the day of birth may manifest agammaglobulinemia, hypogammaglobulinemia, as well as profound immunodeficiencies, including those characteristic of both the cellular and humoral branches of the immune system. Studies in various countries around the world support the conclusion that under field conditions, individuals suffering from malnutrition have profound deficiencies in both T-cell and B-cell dependent immunities (Aref et al., 1970; Abbassy et al., 1974; Jose et al., 1971; Good and Jose, 1975a). However, studies conducted with mice, rats, guinea pigs and a few monkeys in the laboratory in an attempt to mimic the observations made under field conditions of protein-calorie malnutrition yielded different results. Instead of being diminished by protein, protein-calorie, or calorie deprivation, many of the cell-mediated immunologic functions were significantly increased in mice, rats, guinea pigs and monkeys that had been subjected to protein and protein-calorie malnutrition without deprivation of other nutrients (Jose et al., 1971; Good and Jose, 1975a; 1975b; Cooper et al., 1974; 1975; Good et al., 1977a; Kramer and Good, 1978). This kind of nutritional deprivation interferes with antibody-producing capability while at the same time augmenting the tempo of allograft rejection, increasing proliferative responses to phytomitogens as well as enhancing certain types of tumor immunity or delayed-type hypersensitivity (Good and Jose, 1975a; Cooper et al., 1974; 1975). Even the sensitizability of the animals, that is the minimum dose of antigen that can produce a cell-

165

mediated immune response, is significantly increased (Kramer and Good, 1978; Jose and Good, 1972; 1973).

Some of the major earlier investigations concerned this paradox. On the one hand, field analysis reveals immunodeficiency in children who suffer from protein malnutrition or protein-calorie malnutrition, and on the other, more focused immune deficit in animals restricted in protein plus calories or calories alone (Jose et al., 1971; Good and Jose, 1975a; 1975b; Cooper et al., 1974; 1975; Good et al., 1977a; Kramer and Good, 1978). The influences of the element zinc, although not entirely explaining this striking paradox, has contributed greatly to its resolution (Good et al., 1979; 1980a; 1980b; Schloen et al., 1979). Under both field and experimental conditions in the laboratory, restriction of the element zinc (Iwata et al., 1979), or in protein-calorie malnourished patients feeding zinc alone, were shown to exert a most impressive influence on cell-mediated immune functions (Golden et al., 1978). Experiments of nature proved critical. These included the A46 mutation in cattle (Brummerstedt et al., 1971; 1974) and crodermatitis enteropathica in humans (Moynahan and Barnes, 1973; Moynahan, 1975). In both of these experiments of nature, zinc deficiency was attributable to defective zinc absorption which produced profound thymic involution and extreme cell-mediated immunodeficiency completely correctable by giving adequate zinc either orally or parentally. Dietary restriction of zinc alone in mice not only reproduced acrodermatitis enteropathica in the mice (Iwata et al., 1979), but long before producing acrodermatitis enteropathica lesions, produced profound decreases of levels of circulating thymulin, an indicator of full thymic function and profound deficits of T-cell-mediated immune functions, again completely corrected in mice by zinc administration (Iwata et al., 1979). Experiments with children suffering from protein-calorie malnutrition in which profound T- and B-cell immunodeficiency occurs was shown to be dramatically corrected by giving only zinc (Golden et al., 1978). While not concluding that immunological deficits seen in protein-calorie malnutrition are all attributable to zinc deficiency, the above cited research certainly underscores the importance of this element in normal immune system functioning. Vitamins are also important as observed in both animals and humans subjected to protein-calorie malnutrition (Good et al., 1982). Zinc, iron, other trace and not so trace metals, e.g. magnesium, manganese, etc. and several vitamins including vitamin A, vitamin B, especially vitamin B6 and vitamin C can exert profound influences on immune function (Gershwin et al., 1985; Chandra and Newberne, 1977). The deficiencies of each of these nutrients in patients with so-called protein-calorie malnutrition may contribute in a major way to the deficits of immune functions that represent the extreme immunodeficiency and susceptibility to infections observed in humans suffering from so-called protein-calorie malnutrition under field conditions (Good et al., 1982; Chandra and Newberne, 1977).

Undernutrition and Longevity

A number of experimental models have been used to demonstrate that undernutrition can promote longevity (Walford, 1969; 1983; 1986; Weindruch and Walford, 1988). These include genetically short-lived animals which have a high propensity to develop autoimmune disease, a variety of malignancies, and profound immunodeficiency relatively early in their lives. Restricting the amount of calories these animals consume interferes with the development of most, if not all, of these disease processes and greatly increases life span (Good et al., 1976; 1977b; Fernandes et al., 1977; 1978a; 1978b; Izui et al., 1981; Friend et al., 1978). NZB and B/W mice are particularly convenient animals in which to manipulate diet because of the loss of the cellular proliferative responses and immune function in their lymph nodes and spleen that occurs with aging. Manipulating the composition of the diets with respect to protein, fat and carbohydrate by itself has almost no impact upon the death rates of these short-lived animals (Johnson et al., 1986; Kubo et al., 1987). But, if their calories are restricted (Fernandes et al., 1978a; Johnson et al., 1986; Kubo et al., 1987), even when the diets may range from as little as 15% protein to 80% protein (Gajjar et al., 1987), the life span of the animals can readily be doubled. Indeed, under the appropriate circumstances, life span of these short-lived mice can often be tripled or even quadrupled by undernutrition without malnutrition. The same is true of MRL/*lpr/lpr* mice in which it has been found that calorie intake is the factor that controls survival (Kubo et al., 1984; Fernandes and Good, 1984). As long as the animals are full-fed, there are no differences in the death rate curves regardless of diet composition. The animals develop the diseases they are genetically programmed to develop. But if their energy intake is restricted, life span can be doubled, tripled or occasionally quadrupled. If both energy intake and fat intake are restricted, the life span can regularly be tripled under the right experimental circumstance (Johnson et al., 1986; Kubo et al., 1984; 1987; Gajjar et al., 1987; Fernandes and Good, 1984).

Disease Resistance

It is important to realize that even though the animals in such experiments may be undernourished, they are provided, nonetheless, with all of the minerals and vitamins that they need. The only thing that is restricted is the intake of calories or energy (Johnson et al., 1986; Kubo et al., 1984; 1987; Gajjar et al., 1987; Fernandes and Good, 1984; Fernandes et al., 1978b). When energy is the only restriction, the animals live a healthy and very long life compared to those animals that are fed normal laboratory diets *ad libitum*. If the calories in the diet are high in fat content, *ad libitum*-fed animals may be shown to develop coronary vascular disease (Fernandes et al., 1983). Calorie restriction not only increases longevity, it also reduces cholesterol levels as well as blood pressure and also the incidence of coronary lesions. Furthermore, older restricted mice learn to run mazes as quickly as young animals. In addition, the occurrence of tumors, and the incidence of hyalinizing renal disease (Johnson et al., 1986; Kubo et al., 1984; 1987; Gajjar et al., 1987; Fernandes and Good, 1984) that normally develop spontaneously in these short-lived animals or are triggered by viral infection, are minimized or develop much later in life (Izui et al., 1981; Shields et al., 1991). Mammary adenocarcinoma occurring in C3H/Bi (Fernandes et al., 1976), C3H/He (Sarkar et al., 1982) and C3H/Ou (Chen et al., 1990) mice, for example, is almost completely prevented by undernutrition without malnutrition, along with the ability of the breast epithelial cells and cells elsewhere in the body to produce both type A and type B retrovirus particles (Chen et al., 1990) that are associated in full-fed animals with the development of breast tumors. The same has been observed with respect to the leukemia-producing viruses in AKR mice (Shields et al., 1991). It turns out that in the calorie restricted animals, viral mRNA production is minimal (Chen et al., 1990; Engelman et al., 1990).

One possible disadvantage of undernutrition without malnutrition is that the size of the animals' litters is significantly reduced and reproduction may be interfered with if the calories are restricted too much. Consequently, during early development and during the gestation and lactation period, animals can be full-fed while restricted diets are fed both before and after gestation and lactation (Engelman et al., 1993a; 1994). Interestingly, during the periods when such animals are full-fed the cancer-associated viruses are once again produced in abundant quantities (Engelman et al., 1994). When the reproductive cycle has been completed and diets are once again restricted, the viral expression is reduced or goes away entirely. Consequently, it is possible to either turn on or turn off viral production simply by manipulating the energy intake of the animals. Undernutrition without malnutrition almost completely prevents the development of mammary adeno-carcinoma which would be expected to develop in virtually all of the female mice of the C3H/Ou strain fed an *ad libitum* diet (Engelman et al., 1993b; 1994).

Mechanistic Issues

The beneficial effects of undernutrition without malnutrition appear to be mediated, at least in part, through endocrine pathways. For example, prolactin production is reduced in the diet restricted animals. When normal levels of prolactin are restored by transplanting a pituitary gland beneath the kidney capsule (Engelman et al., 1993a; 1993b), the animals once again develop mammary adenocarcinoma. Other endocrine changes include reduced levels of insulin in the circulation as well as low glucose. Intestinal absorption is also altered, however maintenance of all of the immunologic functions continues despite the aging process, and the immunologic involution that occurs in some mouse strains is attenuated by undernutrition without malnutrition. In addition to the endocrine changes, there are changes in the immune system. For example, the loss of the ability to produce certain cytokines like interleukin-2 (IL-2) (Jung et al., 1982) is restored by restricting energy intake. $CD5^+$ B-cells may also be greatly reduced in chronic energy restricted animals (Ogura et al., 1990).

A rather striking influence of undernutrition without malnutrition is to greatly reduce cell proliferation in many tissues of the body. This phenomenon can be observed within populations of cells in each of the normally rapidly replicating cell systems of the body, e.g., in cells of epithelium all along the gastrointestinal tract (Ogura et al., 1989), in the replicating cells of basal layers of skin (Ogura et al., 1989), in unstimulated spleen cells (Ogura et al., 1989), in squamous epithelium cells along the esophagus (Ogura et al., 1989; Lok et al., 1990), and also in cells of bone marrow (Lok et al., 1990). Thus, the vegetative proliferation (Ogura et al., 1989) as well as proliferation that involves reproductive processes, e.g., proliferation of cells in breast tissue, are greatly reduced by undernutrition without malnutrition (Engelman et al., 1993a; 1993b). In striking contrast, however, we discovered that regenerative cellular repair proliferation as seen after removal of two-thirds of the liver parenchyma was not inhibited by undernutrition without malnutrition (Himeno et al., 1992). In short, this very rapid rate of cell replication is not down-regulated, but rather up-regulated significantly by undernutrition without malnutrition. Adaptive immunologic proliferation and restrictive regenerative-based cell proliferation are not only maintained but actually enhanced by undernutrition without malnutrition.

Experiments have been performed to probe the mechanism(s) which underlie these crucial influences of undernutrition without malnutrition. Already studies have associated undernutrition without malnutrition with decreased production of prolactin (Hamada et al., 1990). Reversal of the influence of prolactin on breast development and breast cancer occurrence may be achieved through pituitary transplants that effectively provide a source of prolactin to the prolactin deficient energy restricted mice (Engelman et al., 1991). This hormone increases proliferation within breast tissue. Further, a dopaminomimetic agent, e.g., Sandoz CV 205-502 (Engelman et al., 1993a; 1993b), inhibits breast cancer development in full-fed mice and inhibits cellular proliferation in the breast, just as protein-calorie malnutrition inhibits cellular proliferation in the mammary gland and prevents breast cancer development. Since dopamine can suppress prolactin release, this observation is consistent with those involving prolactin.

We have recently discovered that undernutrition without malnutrition decreases expression of certain genes, e.g., those associated with epidermal growth factor and also the protein product, production of epidermal growth factor in salivary glands as well as in breast tissue itself (Engelman et al., 1995). This influence may be associated with the resistance to breast cancer development in calorie or energy restricted mice (Engelman et al., 1993b; 1995). Additional investigations centering upon the control of proliferation and upon cytokines which regulate proliferation of lymphocytes may help us to gain a better understanding of the incredible influence that undernutrition without malnutrition has upon the immune system (Engelman et al., 1995).

In summary, it is quite clear that undernutrition without malnutrition prevents a number of diseases that have been linked with abnormalities within the immune system. This protocol prevents cancers in certain strains of animals, prevents the diseases commonly associated with aging, including autoimmune disease,

171

and makes genetically short-lived animals live as long as the mice of the genetically longest-lived strains. It is possible that the effects have to do with an energy equation. Instead of reducing energy intake, it would seem likely that the same effects could be accomplished by simply increasing energy expenditure. However, this possibility has been put to the experimental test and while increased exercise does increase median life span, it does not increase maximum life span as is achieved by undernutrition without malnutrition. Thus, it is the undernutrition without malnutrition that represents the most effective method to inhibit proliferation of certain cells in the body while, at the same time, fostering or driving other forms of cell proliferation, e.g., that associated with defense of the body or regenerative repair. To elucidate the controls exerted on cell proliferation well enough to understand this apparent paradox is a major challenge for the future development of this field.

References

Abbassy, A.S., Badr El-Din, M.K., Hassan, A.I., Aref, G.H., Hammad, S.A., El-Araby, I.I. and Badr El-Din, A.A. (1974). Studies of cell-mediated immunity and allergy in protein energy malnutrition. I. Cell-mediated delayed hypersensitivity. J. Trop. Med. Hyg. 77:13-17.

Aref, G.H., Badr El-Din, M.K., Hassan, A.I. and Araby, I.I. (1970). Immunoglobulins in kwashiorkor. J. Trop. Med. Hyg. 73:186-191.

Brummerstedt, E., Flagstad, T., Basse, A. and Andresen, E. (1971). The effect of zinc on calves with hereditary thymus hypoplasia (lethal trait A-46). Acta. Pathol. Microbiol. Scand. 79:686-687.

Brummerstedt, E., Andresen, E., Bawse, A. and Flagstad, T. (1974). Lethal trait A46 in cattle, immunological investigations. Nord. Vet. Md. 26:279-293.

Chandra, R.K. and Newberne, P.M. (Eds.) (1977). Nutrition, Immunity, and Infection. Mechanisms of Interactions. New York: Plenum Press.

Chen, R.F., Good, R.A., Hamada, N., Hellerman, G.R., Bauer-Sardiña, I., Nonoyama, M., Engelman, R.W and Day, N.K. (1990). Prevention of mouse mammary tumor by calorie restriction suppresses MMTV proviral DNA and proto-oncogene expression. Proc. Natl. Acad. Sci. 87:2385-2389.

Cooper, W.C., Good, R.A. and Mariani, T. (1974). Effects of protein insufficiency on immune responsiveness. Am. J. Clin. Nutr. 27:647-664.

Cooper, W.C., Mariani, T.N. and Good, R.A. (1975). The effects of protein deprivation on cell-mediated immunity. In: Immunodeficiency in Man and Animals: Proceedings. (Bergsma, D, Ed.; Good, R.A. and Finstad, J., Scientific Eds.) Sunderland, Massachusetts: Sinauer Associates, Inc. (pp. 223-228) (Birth Defects: Original Article Series, Vol. XI, No. 1, 1975).

Engelman, R.W., Day, N.K., Chen, R.F., Tomita, Y., Bauer-Sardiña, Dao, M.L. and Good, R.A. (1990). Calorie consumption level influences development of C3H/Ou breast adenocarcinoma with indifference to calorie source. Proc. Soc. Exp. Biol. Med. 193:23-30.

Engelman, R.W., Fukaura, Y., Hamada, N., Good, R.A. and Day, N.K. (1991). Dietary restriction permits normal parturition and lactation but suppresses mouse mammary tumor virus proviral transcription even after mammary involution. Cancer Res. 51(19):5123-5128.

Engelman, R.W., Day, N.K. and Good, R.A. (1993a). Calories, parity and prolactin influence mammary epithelial kinetics and differentiation and alter mouse mammary tumor risk. Cancer Res. 53:1188-1194.

Engelman, R.W., Day, N.K. and Good, R.A. (1993b). Calories, cell proliferation and proviral expression in autoimmunity and cancer. (Minireview). Proc. Soc. Exp. Biol. Med. 203:13-17.

Engelman, R.W., Day, N.K. and Good, R.A. (1994). Calorie intake during mammary development influences cancer risk: Lasting inhibition of C3H/HeOu mammary tumorigenesis by peripubertal calorie restriction. Cancer Res. 54:5724-5730.

Engelman, R.W., Owens, U.E., Bradley, W.G., Day, N.K. and Good, R.A. (1995). Mammary and submandibular gland epidermal growth factor expression is reduced by calorie restriction. Cancer Res. 55:1289-1295.

Fernandes, G. and Good, R.A. (1984). Inhibition by restricted-calorie diet of lymphoproliferative disease and renal damage in MRL/*lpr* mice. Proc. Natl. Acad. Sci. USA 81:6144-6148.

Fernandes, G., Yunis, E.J. and Good, R.A. (1976). Suppression of adenocarcinoma by the immunological consequences of calorie restriction. (Letter), Nature 263:504-506.

Fernandes, G., Good, R.A. and Yunis, E.J. (1977). Attempts to correct age-related immunodeficiency and autoimmunity by cellular and dietary manipulation in inbred mice. In: Immunology and Aging. (Makinodan, T. and Yunis, E., Eds.) New York: Plenum (pp. 111-133) (Comprehensive Immunology, Vol. 1).

Fernandes, G., Friend, P., Yunis, E.J. and Good, R.A. (1978a). Influence of dietary restriction on immunologic function and renal disease in (NZBxNZW)F1 mice. Proc. Natl. Acad. Sci. 75:1500-1504.

Fernandes, G., Yunis, E.J., Miranda, M., Smith, J. and Good, R.A. (1978b). Nutritional inhibition of genetically determined renal disease and autoimmunity with prolongation of life in *kdkd* mice. Proc. Natl Acad Sci. 75:2888-2892.

Fernandes, G., Alonso, D.R., Tanaka, T., Thaler, H.T., Yunis, E.J. and Good, R.A. (1983). Influence of diet on vascular lesions in autoimmune-prone B/W mice. Proc. Natl. Acad. Sci. USA 80:874-877.

Friend, P.S., Fernandes, G., Good, R.A., Michael, A.F. and Yunis, E.J. (1978). Dietary restrictions early and late: Effects on the nephropathy of the NZB x NZW mouse. Lab. Invest. 38:629-632.

Gajjar, A., Kubo, C., Johnson, B.C. and Good, R.A. (1987). Influence of extremes of protein and energy intake on survival of B/W mice. J. Nutr. 117:1136-1140.

Gershwin M.E., Beach, R.S. and Hurley L.S. (1985). Nutrition and Immunity. Orlando, FL: Academic Press, Inc.

Golden, M.H.N., Golden, B.E., Harland, P.S.E.G. and Jackson, A.A. (1978). Zinc and immunocompetence in protein-energy malnutrition. Lancet 1:1226-1227.

Good, R.A. and Jose, D. (1975a). Immunodeficiency secondary to nutritional deprivation: clinical and laboratory observations. In: Immunodeficiency in Man and Animals: Proceedings. (D. Bergsma, R.A. Good and J. Finstad, Eds.) Sunderland, Massachusetts: Sinauer (pp. 219-222).

Good, R.A. and Jose, D. (1975b). Immunodeficiency secondary to nutritional deprivation: clinical and laboratory observations. In: Immunodeficiency in Man and Animals: Proceedings. (Bergsma, D., Ed.; Good, R.A. and Finstad, J., Scientific Eds.) Sunderland, Massachusetts: Sinauer Associates, Inc. (pp. 219-222) (Birth Defects: Original Article Series, Vol. XI, No. 1, 1975).

Good, R.A., Fernandes, G., Yunis, E.J., Cooper, W.C., Jose, D.G., Kramer, T.R. and Hansen, M.A. (1976). Nutritional deficiency, immunological function, and disease. Am. J. Pathol. 84:599-614, September.

Good, R.A., Jose, D., Cooper, W.C., Fernandes, G., Kramer, T. and Yunis, E. (1977a). Influence of nutrition on antibody production and cellular immune responses in man, rats, mice and guinea pigs. In: Malnutrition and the Immune Response. (Suskind, M.R., Ed.) New York: Raven Press (pp. 169-183).

Good, R.A., Fernandes, G., Yunis, E.J., Cooper, W.C., Jose, D.G., Kramer, T. and Hansen, M.A. (1977b). Nutrition and immunity under controlled experimental conditions. Symposia of the Swedish Nutrition Foundation XIII. In: Food and Immunology: Proceedings. (Hambraeus, L, Hanson, L.A. and McFarlane, H., Eds.) Stockholm: Almqvist & Wiksell International (pp. 11-22).

Good, R.A., Fernandes, G. and West, A. (1979). Nutrition, immunity, and cancer — a review. Part I: Influence of protein or protein-calorie malnutrition and zinc deficiency on immunity. MSKCC Clin. Bull. 9:3-12.

Good, R.A., West, A. and Fernandes, G. (1980a). Effects of nutritional factors on immunity. International Symposium on Infections in the Immunocompromised Host, 1st, Veldhoven, Netherlands, 1980. In: Infections in the Immunocompromised Host - Pathogenesis, Prevention and Therapy: Proceedings. (Verhoef, J., Peterson, P.K. and Quie, P.G., Eds.) New York, Elsevier/North-Holland Biomedical Press (pp. 95-128).

Good, R.A., West, A. and Fernandes, G. (1980b). Nutritional modulation of immune responses. Fed. Proc. 39:3098-3104.

Good, R.A., Hanson, L.A. and Edelman, R. (1982). Infections and undernutrition. Nutrition Reviews 40(4):119-128.

Hamada, N., Engelman, R.W., Tomita, Y., Chen, R.F., Iwai, H., Good, R.A. and Day, N.K. (1990). Prolactin effects on the dietary regulation of mouse mammary tumor virus proviral DNA expression. Proc. Natl. Acad. Sci. USA 6733-6737.

Himeno, Y., Engelman, R.W. and Good, R.A. (1992). Influence of calorie restriction on oncogene expression and DNA synthesis during liver regeneration. Proc. Natl. Acad. Sci. USA 89:5497-5501.

Iwata, T., Incefy, G.S., Tanaka, T., Fernandes, G., Menendez-Botet, C.J., Pih, K. and Good, R.A. (1979). Circulating thymic hormone levels in zinc deficiency. Cell. Immunol. 47:100-105.

Izui, S., Fernandes, G., Hara, K., McConahey, P.J., Jensen, F.C., Dixon, F.J. and Good, R.A. (1981). Low-calorie diet selectively reduces expression of retroviral envelope glycoprotein gp70 in sera of NZB x NZW F_1 hybrid mice. J. Exp. Med. 154:1116-1124.

Johnson, B.C., Connor, B., Gajjar, A., Kubo, C., Good, R.A. (1986). Calories versus protein in onset of renal disease in NZB x NZW mice. Proc. Natl. Acad. Sci. USA 83:5659-5662.

Jose, D.G. and Good, R.A. (1972). Immune resistance and malnutrition. (Letter), Lancet 1:314.

Jose, D.G and Good, R.A. (1973). Quantitative effects of nutritional protein and calorie deficiency upon immune responses to tumors in mice. Cancer Res. 33:807-812.

Jose, D.G., Cooper, W.C. and Good, R.A. (1971). How protein deficiency enhances cellular immunity. JAMA 218:1428-1429.

Jung, L.K.L., Palladino, M.A., Calvano, S., Mark, D.A., Good, R.A. and Fernandes, G. (1982). Effect of calorie restriction on the production and responsiveness to interleukin 2 in (NZB x NZW)F_1 mice (Brief Communication). Clin. Immunol. and Immunopathol. 25:295-301.

Kramer, T.R. and Good, R.A. (1978). Increased *in vitro* cell mediated immunity in protein-malnourished guinea pigs. Clin. Immunol. Immunopathol. 11:212-228.

Kubo, C., Day, N.K. and Good, R.A. (1984). Influence of early or late dietary restriction on life span and immunological parameters in MRL/Mp-*lpr-lpr* mice. Proc. Natl. Acad. Sci. USA 81:5831-5835.

Kubo, C., Johnson, B.C., Connor, B., Gajjar, A. and Good, R.A. (1987). Crucial dietary factors in maximizing life span and longevity in autoimmune-prone mice. J. Nutr. 117:1129-1135.

Lok, E., Scott, F.W., Mongeau, R., Nera, E.A., Malcolm, S. and Clayson, D.B. (1990). Calorie restriction and cellular proliferation in various tissues of the female Swiss Webster mouse. Cancer Lett. 51:67-73.

Moynahan, E.J. and Barnes, P.M. (1973). Zinc deficiency and a synthetic diet for lactose intolerance. Lancet 1:676-677.

Moynahan, E.J. (1975). Zinc deficiency and cellular immune deficiency in acrodermatitis enteropathica in man and zinc deficiency with thymic hypoplasia in frisian calves. A possible genetic link. Lancet 2:710.

Ogura, M., Ogura, H., Ikehara, S., Dao, M.L. and Good, R.A. (1989). Decrease by chronic energy intake restriction of cellular proliferation in the intestinal epithelium and lymphoid organs in autoimmunity-prone mice. Proc. Natl. Acad. Sci. USA 86:5918-5922.

Ogura, M., Ogura, H., Lorenz, E., Ikehara, S. and Good, R.A. (1990). Undernutrition without malnutrition restricts the numbers and proportions of Ly-1 B lymphocytes in autoimmune (MRL/l and BXSB) mice. Proc. Soc. Exp. Biol. Med. 193:6-12.

Sarkar, N.H., Fernandes, G., Telang, N.T., Kourides, I.A. and Good, R.A. (1982). Low-calorie diet prevents the development of mammary tumors in C3H mice and reduces circulating prolactin level, murine mammary tumor virus expression, and proliferation of mammary alveolar cells. Proc. Natl. Acad. Sci. USA 7758-7762.

Schloen, L.H., Fernandes, G., Garofalo, J.A. and Good, R.A. (1979). Nutrition immunity and cancer — a review. Part II: Zinc, immune function and cancer. Clin. Bull. MSKCC 9:63-75.

Shields, B.A. Engelman, R.W., Fukaura, Y., Good, R.A. and Day, N.K. (1991). Calorie restriction suppresses subgenomic mink cytopathic focus-forming murine leukemia virus transcription and frequency of genomic expression while impairing lymphoma formation. Proc. Natl. Acad. Sci. USA 88:11138-11142.

Walford, R.L. (1969). The Immunologic Theory of Aging. Copenhagen: Munksgaard.

Walford, R.L. (Ed.) (1983). Maximum Life Span. New York-London: W.W. Norton & Company.

Walford, R.L. (Ed.) (1986). The 120 Year Diet. New York: Simon and Schuster.

Weindruch, R. and Walford, R.L. (Eds.) (1988). The Retardation of Aging and Disease by Dietary Restriction. Springfield, IL: Charles C. Thomas.

STRESS AND INFECTION

Presented by

Dedra S. Buchwald, M.D.

Introduction

Observant physicians throughout history have noted the apparent influence of psychological state on the outcome of infectious diseases. Over thirty years ago, Imboden et al. (1959; 1961) demonstrated the influence of emotional distress on the reported duration of brucellosis and influenza. Subsequent investigations show a similar influence on the incidence and severity of other infectious illnesses, including upper respiratory infections (Alexander and Summerskill, 1956; Jacobs et al., 1969; 1970; Parens et al., 1966; Cohen et al., 1991) and genital herpes (Kemeny et al., 1989; Rand et al., 1990; Goldmeier and Johnson, 1982). During the last decade, research has focused on stress-induced immunological changes as the mediators of these psychosocial influences on infection severity. Studies have demonstrated decrements in cellular immune response associated with examination stress (Kiecolt-Glaser et al., 1984; Glaser et al., 1985; 1993), psychiatric disorders (Schleifer et al., 1989; Irwin et al., 1990; 1992), marital discord (Kiecolt-Glaser et al., 1987; 1993), caring for ill family members (Kennedy et al., 1988), and self-reported daily stresses (Moss et al., 1989). Immunological measures examined in these investigations have included natural killer cell activity, lymphocyte response to mitogen stimulation, specific lymphocyte transformation, proliferative response of memory T-cells to Epstein-Barr virus (EBV), and antibody titers to latent viruses.

In general, these previous studies have examined behavioral outcomes as surrogate measures of biological disease activity. Behavioral measures such as self-reported symptom severity and health care-seeking may, in fact, accurately reflect severity of the underlying disease process. Alternatively, the influence of psychosocial factors on these outcomes may result from stress-mediated changes in symptom perception or illness behavior. For example, Imboden et al. (1959; 1961) relied on self-reported symptoms as measures of disease severity and duration. Several studies that examined psychological predictors of upper respiratory infection among college students determined incidence using records of student health service visits (Alexander and Summerskill, 1956; Jacobs et al., 1969; 1970; Parens et al., 1966). Because psychological distress may increase care-seeking for upper respiratory infections independent of any effect on actual disease incidence (Barsky et al., 1986), this method may introduce spurious associations between stress and disease. More recent studies of upper respiratory infections have relied on symptom diaries (Graham et al., 1986; Stone et al., 1987) or retrospective symptom histories (Glaser et al., 1987; Sarason et al., 1985; McClelland et al., 1980; 1982) to examine incidence. Because psychological distress may increase symptom reporting independent of any effect on disease severity (Lane et al., 1988), these methods may not accurately reflect biological disease activity. In an elegant prospective study designed to address these problems, Cohen et al. (1991) demonstrated that following inoculation with respiratory viruses, the overall rate of clinical upper respiratory infections and 'colds' increased in a dose-response manner with the subjects' degree of psychological stress. A curious, unexplained finding was that, despite an overall correlation, stress was not associated with 'colds' among those with a serologically-documented infection. Lastly, in one of the few studies to examine prognosis, Cope et al. (1994) found that the strongest predictors of chronic post-viral fatigue present at the time of illness onset were psychological distress, attributional style, and receiving a less definite diagnosis of a viral syndrome from their physician. A limitation of this study was the lack of any objective verification of infection.

In studies of herpesviruses, Kemeny et al. (1989) found that subjects with depressed mood had a higher incidence of genital herpes recurrence. Only 40% of recurrences were confirmed by clinical examination. Because examination was initiated by subjects' reporting of symptoms, some episodes of recurrence may have gone unreported and unexamined (i.e., were false negatives). Consequently, the results do not clearly indicate whether depression was associated with more frequent actual herpes recurrence or only a greater likelihood that symptoms of recurrence would be reported. A more recent study by Rand et al. (1990), used a similar follow-up method of self-report triggering clinical confirmation. Prospective daily measures of perceived stress showed no temporal relationship to genital herpes recurrence and no relationship was found between negative life events and number of recurrences.

References

Alexander, R.W. and Summerskill, J. (1956). Factors affecting the incidence of upper respiratory complaints among college students. Student Med. 4:61-73.

Barsky, A.J., Wyshak, G. and Klerman, G.L. (1986). Hypochondriasis: An evaluation of the DSM-III criteria in medical outpatients. Arch. Gen. Psychiatry 43:493-500.

Cohen, S., Tyrrell, D.A.J. and Smith, A.P. (1991). Psychological stress and the susceptibility to the common cold. New Engl. J. Med. 325:6060-12.

Cope, H., David, A., Pelosi, A. and Mann, A. (1994). Predictors of chronic "postviral" fatigue. Lancet 344:864-865.

Glaser, R., Keicolt-Glaser, J.K., Speicher, C.E. and Holliday, J.E. (1985). Stress, loneliness, and changes in herpesvirus latency. J. Behav. Med. 8:249-260.

Glaser, R., Rice, J., Sheridan, J., Fertel, R., Stout, J., Speicher, C., Pinsky, D., Kotur, M., Post, A. and Beck, M. (1987). Stress-related immune suppression: Health implications. Brain Behav. Immun. 1:7-20.

Glaser, R., Pearson, G.R., Bonneau, R.H., Esterling, B.A., Atkinson, C. and Kiecolt-Glaser, J.K. (1993). Stress and the memory T cell response to the Epstein-Barr virus in healthy medical students. Health Psychol. 12:435-442.

Goldmeier, K. and Johnson, A. (1982). Does psychiatric illness affect the recurrence rate of genital herpes. Br. J. Ven. Dis. 58:40-43.

Graham, N.M.H., Douglas, R.M. and Ryan, P. (1986). Stress and acute respiratory infection. Am. J. Epidemiol. 124:389-401.

Imboden, J.B., Canter, A., Cluff, L.E. and Trever, R.W. (1959). Brucellosis: III. Psychological aspects of delayed convalescence. Arch. Intern. Med. 103:406-414.

Imboden, J.B., Canter, A. and Cluff, L.E. (1961). Convalescence from influenza: A study of psychological and clinical determinants. Arch. Intern. Med. 108:393-399.

Irwin, M., Patterson, T., Smith, T.L., Caldwell, C., Brown, S.A., Gillin, J.C. and Grant, I. (1990). Reduction of immune function in life stress and depression. Biol. Psychiatry 27:22-30.

Irwin, M., Lacher, U. and Caldwell, C. (1992). Depression and reduced natural killer cytotoxicity: A longitudinal study of depressed patients and control subjects. Psychol. Med. 22:1045-1050.

Jacobs, M.A., Spilken, A. and Norman, M. (1969). Relationship of life change, maladaptive aggression, and upper respiratory infection in male college students. Psychosom. Med. 31:31-44.

Jacobs, M.A., Spilken, A.Z., Norman, M.M. and Anderson, L.S. (1970). Life stress and respiratory illness. Psychosom. Med. 32:233-242.

Kemeny, M.E., Cohen, F., Zegans, L.S. and Conant, M.A. (1989). Psychological and immunological predictors of genital herpes recurrence. Psychosom. Med. 51:195208.

Kennedy, S., Kiecolt-Glaser, J.K. and Glaser, R. (1988). Immunological consequences of acute and chronic stressors: Mediating role of interpersonal relationships. Br. J. Med. Psychol. 61:77-85.

Kiecolt-Glaser, J.K., Speicher, C.E., Holliday, J.E. and Glaser, R. (1984). Stress and the transformation of lymphocytes by Epstein-Barr virus. J. Behav. Med. 7:1-10.

Kiecolt-Glaser, J.K., Fisher, L.D., Ogrocki, P., Stout, J.C., Speicher, C.E. and Glaser, R. (1987). Marital quality, marital disruption, and immune function. Psychosom. Med. 49:13-34.

Kiecolt-Glaser, J.K., Malarkey, W.B., Chee, M., Newton, T., Cacioppo, J.T., Mao, H.Y. and Glaser, R. (1993). Negative behavior during marital conflict is associated with immunological down-regulation. Psychosom. Med. 55:395-409.

Lane, R.S., Barsky, A.J. and Goodson, J.D. (1988). Discomfort and disability in upper respiratory tract infection. J. Gen. Intern. Med. 3:540-546.

McClelland, D.C., Floor, E., Davidson, R.J. and Saron, C. (1980). Stressed power motivation, sympathetic activation, immune function, and illness. J. Hum. Stress 6:11-19.

McClelland, D.C., Alexander, C. and Marks, E. (1982). The need for power, stress, immune function, and illness among male prisoners. J. Abnorm. Psychol. 91:61-70.

Moss, R.B., Moss, H.B. and Peterson, R. (1989). Microstress, mood, and natural killer cell activity. Psychosomatics 30:279-283.

Parens, H., McConville, B.J. and Kaplan, S.M. (1966). The prediction of frequency of illness from the response to separation. Psychosom. Med. 28:162-176.

Rand, K.H., Hoon, E.F., Massey, J.K. and Johnson, J.H. (1990). Daily stress and recurrence of genital herpes simplex. Arch. Intern. Med. 150:1889-1893.

Sarason, I.G., Sarason, B.R., Potter, E.H. and Antoni, M.H. (1985). Life events, social support and illness. Psychosom. Med. 47:156-163.

Schleifer, S.J., Keller, S.E., Bond, R.N., Cohen, J. and Stein, M. (1989). Major depressive disorder and immunity: Role of age, sex, severity and hospitalization. Arch. Gen. Psychiatry 46:81-87.

Stone, A.A., Reed, B.R. and Neale, J.M. (1987). Changes in daily event frequency precede episodes of physical symptoms. J. Hum. Stress 13:70-74.

PREDICTORS OF RECOVERY FROM ACUTE INFECTIOUS MONONUCLEOSIS

Presented by

Dedra S. Buchwald, M.D.

Acute Infectious Mononucleosis and EBV

Initial contact with Epstein-Barr virus (EBV) results in a wide range of clinical syndromes. Childhood exposure typically leads to asymptomatic or mild infection while later exposure more often results in acute infectious mononucleosis (AIM) and significant morbidity. In the United States, AIM has a peak incidence in late adolescence and early adulthood (Heath et al., 1972; Henke et al., 1973). Serological surveys of susceptible young adults have shown EBV seroconversion rates of greater than 10% over 4-8 years with at least half of those infected developing clinical disease (Evans et al., 1968; Niederman et al., 1970). Although common, surprisingly little information exists on the natural history of AIM and the frequency of delayed convalescence. Several surveillance studies noted a 2-4 week duration of illness, but provided no further data (Evans et al., 1968; Niederman et al., 1970). Other studies not specifically designed to evaluate prognosis have found that 7% of patients still complained of pharyngitis at one month (van der Horst et al., 1991) and the average duration of AIM-associated fatigue was 12 days with patients reporting substantially longer recovery times than their physicians (Anderssen et al., 1987). In an older report, 25% of patients had a persistent illness characterized by fatigue, fever, and atypical lymphocytosis three months after AIM (Issacs, 1948). Finally, data from a recent prospective study of AIM estimated a 10% risk of chronic symptoms six months after the initial illness (White, 1990).

Psychosocial Factors

The likelihood of developing symptomatic illness following EBV seroconversion and the duration of symptoms have been linked to psychosocial factors. In a prospective study of seroconversion among West Point cadets, the development of AIM was more common and the length of hospitalization longer among those characterized by high motivation, poor academic performance and overachieving fathers (Kasl et al., 1979). In an outcome study using hematological findings instead of symptoms to prevent bias due to self-report, subjects who recovered rapidly scored higher on MMPI scales measuring ego strength six months after AIM (Greenfield et al., 1959). Lastly, students with a history of documented AIM made greater subsequent use of mental health services than their healthy counterparts and had a post-infectious psychologically-based malaise (Peszke and Mason, 1969). More recently, Bruce-Jones et al. (1994) derived an empirically-based definition of post-AIM fatigue occurring in the absence of psychiatric disease. Social adversity (e.g., divorce) and threatening life events had little correlation with the subsequent development of a post-infectious fatigue syndrome or on delayed physical recovery. However, social adversity was significantly associated with the presence of psychiatric illness at two and six months after the acute illness. In another study of patients with persistent fatigue three months following a viral infection (primarily EBV), symptoms could not be explained by objective measures (Rutherford and White, 1991), suggesting a role for distorted perception or symptom amplification. Taken together, these studies suggest that the relative influence of biological and psychosocial factors during the course of an infectious illness may change over time.

Biological Factors

Most clinically apparent EBV infections are self-limited and only a minority of cases lead to chronic or life-threatening illnesses (Schooley et al., 1986; Tosato et al., 1985; Borysiewicz et al., 1986; Hamblin et al., 1983). Nonetheless, many biological factors might affect disease severity or delayed convalescence from AIM, including the presence of markers of illness severity such as atypical lymphocytosis, hepatitis or physical examination findings and/or the lack of an adequate immunological response to EBV. In this regard, the typical serological response to EBV is the appearance of viral capsid antigen (VCA)-IgM and early antigen (EA) antibodies soon after infection, followed shortly thereafter by antibodies to VCA-IgG (Henle et al., 1974). Although Epstein-Barr nuclear antigen (EBNA) has been said to appear 4-6 weeks after infection (Henle et al., 1974), the presence of EBNA is not uncommon in acute phase sera and may reflect a vigorous immune response (Sumaya and Ench, 1985; Anderssen et al., 1987; Gervais and Joncas, 1979). For example, in a study of acyclovir treatment of AIM, 27% of patients had antibodies to EBNA and VCA-IgM at study entry. Subjects with early-appearing EBNA were less likely to have abnormal liver function tests, atypical lymphocytes, severe pharyngitis and lymphadenopathy than subjects without this finding. Despite the greater severity of the initial illness, the time to recovery was similar in those with and without early-appearing EBNA (van der Horst et al., 1991). In contrast, Borysiewicz et al. (1986) noted reduced or absent EBNA in individuals with persistent symptoms following documented AIM.

AIM has been chosen as a model for several reasons. First, for most viral infections, there is no commonly available screening test. However, for AIM, in the appropriate clinical setting, a positive monospot or heterophile antibody test indicates a high likelihood of infection with EBV. Second, in patients with a positive monospot, primary EBV infection is easily confirmed by the presence of EBV VCA-IgM antibodies. Third, AIM typically affects younger populations, hence the prevalence of medical disorders which could confound the results and influence prognosis is low. Finally, as described above, there is provocative evidence that suggests that recovery from AIM is influenced by both psychosocial factors and biological factors.

Experimental Model

The site of this prospective cohort study is Group Health Cooperative, a large health maintenance organization in Seattle, Washington. The availability of extensive computer records will make it possible to track patients with respect to mental health and medical visits, prescription use and a variety of other parameters, both previous to and following the episode of AIM. When the study is complete, a total of 200 healthy subjects will be enrolled at the onset of acute EBV infection and followed for six months. Subjects are identified by a positive monospot ordered by their primary care provider and enrolled in the study if they are within two weeks of the onset of AIM-associated symptoms. We have chosen this narrow time frame to determine study eligibility to increase the likelihood that data collected at the index visit will reflect the subject's baseline, pre-morbid status. At the index visit, data is collected on potential biological and psychosocial risk factors. Between the index and the one month follow-up visit, the subject's good health is confirmed by review of their medical records and EBV infection is verified by the presence of EBV VCA-IgM. If these two conditions are met, recovery is assessed with repeated measures of symptom severity, biological disease activity, psychosocial factors and illness behavior collected at one, two and six month follow-up visits.

Biological measures include a physical examination, liver transaminases, a complete blood count (with manual count of atypical lymphocytes) and EBV serology (VCA-IgG, VCA-IgM, anti-EA, anti-EBNA). The psychosocial measures consist of the Hopkins Symptom Checklist (Derogatis, 1977) and a structured psychiatric interview to evaluate psychological distress. Functional status is assessed using the Medical Outcomes Study Short Form General Health Survey (SF-36, Stewart et al., 1988). This instrument has eight subscales which measure various domains such as role functioning, physical functioning and body pain. Other measures describe subject's personality (Eysenck Introversion and Neuroticism subscales, Eysenck and Eysenck,

1975), somatization (Barsky Amplification Scale, Barsky et al., 1988), life stressors (Brugha Threatening Life Experiences Inventory, Brugha et al., 1985), social support and health locus of control.

Recovery from EBV infection is being examined as both a categorical outcome and as a continuous variable. For the former, recovery is defined by the subject's endorsement of 'complete recovery' while non-recovery is reported health status being 'better', 'the same', or 'worse'. The second approach defines recovery in terms of the mean length of time to symptom resolution. Finally, because at this writing only a third of the sample has been enrolled and statistical power to detect potentially interesting differences may be limited by the small sample size, both significant associations (level of significance $p < .01$), as well as trends ($p < .05-.09$) will be discussed.

Physical Signs

The findings reported here are based on 79 subjects who have completed the two month follow-up visit. Their mean age is 22 years, 56% are female, and over 80% are single Caucasian students. The average duration of AIM-associated symptoms is 1.4 months. The individual symptoms are typical of AIM: sore throat (76%), fatigue (70%), painful lymph nodes (62%), myalgias (58%), fever (49%), headache (49%) and chills (35%). Likewise, the physical examination findings in this cohort are characteristic of AIM. For example, the most common signs are pharyngitis (90%), anterior (85%) and posterior (68%) lymphadenopathy and fever (84%), with only a minority of patients having either liver or spleen enlargement. The most common laboratory findings have been increases in liver function tests, either SGOT (38%) or SGPT (53%), and not unexpectedly, the presence of EBV-VCA-IgG (100%). One interesting preliminary observation that has emerged, but awaits confirmation, is that the pattern, height and time of appearance of the EBV-associated antibodies may be different than previously described.

Predictors of Recovery

In terms of outcome, 46% of subjects have completely recovered at one month, 58% at two months, and 81% at six months. Of interest, the rate of non-recovery in this sample is about twice that predicted by the existing literature. Of the pre-existing factors influencing subjective recovery, younger age is the most important. The other significant predictor of recovery is less pain (prior to becoming ill with AIM) as measured by the SF-36. In addition, because of the relatively small sample size (less than half the final sample has been recruited), several interesting trends also have been noted which did not achieve statistical significance. These included an association of worse physical and role functioning, less social support from friends and a poorer subjective pre-AIM rating of health with non-recovery. Other psychosocial measures such as life stressors, a tendency to amplify symptoms, the presence of psychiatric disorders (e.g., major depression), psychological distress or health locus of control do not predict outcome at two months. Variables not associated with recovery include gender, race/ethnicity, number of reported disability days prior to being ill, symptom severity and physical examination or laboratory findings.

When prognosis is examined using duration of illness, women have a significantly longer mean length of illness than men (1.6 versus 1.1 months). Again, age is an important predictor, with older individuals taking longer to recover (< 20 years = 1.2 months versus > 20 years = 1.8 months). Furthermore, at the two month follow-up visit, there were no significant factors associated with recovery. However, compared to those with complete symptom resolution, an intriguing trend was noted towards a higher VCA-IgM among the non-recovered group (geometric mean titer = 12.3 versus 25), suggesting prolonged viral activity or a heightened or prolonged immune response.

Conclusion

In conclusion, among individuals exposed to an infectious agent the incidence, severity and duration of symptoms vary widely. The reasons for this variability are not well understood and have not been systematically studied. However, the available evidence suggests that both biological and psychological factors are important. Previous investigations have often combined clinical evaluation of disease activity with psychosocial measures, in which assessments typically are triggered by self-report, thus obscuring the relationship between psychosocial stressors, actual illness severity or incidence, and symptom reporting. Changes in disease severity or duration also have not been clearly distinguished from changes in disease incidence. These studies also typically have focused on psychosocial factors and in most cases did not simultaneously examine biological outcomes or consider pathophysiological mechanisms. Finally, despite the frequency of AIM (and other viral syndromes), its long-term clinical course and the influence of biological and psychosocial factors on outcome have not been described. This later point is crucial since the contributions of biological and psychosocial factors at illness onset may differ from those which affect its ultimate severity and duration.

The study described above offers the opportunity to examine the biological and psychosocial factors influencing convalescence from AIM, one of the few viral infections that have an easily performed, clinically useful marker (monospot). The availability of such a marker allows the rapid identification of potential subjects and thus an evaluation of pre-morbid factors affecting prognosis. Although it is important to emphasize the preliminary nature of the observations described here, it appears that there are both psychosocial and biological risk factors that influence the recovery from AIM. These include age, gender, functional status, social support, self-reported health, and possibly the persistent elevation of the EBV VCA-IgM antibody. Firm conclusions and the determination of the relative contributions of these and other subjective and objective factors will, however, need to await the collection of more data.

References

Anderssen, J., Skoldenberg, B., Henle, W., Giesecke, J., Ortquist, A., Julander, I., Gustavsson, B., Akerlund, B., Britton, S. and Ernberg, I. (1987). Acylovir treatment in infectious mononucleosis: A clinical and virological study. Infection 15:Suppl1:S14-20.

Barsky, A.J., Goodson, J.D., Lane, R.S. and Cleary, P.D. (1988). The amplification of somatic symptoms. Psychosomatic Med. 50:510-519.

Borysiewicz, L.K., Haworth, S.J., Cohen, J.C., Mundin, J., Rickinson, A. and Sissons, J.G.P. (1986). Epstein-Barr virus specific immune defects in patients with persistent symptoms following infectious mononucleosis. Quart. J. Med. 58:111-121.

Bruce-Jones, W.D.A., White, P.D., Thmas, J.M. and Clare, A.W. (1994). The effect of social adversity on the fatigue syndrome, psychiatric disorders and physical recovery, following glandular fever. Psychol. Med. 24:651-659.

Brugha, T., Bebbington, P., Tennant, C. and Hurry, J. (1985). The list of threatening life experiences: A subset of 12 life event categories with considerable long-term contextual threat. Psychol. Med. 15:189-194.

DeRogatis, L.R. (1977). The SCL-90 Manual I: Scoring, administration, and procedure for the SCL-90. Baltimore: Clinical Psychometrics Unit, Johns Hopkins University.

Evans, A.S., Niederman, J.C. and McCollum, R.W. (1968). Seroepidemiologic evidence of infectious mononucleosis with EB virus. New Engl. J. Med. 279:1121-1127.

Eysenck, H.J. and Eysenck, S.B.G. (1975). Manual of the Eysenck personality questionnaire. London: Hodder and Stoughton Ltd.

Gervais, F. and Joncas, J.H. (1979). Epstein-Barr virus infection: Seroepidemiology in various population groups of the greater Montreal area. Comp. Immunol. Microbiol. Infect. Dis. 2:207-212.

Greenfield, N.S., Roessler, R. and Crosley, A.P. (1959). Ego strength and length of recovery from infectious mononucleosis. J. Nerv. Ment. Dis. 129:125-128.

Hamblin, T., Hussain, J., Akbar, A.N., Tang, Y.C., Smith, J.L. and Jones, D.B. (1983). Immunological reason for chronic ill health after infectious mononucleosis. Brit. Med. J. 287:85-88.

Heath, C.W., Brodsky, A.L. and Potolsky, A.I. (1972). Infectious mononucleosis in a general population. Am. J. Epidemiol. 95:46-52.

Henke, C.E., Kurland, L.T. and Elveback, L.R. (1973). Infectious mononucleosis in Rochester, Minnesota, 1950 through 1969. Am. J. Epidemiol. 98:483-490.

Henle, G., Henle, W. and Horwitz, C.A. (1974). Antibodies to Epstein-Barr virus associated nuclear antigen in infectious mononucleosis. J. Infect. Dis. 130:231-239.

Issacs, R. (1948). Chronic infectious mononucleosis. Blood 3:858-861.

Kasl, S.V., Evans, A.S. and Niederman, J.C. (1979). Psychosocial risk factors in the development of infectious mononucleosis. Psychosom. Med. 41:445-466.

Niederman, J.C., Evans, A.S., Subrahmanyan, L. and McCollum, R.W. (1970). Prevalence, incidence and persistence of EB virus antibody in young adults. New Engl. J. Med. 282:361-365.

Peszke, M.A. and Mason, W.M. (1969). Infectious mononucleosis and its relationship to psychological malaise. Connecticut Med. 33:260-266.

Rutherford, O.M. and White, P.D. (1991). Human quadriceps strength and fatiguability in patients with post viral fatigue. J. Neurol. Neurosurg. Psychiatry 54:961-964.

Schooley, R.T., Carey, R.W., Miller, G., Henle, W., Eastman, R., Mark, E.J., Kenyon, K., Wheeler, E.O. and Rubin, R.H. (1986). Chronic Epstein-Barr virus infection associated with fever and interstitial pneumonitis. Ann. Intern. Med. 104:636-643.

Stewart, A., Hays, R.D. and Ware, J.L. (1988). The MOS short-form general health survey: Reliability and validity in a patient population. Med. Care 26:724-735.

Sumaya, C.V. and Ench, Y. (1985). Epstein-Barr virus infectious mononucleosis in children. II. Heterophil antibody and virus-specific responses. Ped. 75:10119.

Tosato, G., Straus, S., Henle, W., Pike, S.E. and Blaese, R.M. (1985). Characteristic T cell dysfunction in patients with chronic active Epstein-Barr virus infection (chronic infectious mononucleosis). J. Immunol. 134:3082-3088.

van der Horst, C., Joncas, J., Ahronheim, G., Gustafson, N., Stei, G., Gurwith, M., Fleisher, G., Sullivan, J., Sixbey, J., Roland, S., Fryer, J., Champney, K., Schooley, R., Sumaya, C. and Pagano, J.S. (1991). Lack of effect of peroral acyclovir for the treatment of acute infectious mononucleosis. J. Infect. Dis. 164:788-792.

White, P. (1990). Psychological symptoms after glandular fever. Abstr. Amer. Psychiatric Assoc. National Meeting, Washington, D.C. May, 1990.

VIRAL MODELS OF NEUROENDOCRINE/ IMMUNE INTERACTIONS

Presented by

John Sheridan, Ph.D.

A viral model of neuroendocrine/immune interactions is the rotavirus. It induces a superficial infection of the epithelial tissue of the gastrointestinal tract and can be used to probe the effects of stress on neuroendocrine interactions within the gastrointestinal tract. For example, in the SCID animal, infection results in an acute clinical infection with diarrhea, but then the virus continues to be expressed but in the absence of overt clinical symptoms. When the animals are restrained they once again re-develop the symptoms (Dharakul et al., 1990).

The same phenomenon has been demonstrated with respect to herpesviruses (Bonneau et al., 1991a; 1991b). These are generally infections of the dermis, however, they can remain in a latent state within the nervous system. Sometimes the virus can be re-activated along with the expression of clinical symptoms. This is a model that has been used to assess the impact that neuroendocrine pathways might have upon viral re-activation. It turns out that both the hypothalamic-pituitary-adrenal (HPA) axis, as well as the sympathetic nervous system can independently influence the pathogenesis of this virus.

Experimental Model

The stress model that has been utilized is that of restraint, which alters plasma glucocorticoid levels and also activates a catecholamine response. Animals are exposed to influenza virus and various parameters of the cellular immune response are assessed. In addition, histopathology occurring within the lung and respiratory tract can be correlated with the immunologic events. It is known that if the natural killer (NK) cell activity is down-regulated it will correspond with increased pathophysiology of an influenza infection (Stein-Streilein et al., 1988). If the T-cell response is diminished it will enhance the pathogenicity of influenza as well as other viruses (Sheridan et al., 1991). What these observations reflect is the fact that no single immunological factor can resolve an infection. Instead, it requires interactions among several mechanisms.

The restraint stress consists of placing animals into a test tube with air holes punched into it. The animals are restrained beginning at 6 PM when the lights are turned out and continues until between 6 and 10 AM the following morning. A series of pilot studies examining the temporal kinetics of the infection relative to the stressor reveal that the stressor exposure must begin one to two days prior to exposure to the infection in order to induce the largest magnitude of effect upon the immune response (Sheridan et al., 1991). If the infection occurs first followed by the restraint, some changes in the immune response can be observed but they are marginal (Sheridan et al., 1991). If exposure to the stressor occurs three days into the infection, the effect is lost. Plasma is collected from the retro orbital plexus and done sufficiently quickly after disturbing the cages that plasma levels of corticosterone are between 40 to 50 ng/ml which is within the non-stress baseline range. Titers of viral replication peak between two and three days. At this time there is also an elevation in plasma corticosterone (Hermann et al., 1994a).

Activation of the HPA axis by antigenic challenge has been demonstrated by a number of investigators, however it is important to note that it is virus-specific. Influenza virus results in this activation (Hermann et al., 1994a) but herpes does not (unpublished). At seven days post-infection there is a peak of the inflammatory response characterized by massive mononuclear infiltration within the lung. It also corresponds with a time period when activated T-cells can be found in the draining lymph nodes as well as at the site of infection. It is also noteworthy that the nature of the stressor includes not only restraint but also food and water deprivation during exposure to the stressor. Undoubtedly, it is a synergistic effect between these components that contributes to the neuroendocrine response. It is important to note that after eight or nine cycles of restraint, the animals habituate and do not exhibit the same degree of glucocorticoid activation (Hermann et al., 1994a).

Norepinephrine and Corticosterone

In addition to changes in neuroendocrine parameters, changes in sympathetic activation can also be detected using this model. Within both the superficial cervical lymph node - which is the node that drains the upper respiratory tract - and the spleen, the restrained animals have elevated patterns of norepinephrine as measured by high pressure liquid chromatography. In addition, after the same seven cycles of restraint there is an elevation in norepinephrine within both the thymus gland and lung (Hermann et al., 1994b). The next question posed was the extent to which the changes in norepinephrine and glucocorticoids could affect the biological activity of the T-lymphocytes. The cells not only have to respond to the pathogen but they have to be capable of migrating to the site where the pathogen is located.

Considerable evidence indicates that the cellular components of the immune system fail to localize at the site of the pathogen upon exposure to stressors. This may be related to the food and water restriction component of the stressor since malnutrition has been correlated with decreased cellularity within lymphoid tissues, including the draining nodes during infection with influenza. Phenotypic analysis has revealed that the reduction in cell types include B-cells, T-cells, as well as antigen-presenting cells (Bonneau et al., 1991a).

A series of experiments has assessed the role of glucocorticoids in mediating the reduction in lymphocyte trafficking. Glucocorticoids are also known to regulate gene expression in cytotoxic T-cells as well as T-helper cells (Dobbs et al., 1993; Hermann et al., 1993). Those genes might be responsible for the expression of interleukin-2 (IL-2) or possibly the IL-2 receptor. It is also known that glucocorticoids can influence the ability of cells to express adhesion molecules (Cronstein et al., 1992). But all of these changes reflect changes in the signals that are needed to activate the cell. Several lines of evidence indicate that glucocorticoids can also interfere with the signal that enables a cell to travel to the inflammatory site (Hermann et al., 1995).

A pharmacologic approach that has been used involves the administration of the glucocorticoid receptor blocker RU-486. Exposure to this drug has been found to restore the cellular density of the draining lymph node in stress-exposed infected animals (Dobbs et al., 1993). Histologic examination of the tissue reveals that compared with the normal mononuclear infiltration that occurs seven days after infection, exposing the animals to stress prevents this migration of cells (Dobbs et al., 1993; Hermann et al., 1995). However, exposure to the stress does not influence the replication of the virus since viral titers are unchanged (Sheridan et al., 1991).

Stress and Interleukin-2

Production of IL-2 is also affected by stress. However, the animals have to be exposed to the stressor repeatedly in order to observe an effect on the IL-2 response. If the animals are restrained for just a single cycle or if very short stress cycles are used, there is what appears to be a dose-response relationship between the degree of the stress and the changes in IL-2 (Sheridan et al., 1991). Using a different model involving herpes exposure, restraint significantly reduces the number of cytotoxic T-cells (Bonneau et al., 1991a). However, the ability to activate these cells can be partially restored by using the beta-adrenergic antagonist Nadolol, which works in the peripheral nervous system but not the central nervous system. This treatment does not influence the cellularity of the draining lymph node or the lung but it does enable the cells to be active. When the beta-adrenergic antagonist is combined with the glucocorticoid receptor blocker RU-486, the cellular response is restored to 100% (Dobbs et al., 1993).

In summary, the evidence reveals that activation of the HPA axis reduces the ability of viral-specific cells to move initially into the draining lymph nodes where activation is required if the cells are to perform their biological function, and this activation process can be blocked by elevated catecholamines within the tissue. Thus, neuroendocrine pathways and the sympathetic nervous system interact within the peripheral immune compartments to impact on the progression of viral infection.

References

Bonneau, R.M., Sheridan, J.F., Feng, N. and Glaser, R. (1991a). Stress-induced suppression of HSV specific cytotoxic T lymphocyte and natural killer cell activity and enhancement of acute pathogenesis following local HSV infection. Brain, Behavior and Immunity 5:170-192.

Bonneau, R.H., Sheridan, J.F., Feng, N. and Glaser, R. (1991b). Stress-induced effects on cell mediated innate and adaptive memory components of the murine immune response to Herpes simplex virus. Brain, Behavior and Immunity 5:274-295.

Cronstein, B.N., Kimmel, S.C., Levin, R.I., Martinuik, F. and Weissmann, G. (1992). A mechanism for the antiinflammatory effects of corticosteroids: The glucocorticoid receptor regulates leukocyte adhesion to endothelial cells and expression of endothelial-leukocyte adhesion molecule 1 and intercellular adhesion molecule 1. Proc. Natl. Acad. Sci. USA 89:9991-9995.

Dharakul, T., Rott, L. and Greenberg, H.B. (1990). Recovery from chronic rotavirus infection in mice with severe combined immunodeficiency: Virus clearance mediated by adaptive transfer of immune CD8+ T lymphocytes. J. Virol. 64:4375-4381.

Dobbs, C.M., Vasquez, M., Glaser, R.M. and Sheridan, J.F. (1993). Mechanisms of stress-induced modulation of viral pathogenesis and immunity. J. Neuroimmunology 48:151-160.

Hermann, G., Tovar, C.A. Beck, F.M., Allen, C. and Sheridan, J.F. (1993). Restraint stress differentially affects the pathogenesis of an experimental influenza viral infection in 3 inbred strains of mice. J. Neuroimmunol. 47:83-94.

Hermann, G., Tovar, C.A., Beck, F.M. and Sheridan, J.F. (1994a). Kinetics of glucocorticoid response to restraint stress and experimental influenza viral infection in two inbred strains of mice. J. Neuroimmunology 49:25-33.

Hermann, G., Beck, F.M., Tovar, C.A., Malarkey, W.B., Allen, C. and Sheridan, J.F. (1994b). Stress-induced changes attributable to the sympathetic nervous system during experimental influenza viral infection in DBA/2 inbred mouse strain. J. Neuroimmunology 53:173-180.

Hermann, G., Beck, F.M. and Sheridan, J.F. (1995). Stress-induced glucocorticoid response modulates mononuclear cell trafficking during an experimental influenza viral infection. J. Neuroimmunology 56:179-186.

Sheridan, J.F., Feng, N., Bonneau, R.H., Allen, C.M., Huneycutt, B.S. and Glaser R. (1991). Restraint-induced stress differentially affects anti-viral cellular and humoral immune response. J. Neuroimmunology 31:245-255.

Stein-Streilein, J., Guffee, J. and Fan, W. (1988). Locally and systemically derived natural killer cells participate in defense against intranasally inoculated influenza virus. Regional Immunology 1:100-105.

THE PITUITARY GLAND ENHANCES HOST RESISTANCE TO BACTERIAL INFECTION

Presented by

Sean Arkins, Ph.D.

Interferon-Gamma and Growth Hormone

Using a bacterial challenge model, we have defined an important role for the pituitary gland and, in particular, for pituitary-derived growth hormone in regulating the activities of phagocytic cells. Hypophysectomized rats, sham hypophysectomized rats, or intact controls were challenged by intraperitoneal inoculation with *Salmonella typhimurium*. The number of bacteria was adjusted so that all of the intact animals survived the dose. At this level of challenge, the hypophysectomized animals had a 27% survival rate on day 7 (Edwards et al., 1991a). This model provided an opportunity to observe the effects of hormonal manipulations on host survival. The administration of the classic macrophage activating factor, interferon-gamma, increased survival rate to 63% in the hypophysectomized animals. The truly novel finding, however, was that administration of growth hormone resulted in a virtually identical increase in the survival rate of hypophysectomized rats. This was a specific effect of growth hormone and not a generalized protein effect since heat inactivation abrogated the ability of this hormone to promote survival. The increase in the survival of hypophysectomized rats treated with either interferon-gamma or growth hormone in this *Salmonella* challenge model was comparable to the increase in the survival of challenged animals treated with the broad spectrum antibiotic, tetracycline (Edwards et al., 1991a).

We have performed other experiments to determine the mechanisms by which growth hormone enhances host resistance to bacterial challenge. Macrophages were isolated from the

205

peritoneal cavities of either intact or hypophysectomized animals and then cultured in the presence of opsonized *Salmonella typhimurium*. Eight hours later the number of viable bacteria remaining in the culture supernatant was assessed by serial dilutions on trypticase soy agar. Macrophages from hypophysectomized animals showed a significant reduction in their ability to kill bacteria. However, the ability of macrophages to kill *Salmonella typhimurium* was significantly enhanced when the hypophysectomized animals were treated with interferon-gamma for six days prior to the isolation of the phagocytic cells. *In vivo* treatment for six days with growth hormone also significantly enhanced the ability of peritoneal macrophages from hypophysectomized rats to kill bacteria (Edwards et al., 1991a; 1992). The effects of growth hormone on host resistance are mediated, at least in part, by modulating the ability of the phagocytic cells to produce reactive oxygen intermediates such as superoxide anion and hydrogen peroxide (Edwards et al., 1988; 1992). We have found that growth hormone also primes another phagocytic cell type, the neutrophil, for enhanced superoxide anion secretion (Fu et al., 1991). By enhancing the release of reactive oxygen intermediates such as superoxide anion, recombinant human growth hormone also significantly enhances the ability of neutrophils to kill *E. Coli* (Fu et al., 1994).

Growth Hormone and Superoxide Anion Secretion

Human growth hormone has the capacity to bind to both the growth hormone and the prolactin receptors (Hughes and Friesen, 1985). This pleiotropic receptor-binding capacity is not a characteristic of growth hormone produced by other species. It was therefore of interest to determine whether human growth hormone operates through the growth hormone or prolactin receptors to prime human neutrophils for enhanced superoxide anion secretion. In one series of experiments, we found that recombinant human growth hormone is able to increase superoxide anion production in primed neutrophils. This was not true, however, of either recombinant porcine growth hormone or bovine growth hormone (Fu et al., 1992). These results suggest that the growth hormone is working through the prolactin receptor, since pre-incubation of human neutrophils with an antibody to the growth hormone receptor had no effect on superoxide anion production following exposure to either growth hormone or prolactin. In contrast, antibodies to the prolactin receptor completely abrogated the induction of superoxide anion secretion by either growth hormone or prolactin. Finally, a series of experiments using synthetic variants of growth hormone, each with varying degrees of specificity for either the growth hormone or prolactin receptors, clearly revealed that growth hormone primes human neutrophils for enhanced superoxide anion secretion by binding to the prolactin receptor (Fu et al., 1992).

We have completed a similar series of studies using tumor necrosis factor alpha (TNF-α) production as the dependent variable. This factor is important in mediating both the anti-tumor and anti-microbial capacity of macrophages. There is a significant reduction in the ability of phagocytic cells from hypophysectomized rats to produce TNF-α *in vitro*. As we established in other models, both interferon-gamma which is a natural priming reagent for TNF-α release, as well as *in vivo* treatment with growth hormone, are able to increase TNF-α synthesis from macrophages (Edwards et al., 1991b).

In summary, the pituitary gland plays an important role in mediating an organism's ability to fight disease. Removal of this gland is associated with a significant reduction in the ability of rats to combat *Salmonella typhimurium* infection *in vivo*. Administration of growth hormone to such hypophysectomized animals significantly increases their ability to withstand bacterial challenge. This increase in resistance is mediated, at least in part, through the phagocytic component of the immune system. Macrophages from growth hormone treated rats produce significantly more superoxide anion upon stimulation *in vitro* and also kill more *Salmonella typhimurium in vitro*. Growth hormone treatment *in vivo* also restores the ability of macrophages from hypophysectomized animals to release TNF-α and primes another phagocytic cell, the neutrophil, for enhanced superoxide anion secretion and increased bactericidal activity. In humans, but not in other species, these actions of growth hormone are mediated by binding to the prolactin receptor.

References

Edwards, C.K. III, Ghiasuddin, S.M., Schepper, J.M., Yunger, L.M. and Kelley, K.W. (1988). A newly defined property of somatotropin: Priming of macrophages for production of superoxide anion. Science 239:769-771.

Edwards, C.K. III, Yunger, L.M., Lorence, R.M., Dantzer, R. and Kelley, K.W. (1991a). The pituitary gland is required for protection against lethal effects of Salmonella typhimurium. Proc. Natl. Acad. Sci. USA 88:2274-2277.

Edwards, C.K. III, Lorence, R.M., Dunham, D.M., Arkins, S., Yunger, L.M., Greager, J.A., Walter, R.J., Dantzer, R. and Kelley, K.W. (1991b). Hypophysectomy inhibits the synthesis of tumor necrosis factor α by rat macrophages: Partial restoration by exogenous growth hormone or interferon-γ. Endocrinology 128:989-996.

Edwards, C.K. III, Ghiasuddin, S.M., Yunger, L.M., Lorence, R.M., Arkins, S., Dantzer, R. and Kelley, K.W. (1992). *In vivo* administration of recombinant growth hormone or gamma interferon activates macrophages: Enhanced resistance to experimental *Salmonella typhimurium* infection is correlated with generation of reactive oxygen intermediates. Infect. Immun. 60:2514-2521.

Fu, Y.-K., Arkins, S., Wang, B.S. and Kelley, K.W. (1991). A novel role of growth hormone and insulin-like growth factor-I: Priming neutrophils for superoxide anion secretion. J. Immunol. 146:1602-1608.

Fu, Y.-K., Arkins, S., fuh, G., Cunningham, B.C., Wells, J.A., Fong, S., Cronin, M.J., Dantzer, R. and Kelley, K.W. (1992). Growth hormone augments superoxide anion secretion of human neutrophils by binding to the prolactin receptor. J. Clin. Invest. 89:451-457.

Fu, Y.-K., Arkins, S., Li, Y.M., Dantzer, R. and Kelley, K.W. (1994). Reduction in superoxide anion secretion and bactericidal activity of neutrophils from aged rats: Reversal by the combination of gamma interferon and growth hormone. Infect. Immun. 62:1-8.

Hughes, J.P. and Friesen, H.G. (1985). The nature and regulation of the receptors for pituitary growth hormone. Ann. Rev. Physiol. 47:469-482.

EFFECTS OF STRESS ON THE COURSE
OF MYCOBACTERIAL INFECTIONS
INCLUDING TUBERCULOSIS

Presented by

Bruce Zwilling, Ph.D.

Epidemiology

Stress by itself does not cause disease. Stress creates a micro-environment within the body which then makes it easier for other things to trigger specific symptoms. This is clearly the case with respect to susceptibility to tuberculosis, a disease that infects 1.8 billion individuals or one-third of the world population. It also accounts for approximately 3 million deaths per year with 8 million new cases being diagnosed annually (Snider et al., 1994). This represents more deaths than caused by any other infectious disease, making further understanding of the progression of tuberculosis a high priority for any health agency. Yet not all individuals exposed to tuberculosis have the same prognosis. Genetic predisposition, exposure to the pathogen and stress each contribute to the display of clinical symptoms.

Transmission

Tuberculosis is spread when the microorganisms are inhaled into the lung and are then picked up by alveolar macrophages. Eventually a specific immune response is induced which then results in the activation of T-cells and various cytokines (Kaufman, 1993; Caan and Kaufman, 1994; Ellner et al., 1990). These serve as chemical magnets causing more macrophages to infiltrate the site of infection. These cellular responses represent an initial attempt by the body to control the growth of the microorganism and to isolate it in the form of a granuloma. While some viable organisms will be present, the micro-environment is not favorable

211

to their growth. For most individuals who are infected with tuberculosis this steady state infection can last the rest of their lives without necessarily causing a significant health problem, however, there is a 10% lifetime chance that the disease will reactivate (Snider et al., 1994). When that happens, the control mechanisms that keep the growth of the organism under control lose their effectiveness and the organisms begin to grow and disseminate. This results in active disease and the spread of the bacteria in the form of droplet aerosols to other members of the population. What are the events that can alter the immune system's ability to keep the organism in remission? They include stress, protein malnutrition, aging, as well as chronic alcoholism. The link between stressful events and the progression of active tuberculosis has been documented in many published reports (Ishigami, 1919; Wiegeshaus et al., 1989; Collins, 1989). The importance of one's genetic code in affording protection against infectious agents is also quite apparent when considering the growth of mycobacterium. Resistance to this and other pathogens is autosomally dominant and maps to a gene on chromosome 1. There is also a group of genes on human chromosome 2q. The resistance gene in man is probably responsible for the documented differences in resistance and susceptibility among different populations of individuals (Bushman and Skamene, 1988; Zwilling and Hilburger, 1994).

Role of Stress

There is clearly a link between genetic predisposition to mycobacterium and stress. The experimental model that has been used to demonstrate this utilizes mice that are injected with *Mycobacterium avium* and then stressed using restraint for ten 18 hour cycles, interrupted after five cycles by two days of rest. Following each cycle the mice are returned to their regular cages. Twelve days later the animals are sacrificed following exposure to the final stressor. The number of microorganisms in the spleen and the lungs is then counted. Using this model it is apparent that increasing the amount of stress results in an increase in susceptibility to mycobacterial growth (Brown et al., 1993; Brown and Zwilling, 1995). There are many more mycobacterial colony-forming units in the spleens of those mice that are stressed for 10 cycles as compared to those mice that are stressed for less than 10 cycles. In addition, more colony-forming units can be isolated from the spleens of genetically-susceptible mice compared to non-susceptible animals (Brown et al., 1993). Interestingly, activation of the hypothalamic-pituitary-adrenal (HPA) axis increases infection in the susceptible mice but not in the resistant mice (Brown et al., 1993; 1995a; Brown and Zwilling, 1994). This increased infection rate can be abrogated by adrenalectomy or the administration of the glucocorticoid receptor antagonist RU-486 (Brown et al., 1993). These data clearly demonstrate that the increased mycobacterium growth secondary to stress is mediated in large part through activation of the HPA axis. However, the difference in susceptibility between the two different strains is not due to a difference in HPA axis activation. Both groups of mice exhibit comparable changes in plasma glucocorticoids and it is possible to suppress other macrophage functions using the restraint stress paradigm (Brown et al., 1993). It is evident that three factors are necessary for infection to occur: exposure to the pathogen, a genetic predisposition, and exposure to a stressor (Brown et al., 1995b).

References

Brown, D.H. and Zwilling, B.S. (1994). Activation of the hypothalamic-pituitary-adrenal axis differentially affects the anti-mycobacterial activity of macrophages from BCG-resistant and -susceptible mice. J. Neuroimmunol. 53:181-187.

Brown, D.H. and Zwilling, B.S. (1995). Neuroimmunology of host-microbial interactions. In: Psychoneuroimmunology, Stress and Infection. (Friedman, H., Klein, T.W. and Friedman, A.L., Eds.) New York: CRC Press (pp. 153-172).

Brown, D.H., Sheridan, J., Pearl, D. and Zwilling, B.S. (1993). Regulation of mycobacterial growth by the hypothalamus-pituitary-adrenal axis: Differential responses of Mycobacterium bovis BCG-resistant and -susceptible mice. Infect. Immun. 61:4793-4800.

Brown, D.H., Lafuse, W. and Zwilling, B.S. (1995a). Cytokine mediated activation of macrophages from Mycobacterium bovis BCG resistant and susceptible mice: Differential effects of corticosterone on antimycobacterial activity and expression of the Bcg gene (candidate Nramp). Infect. Immun. 63:2983-2988.

Brown, D.H., Miles, B.A. and Zwilling, B.S. (1995b). Growth of Mycobacterium tuberculosis in BCG-resistant and -susceptible mice: Establishment of latency and reactivation. Infect. Immun. 63:2243-2247.

Bushman, E. and Skamene, E. (1988). Genetic background of the host, expression of natural resistance and acquired immunity to tuberculosis. In: Mycobacterium tuberculosis: Interactions with the Immune System. (Benedinelli, M. and Friedman, H., Eds.) New York: Plenum Press (pp. 59-79).

Caan, J. and Kaufman, S.H.E. (1994). Immune mechanisms in protection. In: Tuberculosis: Pathogenesis, Protection and Control. (Bloom, B.R., Ed.) Washington, DC: ASM Press (pp. 389-415).

Collins, F.M. (1989). Mycobacterial disease, immunosuppression and acquired immunodeficiency. Clin. Microbiol. Rev. 2:360-377.

Ellner, J.J., Boom, W.H., Edmonds, K.L., Ruh, E.A., Tossi, Z. and Wallis, R.S. (1990). Regulation of immune responses to Mycobacterium tuberculosis. In: Microbial Determinants of Virulence and Host Response. (Ayoub, E.M., Cassell, G.H.,

Branch, W.C. Jr. and Henry, T.J., Eds.) Washington, DC: ASM Press (pp. 77-91).

Ishigami, T. (1919). The influence of psychic acts on the progress of pulmonary tuberculosis. Amer. Rev. Tuberculosis Pulmonary Disease 2:470-484.

Kaufman, S.H.E. (1993). Tuberculosis. The role of the immune system. The Immunologist 1:109-114.

Snider, D.E., Raviglione, M. and Kochi, A. (1994). Global burden of tuberculosis. In: Tuberculosis: Pathogenesis, Protection and Control. (Bloom, B.R., Ed.) Washington, DC: ASM Press (pp. 3-11).

Wiegeshaus, E., Balasubramaniam, V. and Smith, D.W. (1989). Immunity to tuberculosis from the perspective of pathogenesis. Infect. Immun. 57:3671-3676.

Zwilling, B.S. and Hilburger, M.H. (1994). Macrophage resistance genes: Bcg/Ity/Lsh. In: Macrophage-Pathogen Interactions. (Zwilling, B.S. and Eisenstein, T.K., Eds.) New York: Marcel-Dekker (pp. 233-245).

NOREPINEPHRINE AND OTHER HORMONAL FACTORS THAT MAY AFFECT BACTERIAL GROWTH

Presented by

Mark Lyte, Ph.D.

Neurohormones and Microbes

There is a tendency to view neurotransmitters and neurohormones, especially those activated by stress, within the context of the organism in which they are being studied. For example, the role that catecholamines and glucocorticoids may play in modulating the immune system of the host is frequently a focal point of research assessing the effects of stress on immunity. It is important to recognize, however, that many of the biogenic amines and neurohormones exist in non-mammalian species as well. These include plants, insects, and even microorganisms (Smith, 1971; Pitman, 1971; Lenard, 1992). For example, insulin has been found in virtually all microorganisms that have been examined to date (Lenard, 1992). Corticotropin has been identified in some species of bacteria while other bacteria have receptors for neurohormones and are capable of responding to these hormones (LeRoith et al., 1986). Therefore, in studying the course of disease one has to consider not only the impact that neurochemicals produced by the host might have upon its immune system, but also the impact that these substances might have upon the direct growth and proliferation of the microbial organism.

Catecholamines and Bacterial Growth

Several clues that there may be a link between neurochemicals produced by the host and the proliferation of microbes are to be found in the literature. It has long been known that in both dogs and humans overwhelming sepsis is frequently accompanied by elevated levels of catecholamines (Groves et al., 1973; Benedict

217

and Grahame-Smith, 1978). Others have demonstrated an inverse relationship between plasma norepinephrine levels and survival, with increased levels of this catecholamine being correlated with decreased survival (Jones et al., 1988). Research has revealed that norepinephrine, when added to culture media, can significantly increase the growth of bacteria (Lyte and Ernst, 1992; 1993). Importantly, experiments were conducted utilizing a serum-based medium coupled with very low bacterial inoculums to more closely approximate *in vivo* conditions accompanying actual infection. Neither dopamine nor epinephrine are able to stimulate such growth to the same degree achieved with norepinephrine. The mechanisms governing the ability of norepinephrine to increase bacterial growth are non-nutritional in nature since incubation of gram-negative bacteria with metabolites of norepinephrine such as normetanephrine, which contains one more methyl group than norepinephrine and hence would serve as a better energy source for growth, are without effect on growth. An argument can always be made that the amounts of catecholamine being added in tissue culture media may not reflect the levels that would exist *in vivo*. But when taking into consideration the increased levels within the micro-environment of tissue rather than in plasma, it is probably correct to conclude that the levels being used do accurately reflect levels that would exist within the host (Meirieu et al., 1986). Other experiments have revealed that not only does norepinephrine promote the growth of bacteria but also the expression of virulence-related factors (Lyte et al., in press).

Bacterial growth has been examined in a pilot study with mice but using a design that does not enable the immune system to respond. A predetermined amount of bacteria is introduced into a chamber surrounded by filter material that does not allow the bacteria to escape (Day et al., 1980). However, the mesh of the filter is such that norepinephrine from the host is able to enter. But bacteria cannot exit and immune cells cannot enter the chamber. These chambers are then implanted into mice that are subsequently exposed to stress. A social conflict stress model is used with a significant increase in the growth of bacteria as a result of the micro-environment created by the stress. However, the model does not rule out that substances produced by the bacteria such as endotoxin might not leak out and somehow stimulate the immune system. The primary point of these studies is that the growth of bacteria within the chamber may be due to direct interactions with the neurohormonal components mediating the stress response. In summary, while these experiments are preliminary, they do provide the rationale for viewing the impact of stress not only from the perspective of the host but also from that of the microbe, and that the pathogenicity of infectious microorganisms may, in part, be due to direct interactions between the infectious microorganism and the neurohormonal environment of the host (Lyte, 1993).

References

Benedict, C.R. and Grahame-Smith, D.G. (1978). Plasma noradrenaline and adrenaline concentrations and dopamine-beta-hydroxylase activity in patients with shock due to septicemia, trauma and haemorrhage. Quarterly Journal of Medicine 185:1-20.

Day, S.E.J., Vasli, K.K., Russell, R.J. and Arbuthnott, J.P. (1980). A simple method for the study *in vivo* of bacterial growth and accompanying host response. Journal of Infection 2:39-51.

Groves, A.C., Griffiths, J., Leung, F. and Meek, R.N. (1973). Plasma catecholamines in patients with serious postoperative infection. Annals of Surgery 178:102-107.

Jones, S.B., Westfall, M.V. and Sayeed, M. (1988). Plasma catecholamines during *E. coli* bacteremia in conscious rats. American Journal of Physiology 254:R470-477.

Lenard, J. (1992). Mammalian hormones in microbial cells. Trends in Biochemical Sciences 17:147-150.

LeRoith, D., Roberts, C. Jr., Lesniak, M.A. and Roth, J. (1986). Receptors for intracellular messenger molecules in microbes: Similarities to vertebrate receptors and possible implications for diseases in man. Experientia 42:782-788.

Lyte, M. and Ernst, S. (1992). Catecholamine induced growth of gram negative bacteria. Life Sciences 50:203-212.

Lyte, M. and Ernst, S. (1993). Alpha and beta adrenergic receptor involvement in catecholamine-induced growth of gram-negative bacteria. Biochemica Biophysica Research Communication 190:447-452.

Lyte, M., Arulanandam, B., Nguyen, K., Frank, C., Erickson, A. and Francis, D. Norepinephrine induced growth and expression of virulence associated factors in enterotoxigenic and enterohemorrhagic strains of *Escherichia coli*. In: Mechanisms in the Pathogenesis of Enteric Diseases. (Paul, P.S., Francis, D.H. and Benfield, D., Eds.) New York: Plenum Press (in press).

Lyte, M. (1993). The role of microbial endocrinology in infectious disease. Journal of Endocrinology 137:343-345.

Meirieu, O., Pairet, M., Sutra, J.F. and Ruckebusch, M. (1986). Local release of monoamines in the gastrointestinal tract: An *in vivo* study in rabbits. Life Sciences 38:827-834.

Pitman, R.M. (1971). Transmitter substances in insects: A review. Comparative and General Pharmacology 2:347-371.

Smith, T.A. (1971). The occurrence, metabolism and functions of amines in plants. Biological Reviews of the Cambridge Philosophical Society 46:201-241.

RHEUMATOID ARTHRITIS

Presented by

Esther Sternberg, M.D.

Animal Model

In any disease process, one has to consider the antecedent events as well as those which occur following the initiation of symptoms. An important advantage of working with animal models is that they can be studied before exposure to the disease-triggering stimulus. After that exposure, the very delicate balance between the immune system and the stress response becomes altered. Consequently, when studying humans it is difficult to differentiate between those aspects of the hypothalamic-pituitary-adrenal (HPA) axis response that are secondary to the chronic stress of inflammation, and those that existed prior to the inflammation which in turn might have predisposed the person to develop the disease. The model that has been used extensively in studying inflammatory disease mechanisms is the Lewis rat which remains disease-free until exposed to any one of a variety of inflammatory triggers. The pattern of inflammatory disease which develops depends upon the inflammatory trigger to which they are exposed. For example, exposing the Lewis rat to a single injection of streptococcal bacterial cell wall intraperitoneally results in severe arthritis, which peaks at 48 hours, decreases and then peaks again at three to four weeks and persists thereafter (Sternberg et al., 1989a; 1992).

Fischer rats, on the other hand, develop minimal, if any, acute arthritic response and no chronic response (Sternberg et al., 1989a). The acute response is thymic independent, and the chronic response is thymic dependent as evidenced by the fact that nude athymic Lewis rats develop a full blown acute response and no chronic response (Sternberg et al., 1989a). This suggests that early events in the immune response may play an important role in chronic disease. Since most patients report to their physician after the inflammation has already developed and in all likelihood persisted for some time, interventions may be less effective. Although not yet proven, stress response-related interventions may be most beneficial during the very early stages of the disease.

Hypothalamic-Pituitary-Adrenal Axis

It is quite clear that Lewis rats, even before developing symptoms, have an altered endocrine system. Compared to Fischer rats, their adrenocorticotropin hormone (ACTH) and corticosterone response is significantly reduced in response to a variety of inflammatory stimuli, including streptococcal cell walls, or interleukin-1 (IL-1) alpha (Sternberg et al., 1989a; 1989b). Gaining an understanding of the link between brain-controlled endocrine responses known to mediate the inflammatory response in rats will provide insights regarding disease mechanisms in humans.

A number of lines of evidence indicate that the primary endocrine dysregulation in Lewis rats is within the brain, and specifically in neurons that produce corticotropin releasing factor (CRF). After a single intraperitoneal injection of streptococcal cell walls, Fischer rats express a large amount of hypothalamic CRF mRNA, while Lewis rats' CRF and mRNA remains at baseline levels (Sternberg et al., 1989b). Lewis rats also have a problem expressing enkephalin mRNA, which is usually co-expressed in the same paraventricular neurons as CRF (Sternberg et al., 1989b). This suggests that the problem is not in the CRF gene itself, but instead something that controls CRF secretion or production. Consequently, a number of neurotransmitters known to regulate CRF have been examined. These include adrenergic systems, serotonin, as well as acetylcholine, all up-regulators of CRF (Calogero et al., 1992). The down regulators include GABA benzodiazepine, the opiates, and glucocorticoids (Smith et al., 1992). Our studies revealed no differences in the binding and affinity characteristics of alpha adrenergic, beta adrenergic, 5-HT$_2$

or muscarinic acetylcholine receptors between Fischer and Lewis rats (Calogero et al., 1992). However, there were differences between these two types of rats with respect to hypothalamic GABA benzodiazepine receptors (Smith et al., 1992). The number of benzodiazepine GABA receptors in the Lewis rats are significantly higher than in the Fischers, however, adrenalectomizing the Fischer rats abolishes this difference. Since adrenalectomy had this effect, it is quite clear that the change in the number of receptors is secondary to the effects of corticosterone in these animals. This difference in the number of GABA benzodiazepine receptors has behavioral implications since this neurotransmitter system might very well have a calming effect on these animals (Smith et al., 1992). There are no differences in the glucocorticoid type II receptors, except in the thymus gland, and this difference is probably secondary to the differential levels of corticosterone in the two strains. There are also differences in the 5-HT$_1\alpha$ receptor with respect to both content and expression of mRNA in the hippocampus of the Lewis rat compared with the Fischer (Burnet et al., 1992). Sprague Dawley rats are intermediate. However, the role these differences play in the increased susceptibility of the animals to inflammatory disease is not clear. For example, the differences in the 5-HT$_1\alpha$ could lead to a clamped down CRF response, or it could be that glucocorticoid-related GABA differences lead to CRF hyporesponsiveness. So simply analyzing the differences in these receptors reveals little, except that the entire pattern of receptor number in a variety of neurotransmitter systems that are known to control CRF is consistent with a down-regulated CRF system in Lewis rats.

Intervention Strategies

Instead of focusing on individual neurotransmitters, intervention strategies have been adopted as a means of identifying the contribution of these differences to the etiology of the symptoms. One such intervention strategy has been implanting normal hypothalamic tissue into the third ventricle of Lewis rats. This significantly reduces Lewis rats' susceptibility to inflammation (Misiewicz-Poltorak et al., 1993). The simplest interpretation is that the transplants are providing a source of CRF. However, histologic analyses of the transplants does not support this conclusion since CRF production is variable. Whether the effect of transplantation is due to CRF or whether there is some factor within the transplanted tissue which is capable of activating host CRF is not clear. Regardless of the mechanism, research using the Lewis rat model has clearly demonstrated the important role that stress-related hormones can play in modulating the course of inflammatory disease.

References

Burnet, P.W., Mefford, I.N., Smith, C.C., Gold, P.W. and Sternberg, E.M. (1992). Hippocampal 8-[3H]hydroxy-2-(di-n-propylamino) tetralin binding. J. Neurochem. 59(3):1062-1070.

Calogero, A.E., Sternberg, E.M., Bagdy, G. et al. (1992). Neurotransmitter-induced hypothalamic-pituitary-adrenal axis responsiveness is defective in inflammatory disease-susceptible Lewis rats: *In vivo* and *in vitro* studies suggesting globally defective hypothalamic secretion of corticotropin-releasing hormone. Neuroendocrinology 55(5):600-608.

Misiewicz-Poltorak, B., Zelazowska, E., Gomez, M., Gold, P.W. and Sternberg, E.M. (1993). Intra-cerebroventricular transplantation of F344/N rat embryonic hypothalamic tissue is associated with reduction of peripheral inflammatory responses in inflammatory disease susceptible LEW/N rats. Soc. for Neurosci. Abstracts 19:763.

Smith, C.C., Hauser, E., Renaud, N.D. et al. (1992). Increased hypothalamic [3H]flunitrazepam binding in hypothalamic-pituitary-adrenal axis hyporesponsive Lewis rats. Brain Res. 569(2):295-299.

Sternberg, E.M., Hill, J.M., Chrousos, G.P. et al. (1989a). Inflammatory mediator-induced hypothalamic-pituitary-adrenal axis activation is defective in streptococcal cell wall arthritis-susceptible Lewis rats. Proc. Natl. Acad. Sci. USA 86(7):2374-2378.

Sternberg, E.M., Young, W., Bernardini, R. et al. (1989b). A central nervous system defect in biosynthesis of corticotropin-releasing hormone is associated with susceptibility to streptococcal cell wall-induced arthritis in Lewis rats. Proc. Natl. Acad. Sci. USA 86(12):4771-4775.

Sternberg, E.M., Chrousos, G.P., Wilder, R.L. and Gold, P.W. (1992). The stress response and the regulation of inflammatory disease. Ann. Intern. Med. 117(10):854-866.

EFFECTS OF STRESS ON EXPERIMENTAL ALLERGIC ENCEPHALOMYELITIS

Presented by

Caroline Whitacre, Ph.D.

Relationship to Multiple Sclerosis

Experimental autoimmune encephalomyelitis (EAE) is frequently studied as an animal model for the human demyelinating disease, multiple sclerosis. EAE is induced by injecting myelin basic protein (MBP) into the Lewis rat or some strains of mouse. During the 10 to 12 days following the injection of MBP, the expansion of MBP-reactive T-cells occurs in the lymph node compartment followed by trafficking of such cells to the central nervous system (CNS) (Paterson and Swanborg, 1988). EAE is manifested as an ascending paralysis, beginning with a loss of tonicity in the tail, followed by complete hind leg paralysis. The animals spontaneously recover and are refractory to subsequent disease reinduction. At the microscopic level, the disease is characterized by perivascular cuffing, with lymphocytes and macrophages surrounding CNS blood vessels. The disease involves proliferation of CD4 T-helper 1 (Th-1) lymphocytes as well as antibody responses. However, the antibody does not appear to play a significant role in disease pathogenesis. Cytokines important to disease induction include interleukin-2 (IL-2), interferon-gamma, and tumor necrosis factor.

Stress and EAE

A link between EAE and stress was first demonstrated in the early 1960's by Seymour Levine, who reported that the disease symptoms could be suppressed by exogenously administered glucocorticoids and restraint stress (Levine et al., 1962). Although the male Lewis rat has reduced levels of corticosterone as reflected

227

in the circadian rhythm, the female Lewis rat has somewhat higher levels of this steroid (Griffin and Whitacre, 1991). Thus, female Lewis rats were subjected to restraint stress beginning five days prior to the injection of MBP, and extending through the recovery period. In the male rats, stressing them for one hour per day actually resulted in a significantly increased amount of disease activity, whereas stressing them for nine hours per day resulted in a decrease in disease activity (Griffin et al., 1993). The female Lewis rats, however, which have higher levels of basal and stress-induced glucocorticoid levels compared with the males, showed a different type of response. They not only had a much greater degree of suppression of disease activity, but there was no evidence of enhancement of symptoms after just one hour of stress. Instead, a more profound decrease in disease was observed (Griffin et al., 1993).

It is important to recognize that many diseases are, in and of themselves, stressful. This is certainly true of the EAE model in rats. At the time of appearance of clinical disease, there is an abrupt rise in corticosterone (MacPhee et al., 1989). This rise in corticosterone can be observed in male and female rats but the response is blunted in animals exposed to stress for nine hours. There is also a correlation with IL-2 levels produced by lymphocytes derived from the lymph node. In the control animals, there is a peak in IL-2 production on days 12 and 15, whereas the levels remain lower and constant throughout the disease course in female Lewis rats exposed to stress for nine hours (Griffin et al., 1993).

Immunologic Mechanisms

Some studies have addressed the nature of the processing of MBP. It is known that the MBP amino acid sequence capable of inducing disease in the rat resides between amino acids 68 and 88. This 20 amino acid sequence does not require further processing, while the entire molecule does. The disease suppressing effects of stress are observed only when animals are exposed to the entire MBP molecule, whereas no suppressive effects of stress are observed when the 20 amino acid epitope is injected (Griffin et al., 1993). Two possible explanations can be entertained. One is that the stress effects are mediated via antigen processing. The other is that there is a differential effect of stress on various T-cell populations.

Other studies have focused on a mouse model of EAE since the mouse, in contrast to the rat, will often have a relapsing course of disease which is more relevant to the multiple sclerosis disease process. B10.PL mice have been exposed to stress in the form of restraint for 12 hours per day. Compared with control animals which exhibit all of the manifestations of the disease, the stressed animals have no symptoms. This is also reflected in the lymph nodes and spleen, which are dramatically smaller in size. There is also a profound decrease in the number of antigen reactive cells in the stressed mice compared with the controls.

In summary, stress has an inhibitory effect on EAE in both male and female Lewis rats, with female rats exhibiting much greater suppression. This would be expected since the females have higher levels of glucocorticoids compared with males. Evidence has also been generated suggesting that stress works through antigen processing or possibly has a differential effect on T-cell populations since EAE induced with MBP but not with the 68-88 peptide is suppressed. In a relapsing mouse model of EAE, suppression of long term disease as well as reduced cellularity and diminished frequency of MBP-reactive cells can be observed.

References

Griffin, A.C. and Whitacre, C.C. (1991). Sex and strain differences in the circadian rhythm fluctuation of endocrine and immune function in the rat: Implications for rodent models of autoimmune disease. J. Neuroimmunol. 35:53-64.

Griffin, A.C., Lo, W.D., Wolny, A.C. and Whitacre, C.C. (1993). Suppression of experimental autoimmune encephalomyelitis by restraint stress: Sex differences. J. Neuroimmunol. 44:103-116.

Levine, S., Strebel, R., Wenk, E. and Harman, P. (1962). Suppression of experimental allergic encephalomyelitis by stress. Proc. Soc. Exp. Biol. Med. 109:294-298.

MacPhee, I., Antoni, F. and Mason, D. (1989). Spontaneous recovery of rats from experimental allergic encephalomyelitis is dependent on regulation of the immune system by endogenous adrenal corticosteroids. J. Exp. Med. 169:431-445.

Paterson, P.Y. and Swanborg, R.H. (1988). Demyelinating diseases of the central and peripheral nervous systems. In: Immunological Diseases (Samter, M., Talmage, D.W., Frank, M.M., Austen, K.F. and Claman, H.N., Eds.) Boston: Little Brown & Co. (pp. 1877-1916).

DEVELOPMENTAL INFLUENCES
UPON RESPIRATORY DISEASE

Presented by

Thomas Boyce, M.D.

The effects of stress in adults can be far-reaching. But this represents the tip of a much larger biological iceberg when considering the impact that stress may have during early development. Physiological processes which are taking place may be altered in ways that will have long-lasting, if not permanent effects on the ability of the host to respond to a number of environmental factors.

There are a number of events that occur during childhood that are challenging and sometimes stressful. These early stressful events in the life of both the child and the family are associated in a modest, but nonetheless graded, dose-response manner with a variety of morbidities, including streptococcal illnesses, injuries, respiratory infections, and all-cause illness and hospitalizations (Meyer and Haggerty, 1962; Horwitz et al., 1988; Padilla et al., 1976; Boyce et al., 1977; Graham et al., 1986; Beautrais et al., 1982). One of the reasons for the unevenness in stress-illness associations is probably the large amount of variability inherent in individuals' psychobiologic responses to stressful or challenging circumstances. Some conceive of the variability as 'noise'; others as 'music'. The latter seek to characterize and explore the differences in biological responsiveness in order to understand better the multitude of organismic variables that can have an impact on the link between mind and disease resistance.

Starting School and Respiratory Illness

The model often chosen for studies examining the impact of early stressful developmental events and health is the transition associated with starting school. This is an event that happens to virtually all five year olds and is often accompanied by an abrupt increase in respiratory illness in the months following school entry. Undoubtedly, this is related at least in part to a host of new pathogenic agents to which children are exposed upon entering primary school. It may also be related, however, to the observation that salivary cortisol is significantly increased from one week prior to kindergarten entry to one week following kindergarten entry (Boyce et al., 1995a). Part of the increased respiratory illness susceptibility could thus be triggered by the changes in a potentially immunosuppressive steroid hormone. An operating assumption is that the phenomenon of kindergarten entry is a normative and universal childhood stressor. The working study hypothesis is that children will show extensive individual differences in their immune responses to the stress of starting school, and that the individual differences in immune "reactivity" will be associated with subsequent respiratory illness incidence.

Immunologic Changes

Specifically, it has been proposed that children showing the greatest immunoresponsivity to the stress of starting school will have higher respiratory illness incidence in the 12 weeks following school entry. One week prior to kindergarten entry, a blood sample was obtained for the purpose of measuring CD4, CD8 and CD19 cells. In addition, the ability of lymphocytes to respond to pokeweed mitogen was assessed and antibody titers against the pneumococcal vaccine were measured. Two weeks later the children were brought back, during which time they were carefully assessed for their degree of stress associated with this life transition. This was then followed by a 12 week period of respiratory illness surveillance using questionnaires and interviews with parents on an every-other-week basis, for a total of six reports. Unexpectedly, a natural stressor occurred during the mid-point of the study when an earthquake registering 7.2 on the Richter scale occurred in the Bay area of San Francisco. The effects of this stressor have been assessed in conjunction with the more normative event.

As would be expected, there was a great deal of variability with respect to the various immune system measures. There was, however, a change in the incidence of respiratory illness from before to after the earthquake (Boyce et al., 1993). There was also considerable variability with respect to this measure, as well as changes in behavioral problems from before to after the earthquake. When the immune measures are combined into an immune reactivity score, there is a highly significant correlation of .58 between such scores and post-earthquake illness incidence. When the change in respiratory illness incidence is examined as a function of the earthquake's impact upon parents, it has been found that children with high immune reactivity differ strikingly from those with low immune reactivity. High immune reactivity subjects whose parents report high stress from the earthquake have the greatest accelerations in respiratory illness incidence of any of the children in the study. On the other hand, children with low immune reactivity show a slight decline in respiratory illness incidence when the impact on the parent has been high (Boyce et al., 1993).

Stress Intensity and Host Responsiveness

This ongoing study reveals that there is considerable variability in immune function measures following kindergarten entry, although no child had immunologic measures outside the normal range. Second, there is substantial variability in respiratory illness incidence surrounding the earthquake, although no increase in illness incidence has been found in the post-earthquake period for the sample taken as a whole. However, controlling for the effect of immune reactivity, the degree of earthquake-related parental stress is significantly predictive of alterations in illness incidence (Boyce et al., 1993). There is also up-regulation of helper-suppressor ratios and lymphocyte responsiveness to pokeweed mitogens, which together are significantly predictive of increases in illness incidence (Boyce et al., 1995b). The implication of these studies is that the health effects of psychologically stressful events are best predicted by an interaction between the intensity of the environmental stressor and biological reactivity of the individual host.

With respect to the more general study findings independent of the earthquake, it has been shown that the highest illness incidences are found in children with the combination of high immune responsivity and high stress families (Boyce et al., 1995b). What has been unexpected is that the lowest illness rates in the study are in those children with high immune responsivity and low stress, but living in highly supportive family environments. Thus, children with high immune reactivity experienced either the highest rates of respiratory illness or the lowest rates of respiratory illness, depending upon the inherent stressfulness of their family environment.

Cardiovascular Changes and Immunity

There is evidence of a link between immune system changes and cardiovascular parameters. The literature reveals that there may be a relationship between immune responsiveness in a laboratory setting and cardiovascular responsiveness in this setting. A decline in mitogen responsiveness following a period of laboratory stress is correlated, for example, with high cardiovascular reactivity (Manuck et al., 1991). This linkage between the cardiovascular and immune system has been assessed experimentally. Children have been exposed to a series of developmentally challenging tasks during a 20 minute period, and during that time, heart rate and blood pressure have been assessed to allow grouping into either high or low reactivity groups. The degree of stress experienced within the childcare setting has also been measured. Respiratory illness incidence has been determined over a six month period in children experiencing low versus high levels of stress within the childcare setting. Among the children showing high mean arterial pressure reactivity, there is a positive slope going from low to high stress situations, and among the low arterial pressure reactivity children, a negative slope going from low to high stress settings.

In summary, these data would suggest that school is a normative developmental transition that is capable of activating the hypothalamic-pituitary-adrenal axis and producing other stress-related physiological effects. Second, individual differences are quite striking in the degree of immune responsiveness to a normative stressor. Third, the differences in immune responsivity seem to be predictive of respiratory illness incidence in a context-specific manner. And fourth, the exaggerated immune responsivity seems to increase illness incidence in high stress settings, but may actually decrease illness in low stress settings.

References

Beautrais, A., Fergusson, D. and Shannon, F. (1982). Life events and childhood morbidity: A prospective study. Pediatrics 70:935-940.

Boyce, W.T., Jensen, E.W., Cassel, J.C., Collier, A.M., Smith, A.H. and Ramey, C.T. (1977). Influence of life events and family routines on childhood respiratory tract illness. Pediatrics 60:609-615.

Boyce, W.T., Chesterman, E.A., Martin, N., Folkman, S., Cohen, F. and Wara, D. (1993). Immunologic changes occurring at kindergarten entry predict respiratory illnesses following the Loma Prieta earthquake. J. Dev. Behav. Pediatr. 14:296-303.

Boyce, W.T., Adams, S., Tschann, J.M., Cohen, F., Wara, D. and Gunnar, M.R. (1995a). Adrenocortical and behavioral predictors of immune responses to starting school. Pediatrics Res. 38:1009-1017.

Boyce, W.T., Chesney, M., Alkon-Leonard, A. et al. (1995b). Psychobiologic reactivity to stress and childhood respiratory illnesses: Results of two prospective studies. Psychosomatic Medicine 57:411-422.

Graham, N., Douglas, R.M. and Ryan, P. (1986). Stress and acute respiratory infection. Epidemiol. 124:389-401.

Horwitz, S.M., Morgenstern, H., DiPietro, L. and Morrison, C.L. (1988). Determinants of pediatric injuries. AJDC 142:605-611.

Manuck, S.B., Cohen, S., Rabin, B.S., Muldoon, M.F. and Bachen, E.A. (1991). Individual differences in cellular immune response to stress. Psychol. Sci. 2:111-115.

Meyer, R.J. and Haggerty, R.J. (1962). Streptococcal infections in families: Factors altering individual susceptibility. Pediatrics 29:539-549.

Padilla, E.R., Rohsenow, D.J. and Bergman, A.B. (1976). Predicting accident frequency in children. Pediatrics 58:223-226.

BEHAVIORAL EFFECTS OF VIRUS INFECTIONS

Presented by

Linda S. Crnic, Ph.D.

Mechanisms of Action

It is well documented that viruses can influence behavior (reviewed in Hart, 1988; Crnic, 1991). Several mechanisms for the effects are possible. Some viruses are neurotrophic and are capable of destroying tissue in the brain, via either a direct cytopathic effect of the virus or the immune response to the virus. Viruses can also disrupt normal development, altering neuron migration and structure. Viral products, such as proteins, can alter brain function, either directly or through alteration of host gene expression. Viruses can also alter behavior via their effects upon endocrine organs. Finally, the immune system can alter behavior through the generation of autoantibodies or via cytokines released in response to infection.

Direct Effects

Encephalitis produced by herpes simplex virus alters the brain and behavior differently depending upon the genetic make-up of the host. Thus, NYA:Nylar mice develop hyperactivity while NYA:SW mice develop learning deficits (McFarland and Hotchin, 1983). While destruction of tissue in adult mice is dramatic, in immature animals the development of the brain can be altered by virus infection (e.g., Oster-Granite and Herndon, 1976). Neuronal migration, branching and spine number can be affected. For example, GP120 from HIV retards behavioral development and decreases branching of corticopyramidal neurons (Hill et al., 1993). Herpesviruses can interfere with cerebellar development and induce hyperactivity (Crnic and Pizer, 1988). Viral interference with granule cell migration in the cerebellum is not confined to herpesviruses, for example, Tamiami virus in rats produces even more extreme effects (Gilden et al., 1974), as do many perinatal toxins.

Toxic Effects of Virus Gene Products

When a cell is infected by a virus, the virus shuts off the host cell protein production and directs the cell to make viral proteins and nucleic acids. Some of these products can have adverse effects on cells even in the absence of whole virus particles. For example, using transgenic models, expression of the bel region of the human foamy retrovirus leads to encephalopathy in the CA-3 layer of the hippocampus and telencephalic cortex in mice (Bothe et al., 1991). Expression of an envelope gene of the Cas Br E murine retrovirus in transgenic mice led to compromised balance and muscle strength (Kay et al., 1993). Giulian et al. (1993) demonstrated that the HIV-1 GP120 binding to CD4 on mononuclear phagocytes causes them to release a neurotoxin which acts through NMDA receptors to damage the brain. Viral proteins can also mimic host proteins to alter function of the brain (e.g., Komiyama et al., 1994). In each of these examples, it is clear that a single viral product is responsible for the toxic effects.

Virus Effects on Gene Regulation

As noted above, viruses subvert the cells' machinery to replicate themselves, but even non-replicating viruses can alter a cell's gene expression and thus phenotype. For example, beta-adrenergic receptors are reduced 50% in C6 rat glioma cells following exposure to lymphocytic choriomeningitis virus (LCMV) (Koschel and Muenzel, 1980). In animals, this virus produces a chronic persistent infection that does not kill the cell but changes its production of growth factors. For example, this virus, in some strains of mice, reduces somatostatin levels. In other strains of mice, LCMV decreases the ability of pituitary cells to secrete growth hormone (Oldstone et al., 1985), resulting in extremely small mice. In other cases, viruses can trigger the expression of certain peptides. For example, the expression of the neuropeptide galanin is increased in dorsal root ganglion cells during infection with herpes simplex virus (Henken and Martin, 1992). Since viruses can regulate gene expression, they can impact neurotransmitter expression and the behavior of the organism. Lycke and Roos (1974) demonstrated many years ago that herpes encephalitis resulted in animals becoming hyperactive as the infection progressed. This was correlated with increased neurotransmitter metabolites. Thus, in this instance up- and not down-regulation of neurotransmitters was observed.

Autoantibodies

Another means by which viruses can influence the central nervous system (CNS) and behavior is through the generation of autoantibodies. Several possible mechanisms might enable viruses to trigger autoimmune disease. Molecular mimicry might occur when there is cross-reactivity between viral and host antigens (e.g., Oldstone, 1989). In addition, viruses might display normally sequestered host antigens, thereby enabling them to elicit an immune response. This mechanism might explain some of the demyelinating diseases, since enveloped viruses bud through the host cell membrane, thus carrying with them host membrane (e.g., myelin) proteins on their surface. Viruses might modify antigens to render them more antigenic, or block tolerance to them.

Autoantibodies can alter behavior by leading to immune attack on CNS tissue, by promoting the expression of cytokines that can alter behavior, and by attacking peripheral organs, such as endocrine organs, that may influence behavior.

Direct cytopathic effects on endocrine organs, or immune attack on endocrine organs due to autoantibody formation can lead to altered hormone levels and thus altered behavior. As noted above, effects of viruses on gene expression can also alter the production of peptides such as growth hormone (e.g., de la Torre and Oldstone, 1992). It is also well documented that glucocorticoids can be activated by virus infection via cytokine release (e.g., Dunn et al., 1989). Cytokines can also alter thyroid and gonadal hormones.

Cytokines

Cytokines released by the body to fight virus infections can have profound effects on behavior, especially the set of evolutionarily conserved 'sickness behaviors'. Benjamin Hart (1988) viewed these changes in behavior as integral to fighting pathogens. Organisms must generate a fever and decrease plasma iron concentrations to impede the multiplication of bacteria and viruses. Food intake must be decreased to lower plasma nutrient concentrations at the same time that an energy demanding fever is mounted. Thus, to conserve energy, activity and non-essential energy expenditures such as grooming are minimized and time spent asleep is increased. This integrated system of behavioral changes, while it enables us to fight pathogens, has implications for human mental health. This set of sickness behaviors in many ways resemble those behavioral changes seen during depression. Thus, it might be useful to consider clinical depression not as a malfunction of the brain, but rather as the inappropriate activation of a pattern of behavioral changes that have evolved to help us survive infection.

Depression of behavior is quite evident following the injection of interferon-alpha, a prominent antiviral cytokine (e.g., Segall and Crnic, 1990). Injecting this cytokine in amounts that typically occur during infection both lowers the amount of activity and shifts the daily peak of activity. The onset of REM sleep is advanced in experimental primates exposed to interferon-alpha (Reite et al., 1987), a finding seen in humans during clinical depression. In human subjects a profound change in mood state occurs following exposure to interferon-alpha (Crnic et al., unpublished data) that is similar to the mood changes that occur during illness. It is noteworthy that interferon-alpha is able to produce a delayed and dose-dependent increase in corticosteroid levels in mice that is observable only with species appropriate interferon.

Cytokines can also have toxic effects. Melvin Heyes (e.g., Heyes et al., 1990) has shown that the interferons produced in response to virus infection up-regulate indoleamine dioxygenase, which shunts tryptophan down the kynurenin pathway, leading to the production of quinolinic acid, a neurotoxin.

Finally, it is important to consider the possibility that some of the cytokines may affect behavior by acting not within the CNS but in the periphery of the body, either by signaling via the peripheral nervous system (e.g., Watkins et al., 1994) or via direct effects upon tissue. Muscles isolated from mice that had been exposed to interferon-alpha as well as muscles from untreated mice that had interferon-alpha added to the testing bath had altered responses to electrostimulation. Both contraction force and the rate of fatigue of the muscles was altered, suggesting that the cytokine might produce fatigue by acting in the periphery as well as in the brain (Crnic, unpublished data).

Cytokines have a wide variety of effects on physiological and behavioral processes. Had they not been discovered first in the context of the immune system, they might be considered neuromodulators, reproductive hormones or embryonic growth factors. They clearly serve as a conduit via which viruses can influence many aspects of behavior.

References

Bothe, K., Aguzzi, A., Lassmann, H., Rethwilm, A. and Horak, I. (1991). Progressive encephalopathy and myopathy in transgenic mice expressing human foamy virus genes. Science 253:555-557.

Crnic, L.S. and Pizer, L.I. (1988). Behavioral effects of neonatal herpes simplex type 1 infection of mice. Neurotoxicology and Teratology 10:381-386.

Crnic, L.S. (1991). Behavioral consequences of virus infection. In: Psychoneuroimmunology, 2nd Ed. (Ader, R., Felten, D.L. and Cohen, N., Eds.) San Diego: Academic Press (pp. 749-769).

de la Torre, J.C. and Oldstone, M.B.A. (1992). Selective disruption of growth hormone transcription machinery by viral infection. Proc. Natl. Acad. Sci. USA 89:9939-9943.

Dunn, A.J., Powell, M.L., Meitin, C. and Small, P.A. Jr. (1989). Virus infection as a stressor: Influenza virus elevates plasma concentrations of corticosterone, and brain concentrations of MHPG and tryptophan. Physiol. Behav. 45:591-594.

Gilden, D.H., Friedman, H.M. and Nathanson, N. (1974). Tamiami virus induced cerebellar heterotopia. J. Neuropathol. Exp. Neurol. 33:29-41.

Giulian, D., Wendt, E., Vaca, K. and Noonan, C.A. (1993). The envelope glycoprotein of human immunodeficiency virus type 1 stimulates release of neurotoxins from monocytes. Proc. Natl. Acad. Sci. USA 90:2769-2773.

Hart, B.L. (1988). Biological basis of the behavior of sick animals. Neurosci. Biobehav. Rev. 12:123-137.

Henken, D.B. and Martin, J.R. (1992). Herpes simplex virus infection induces a selective increase in the proportion of galanin-positive neurons in mouse sensory ganglia. Exp. Neurol. 118:195-203.

Heyes, M.P., Brew, B.J., Price, R.W. and Markey, S.P. (1990). Cerebrospinal fluid quinolinic acid and kynurenic acid in HIV-1 infection. Neurotoxicity of Excitatory Amino Acids 4:217-221.

Hill, J.M., Mervis, R.F., Avidor, R., Moody, T.W. and Brenneman, D.E. (1993). HIV envelope protein-induced neuronal damage and retardation of behavioral development in rat neonates. Brain Res. 603:222-233.

Kay, D.G., Gravel, C., Pothier, F., Laperriere, A., Robitaille, Y. and Jolicoeur, P. (1993). Neurological disease induced in transgenic mice expressing the *env* gene of the Cas-Br-E murine retrovirus. Proc. Natl. Acad. Sci. USA 90:4538-4542.

Komiyama, T., Ray, C.A., Pickup, D.J., Howard, A.D., Thornberry, N.A., Peterson, E.P. and Salvesen, G. (1994). Inhibition of interleukin-1 beta converting enzyme by the cowpox virus serpin CrmA - An example of cross-class inhibition. J. Biol. Chem. 269:19331-19337.

Koschel, K. and Muenzel, P. (1980). Persistent paramyxovirus infections and behaviour of beta-adrenergic receptors in C-6 rat glioma cells. J. Gen. Virol. 47:513-517.

Lycke, E. and Roos, B.-E. (1974). Influence of changes in brain monoamine metabolism on behavior of herpes simplex-infected mice. J. Neurol. Sci. 22:277-289.

McFarland, D.J. and Hotchin, J. (1983). Host genetics and the behavioral sequelae to herpes encephalitis in mice. Physiol. Behav. 30:881-884.

Oldstone, M.B.A., Ahmed, R., Buchmeier, M.J., Blount, P. and Tishon, A. (1985). Perturbation of differentiated functions during viral infection *in vivo* I. Relationship of lymphocytic choriomeningitis virus and host strains to growth hormone deficiency. Virol. 142:158-174.

Oldstone, M.B. (1989). Molecular mimicry as a mechanism for the cause and a probe uncovering etiologic agent(s) of autoimmune disease. Curr. Top. Microbiol. Immunol. 145:127-135.

Oster-Granite, M.L. and Herndon, R.M. (1976). The pathogenesis of parvovirus-induced cerebellar hypoplasia in the Syrian hamster, *Mesocricetus auratus*. Fluorescent antibody, foliation, cytoarchitectonic, golgi and electron microscopic studies. J. Comp. Neurol. 169:481-522.

Reite, M., Laudenslager, M., Jones, J., Crnic, L. and Kaemingk, K. (1987). Interferon decreases REM latency. Biol. Psychiatry 22:104-107.

Segall, M.A. and Crnic, L.S. (1990). An animal model for the behavioral effects of interferon. Behav. Neurosci. 104:612-618.

Watkins, L.R., Wiertelak, E.P., Goehler, L.E., Mooney-Heiberger, K., Martinez, J., Furness, L., Smith, K.P. and Maier, S.F. (1994). Neurocircuitry of illness-induced hyperalgesia. Brain Res. 639:283-299.

NEGATIVE EMOTIONS AS PREDICTORS OF RESPIRATORY SYMPTOMS

Presented by

Sheldon Cohen, Ph.D.

Design Issues

Research investigating the role of negative emotions in immune system-mediated diseases has seldom distinguished between emotions as states and emotions as traits. For example, when people report that they are depressed, does it simply mean that they are depressed only at that moment, or are they depressed most of the time? The former is a state condition, while the latter a trait condition. State and trait conditions may have different implications for the immune response, and it is only by distinguishing between them that we will be able to understand how an emotional response influences immune-mediated diseases.

In addition to distinguishing between the nature of the psychological variables, it is important that disease outcomes be assessed with biological markers of pathology rather than subject self-report. This is because psychological characteristics can result in biases in sensitivity to and reporting of symptoms of an illness (Cohen and Williamson, 1991). People experiencing negative emotions are more likely to pay attention to their bodies and to define ambiguous physical sensations as symptoms indicative of disease (Cohen and Williamson, 1991; Pennebaker, 1982). This can be independent of any pathophysiology and be attributable entirely to how people view their symptoms. Thus, it is important for studies to provide biological markers of disease and hence allow researchers to distinguish between psychological effects on self-report versus effects on underlying pathophysiology.

245

Negative Emotions and Symptom Reporting

Negative emotional states and traits have been assessed in healthy individuals who were then exposed to either an influenza virus or a rhinovirus to determine whether these psychological characteristics influence the severity of upper respiratory infections (Cohen et al., 1995). Only those who were both infected and exhibited symptoms were considered. The questions that were posed were (a) do negative emotions influence symptom reporting for people who have colds, and (b) if they do, is it because of an underlying emotional trait or because of a current emotional state? Another issue is whether the emotional influences that correlate with progression of illness are due to biases in symptom reporting or to pathophysiological changes.

The experimental model is as follows. Prior to being exposed to a virus, trait and state negative emotions (anxiety, depression, anger and fatigue) and upper respiratory symptoms were measured by questionnaire, antibodies to the inoculation virus were assessed in blood samples, and current infectious status determined by looking for the inoculation virus in nasal secretions. Following the collection of these samples and information, each subject was exposed (using nasal drops) to either the rhinovirus or influenza virus. Daily for six days following viral inoculation, follow-up nasal washes and self-reported symptoms were collected, as well as the amount (weight) of mucous the subject produced. Twenty-one days later, a second blood sample was taken to assess the production of antibody to the inoculation virus. Seventy-one subjects were used with a mean age of 25.8 and 51% being female. All were physically healthy, not pregnant, and HIV negative.

To assess 'trait' negative emotion, people were asked to what extent each of a series of adjectives described how they are "most of the time." To assess 'state' emotion they rated the same adjectives but instead were asked the degree to which they experienced these feelings within "the past 24 hours." Since the measures of anxiety, depression, fatigue, and anger were all highly intercorrelated, they were combined into single measures of state and trait negative emotion. Eight symptoms were used in the symptom protocol, including congestion, runny nose and sneezing. Daily mucous weights were used as a marker of how sick the subjects were. By comparing their symptom reports with mucous weights, it was possible to compare individuals' self-reports with an objective marker of pathophysiology. In order to meet criteria to be included in the study, all subjects had to report at least two more symptoms than they reported before they were exposed to a virus, and had to be positive on one of the two biological indicators of infection -- antibodies produced against the particular virus that they had been exposed to, or viral replication (shedding) in nasal secretions. In the analysis, we controlled for a number of factors including whether or not the person had been exposed previously to the virus, their age, gender, level of education, and whether they received the rhinovirus or the influenza virus.

The results revealed that people who score higher on trait negative emotion report more symptoms over the course of the cold. This is also true of those individuals who are high with respect to state negative emotion. A regression analysis revealed that state and trait are independent predictors of symptoms, even though their associations with symptom reporting are basically the same. Moreover, state and trait emotion were not associated with symptom reporting before exposure to the virus, only after persons were infected. This indicates that these psychological variables influence response to illness but do not result in reports of upper respiratory symptoms outside of the illness.

A remaining question is whether the negative emotion is associated with increased sensitivity to true symptoms of illness or simply with reports of symptoms with no pathophysiological basis. Those with higher levels of state negative emotion produced more mucous over the course of the trial than those with lower levels. However, trait negative emotion was not associated with this marker of pathophysiology. Moreover, path analysis was consistent with a model in which state negative emotion influenced symptom reporting through its effects on the pathophysiology of the disease (as indicated by mucous weights), but that the effect of trait negative emotion on mucous weights was independent of disease pathophysiology and hence attributable to biases in symptom reporting.

In summary, trait and state negative emotion were both associated with more health complaints of people with respiratory illness. In the case of state negative emotion, the association is attributable to underlying illness, and in the case of trait negative emotion, the association is attributable to psychological or cognitive biases in reporting symptoms.

References

Cohen, S. and Williamson, G. (1991). Stress and infectious disease in humans. Psychological Bulletin 109:5-24.

Cohen, S., Doyle, W.J., Skoner, D.P., Fireman, P., Gwaltney, J. and Newsom, J. (1995). State and trait negative affect as predictors of objective and subjective symptoms of respiratory viral infections. Journal of Personality and Social Psychology 68:159-169.

Pennebaker, J.W. (1982). The Psychology of Physical Symptoms. New York: Springer-Verlag.

IMMUNOLOGIC DEFENSES AGAINST CANCER

Presented by

Ronald B. Herberman, M.D.

Cellular Mechanisms

Before understanding how stress might impact upon the progression of cancer, it is first necessary to understand those aspects of the immune system that are integral in modulating the progression of this disease.

If one considers all of the various components of the immune system that might be involved in defense against tumors, then one could postulate a variety of potential mechanisms. There are the specific adaptive components of the immune response mediated by T-cells and by antibodies. There are also non-specific natural components which would include macrophages, monocytes, and natural killer (NK) cells. It is quite clear that when tumor associated antigens are present and the tumor is immunogenic, a T-cell-mediated immune response will be elicited (Herberman, 1991). This, in fact, is probably the most potent mechanism that exists for the resistance against both the development of tumors as well as the progression and metastatic spread. It should be noted, however, that it has been very difficult despite using a wide variety of tumor models to conveniently and reproducibly demonstrate T-cell-mediated immunity against tumors in humans (Herberman, 1991). In addition, there currently is a paucity of evidence that neuroendocrine or central nervous system effects can influence tumor growth via their effects on T-lymphocytes.

Macrophages are capable of killing tumors, especially when the macrophages are activated by various cytokines such as interferon-gamma (Herberman, 1991). These phagocytic cells may also interact with T-cells to induce more specific killing. But it is important to realize that macrophages can be viewed as a double-edged sword and that under certain circumstances they can be counterproductive and function essentially as suppressor cells (Kirchner et al., 1976). As was true with T-lymphocytes, there is very little evidence that neuroendocrine mediators may impact in a significant way upon the ability of macrophages to combat tumors, but such a possibility cannot be ruled out.

Natural Killer Cells

Of the various cell types that have been implicated in combating tumors, the one that is most likely to be influenced by psychological variables and by the conduits that link the brain with the immune system is the NK cell. These are lymphocytes that have characteristic morphology of large granular cells. However, they have unique genetic and cell surface characteristics which clearly distinguish them from both T-cells and B-cells (Whiteside and Herberman, 1994). They can be sub-categorized on the basis of various cell surface markers as well as biological function. They can act as killers against various tumor cells including those which T-cells are not capable of acting against. They also are capable of producing cytokines. However, the bulk of evidence suggests that they play an important role against metastatic spread of tumors (Whiteside and Herberman, 1994). These data have been forthcoming from studies that have shown that whenever there is low NK activity there is more aggressive metastasis of tumors (Whiteside and Herberman, 1994). Conversely, when there is evidence of increased NK activity there tends to be resistance against metastasis. This has been convincingly demonstrated by using adoptive transfer of purified NK cells into animals with low NK activity. In an animal model of malignant melanoma in which the NK cell activity is selectively depressed by an antibody, multiple metastatic lesions occur on the surface of the liver. Adoptive transfer of NK cells reduces this metastasis (Whiteside and Herberman, 1994). While this is an experimental model using the B16 melanoma in mice, there is increasing evidence to indicate that the same type of relationship holds for clinical populations as well. In patients with breast cancer as well as head and neck cancer, there is an inverse correlation between levels of NK activity and the development of metastasis (Whiteside and Herberman, 1994). Upon long-term follow-up, those individuals who have problems with metastasis are usually those with low NK cell activity.

Immuno-Surveillance

A focus of intense research over the years has been the role that cells of the immune system play in immune surveillance (Herberman, 1983). These would include a variety of cell types, not just NK cells. The hypothesis is that the immune system plays a central role in resistance against the development of tumors. Consequently, one would predict that under conditions of immune deficiency there will be more tumors developing and that the immune deficiency would precede tumor development. Addressing this question is logistically very difficult. This is especially true of human models because of the long period of time that one would have to survey a population in order to obtain adequate data. It has been possible to partially address this question in a population of individuals immunosuppressed for organ transplant. In such individuals there is a very high incidence of post-transplant lymphoproliferative disease (Ho, 1995). This has been observed in 10-25% of children and between 3-5% of adults. Interestingly, the primary risk factor is being seronegative for Epstein-Barr virus (EBV) at the time of transplant (Ho, 1995). This suggests that EBV plays a central role in the pathogenesis of lymphoproliferative disorders. That is, if a transplant patient has not been previously exposed to this virus, they will be at very high risk for lymphoproliferative disease when they are immunosuppressed in order to minimize rejection of their transplanted organ. From 10 to 30% of these individuals will develop tumors within one year. It is interesting that when the immunosuppression is stopped, in about half the cases the tumor spontaneously regresses (Ho, 1995). This observation has given rise to a series of studies to search for psychological variables that might help predict who is more likely to benefit by having the immunosuppression stopped. There are several potential mechanisms whereby the central nervous system might impact upon the progression of tumors. Virtually all of the neuroendocrine and autonomic pathways which are known to impact on various aspects of the immune system have to be considered, especially since NK cells not only bear receptors for but also are responsive to a number of brain controlled chemicals (Weigent and Blalock, 1987).

References

Herberman, R.B. (1983). Immune surveillance hypothesis: Updated formulation and possible effector mechanisms. In: Progess in Immunology, V. (Tada, T., Ed.) Japan: Academic Press (pp. 1157-1167).

Herberman, R.B. (1991). Principles of tumor immunology. In: American Cancer Society Textbook of Clinical Oncology. (Holleb, A.I., Fink, D.J. and Murphy, G.P., Eds.) Atlanta: American Cancer Society (pp. 69-79).

Ho, M. (1995). Risk factors and pathogenesis of posttransplant lymphoproliferative disorders. Transplantation Pro. 27:38-40.

Kirchner, H., Glaser, M., Holden, H.T., Fernbach, B.R. and Herberman, R.B. (1976). Suppressor cells in tumor bearing mice and rats. Biomedicine 24:371-374.

Weigent, D.A. and Blalock, J.E. (1987). Interactions between the neuroendocrine and immune systems: Common hormones and receptors. Immunol. Rev. 100:79.

Whiteside, T.L. and Herberman, R.B. (1994). Human natural killer cells in health and disease: Biology and therapeutic potential. In: Clinical Immunotherapeutics, 1st Edition. (Adis, E., Ed.) Adis International Ltd. (pp. 56-66).

THE EFFECTS OF CLASSICAL CONDITIONING AND STRESS ON IMMUNE FUNCTION IN CANCER PATIENTS

Presented by

Dana Bovbjerg, Ph.D.

Historical Perspective

The seminal experiments of Pavlov early in the century established that physiological processes can be altered by associative learning (Pavlov, 1927). In Pavlov's classic experiments, dogs learned to associate the ringing of a bell with presentation of meat, such that after several pairings, they began to salivate at the sound of the bell. In Pavlov's terminology, the bell served as a conditioned stimulus which, after pairing with an unconditioned stimulus (the meat) for salivation (the unconditioned response) began to elicit a conditioned response (salivation). It should be noted that this conditioned salivation occurred in anticipation of the meat and served to wet the mouth of the dog in preparation for the ingestion of food.

Conditioning in Patients Receiving Chemotherapy

The basic principles of conditioning established by Pavlov have applicability well beyond the dog laboratory. For example, many individuals receiving repeated outpatient chemotherapy for cancer develop what has been called "anticipatory" nausea. After several experiences of nausea and vomiting following chemotherapy infusions, these patients experience nausea in the clinic as they await subsequent infusions. Considerable research now supports the view that this anticipatory nausea is a conditioned response to clinic cues (conditioned stimuli) previously paired with cytotoxic chemotherapy (unconditioned stimulus) that induced nausea

(Carey and Burish, 1988; Morrow and Dobkin, 1988; Bovbjerg et al., 1992).

The literature on conditioned nausea raised the possibility that patients may also develop conditioned changes to other side effects of chemotherapy, including changes in immune function, as a result of the pairing of clinic cues with the immunosuppressive side effects of the cytotoxic agents typically used in treatment. If so, one would expect to see "anticipatory" changes in immune measures when patients return to a clinic where they previously received treatment. As a first test of this hypothesis, we compared immune measures in blood samples obtained in the clinic to samples collected in the patients' homes several days before their fourth infusion of chemotherapy for ovarian cancer (Bovbjerg et al., 1990). Results indicated that patients not only experienced higher levels of nausea in the clinic, but they also showed changes in measures of immune function such as *in vitro* proliferative responses to mitogenic challenge. Because patients also experienced higher levels of anxiety in the clinic, we considered the possibility that stress-induced immune suppression could have been responsible for the anticipatory immune changes, but found no statistical support for this alternative mechanism (Bovbjerg et al., 1990). These results are consistent with a now voluminous literature based upon animal models, which has conclusively demonstrated that a wide range of immunologic activity can be modified by classical conditioning (Ader and Cohen, 1994).

Based on the conditioning literature in animals, we have recently developed a conditioning model with which to explore the impact of associative learning on a variety of side effects of chemotherapy for cancer. In this experimental model, patients are randomly assigned to either receive a distinctive beverage immediately before each chemotherapy infusion (Experimental Group) or not (Control Group). After several such pairings of the beverage (putative conditioned stimulus) with chemotherapy (putative unconditioned stimulus), we have found strong evidence that patients develop several independent conditioned responses, including: conditioned taste aversion (Schwartz et al., in press), conditioned nausea (Bovbjerg et al., 1992), conditioned emotional distress (Jacobsen et al., 1995), and initial results also indicate conditioned changes in immune function. The relations among these conditioned responses and their relations to other psychological variables (e.g., emotional distress) have yet to be elucidated, but are likely to prove complex. Immune defenses in patients receiving chemotherapy for cancer may be altered by the cancer itself, by chemotherapy, by stress, by conditioned emotional distress, by conditioned immune effects, as well as a host of other demographic, behavioral, and medical variables. Experimental models of conditioned effects and stress effects, which can be investigated under controlled conditions may provide a strong approach to unraveling some of these complexities. Our ongoing studies are now focusing on the neuroendocrine mechanisms that may be responsible for conditioned effects in chemotherapy patients, as well as the cellular mechanisms underlying the conditioned changes in immune function.

Clinical Implications of Psychobehavioral Influences

Cancer researchers have speculated for some time that psychological and behavioral influences on immune defenses may have an impact on the incidence and progression of neoplastic disease (Bovbjerg, 1991). As yet, data are scant (Bovbjerg, 1994); although independent research has demonstrated: 1) psychological effects on cancer, 2) psychological effects on immune function, and 3) relations between immune defenses and cancer, few studies have attempted to concurrently assess all three domains. There has also been little research attention paid to the possibility that psychobehavioral effects on the immune system may have clinical implications for infectious complications associated with cancer and its treatment, which remain an important source of morbidity and mortality in these patients (Chanock, 1993). The potential clinical significance of psychobehavioral influences on infection in cancer patients, who are typically immunocompromised by treatment, is supported by the large literature linking psychobehavioral variables to infection in otherwise healthy individuals (Bovbjerg and Stone, 1995).

The evidence thus strongly suggests that psychobehavioral influences on immune function in cancer patients may prove to have important clinical consequences both for cancer and for the infectious complications of cancer and its treatment. We must now await the results of rigorous interdisciplinary research to know the full impact of psychobehavioral influences.

References

Ader, R. and Cohen, N. (1994). CNS-immune system interactions: Conditioning phenomena. Behavioral and Brain Sciences 8:379-394.

Bovbjerg, D.H. (1991). Psychoneuroimmunology - Implications for Oncology? Cancer 67:828-832.

Bovbjerg, D.H. (1994). Psychoimmunology: A critical analysis of the implications for clinical oncology in the 21st century. In: The Psychoimmunology of Human Cancer. (Lewis, C.E., O'Sullivan, C. and Barraclough, J., Eds.) Oxford: Oxford University Press (pp. 417-426).

Bovbjerg, D.H. and Stone, A.A. (1995). Stress and upper respiratory infection. In: Psychoneuroimmunology and Infection. (Friedman, H., Klein, T. and Friedman, A.L., Eds.) Boca Raton, FL: CRC Press (pp. 195-213).

Bovbjerg, D.H., Redd, W.H., Maier, L.A., Holland, J.C., Lesko, L.M., Niedzwiecki, D. and Hakes, T.B. (1990). Anticipatory immune suppression and nausea in women receiving cyclic chemotherapy for ovarian cancer. Journal of Consulting and Clinical Psychology 58:153-157.

Bovbjerg, D.H., Redd, W.H., Jacobsen, P.B., Manne, S.L., Taylor, K.L., Surbone, A., Norton, L., Gilewski, T.A., Hudis, C.A. and et al. (1992). An experimental analysis of classically conditioned nausea during chemotherapy [see comments]. Psychosomatic Medicine 54:623-637.

Carey, M.P. and Burish, T.G. (1988). Etiology and treatment of the psychological side effects associated with cancer chemotherapy. A critical review and discussion. Psychol. Bull. 104:307-325.

Chanock, S. (1993). Evolving risk factors for infectious complications of cancer therapy. Hematology/Oncology Clinics of North America 7:771-793.

Jacobsen, P.B., Bovbjerg, D.H., Schwarts, M.D., Hudis, C.A., Gilewski, T.A. and Norton, L. (1995). Conditioned emotional distress in women receiving chemotherapy for breast cancer. Journal of Consulting and Clinical Psychology 63:108-114.

Morrow, G.R. and Dobkin, P.L. (1988). Anticipatory nausea and vomiting in cancer patients undergoing chemotherapy treatment: Prevalence etiology and behavioral interventions. Clinical Psychology Review 8:517-556.

Pavlov, I.P. (1927). Conditioned Reflexes: An Investigation of Physiological Activity of the Cerebral Cortex (Lecture III). Oxford: Oxford University Press.

Schwartz, M.D., Jacobsen, P.B. and Bovbjerg, D.H. The role of nausea in the development of taste aversion among cancer chemotherapy patients. Physiology and Behavior (in press).

DEPRESSION IN BREAST AND PANCREATIC CANCER

Presented by

Dominique L. Musselman, M.D.

It is not uncommon to find significant rates of depression in any outpatient medical setting. However, amongst those with cancer the rates of depression skyrocket. In particular, patients diagnosed with pancreatic tumors have one of the highest rates in comparison with all of the other cancers (Fras et al., 1967; Joffe et al., 1986). Furthermore, the incidence of depression can precede the onset of pancreatic cancer symptoms so it is not simply an exogenous or reactive depression to the medical condition (Yaskin, 1931).

Biological Correlates of Depression

It is important to consider the various biological changes that have now been associated with depression. Over the past 20 years a number of neuroendocrine alterations have been characterized. These include deficient serotonergic neurotransmission, altered sleep patterns, as well as anatomical abnormalities (McDaniel et al., 1995), especially within the caudate nucleus which is necessary for effective processing of information (Schneider, 1984; Reisine et al., 1977; Tolosa, 1981). In geriatric populations there is a tendency to detect large ventricles (Abas et al., 1990; Jacoby and Levy, 1980; Pearlson et al., 1989; Rabins et al., 1991), as well as an enlargement of structures that are essential to the hypothalamic-pituitary-adrenal (HPA) axis. Specifically, the pituitary (Krishnan et al., 1991) and adrenal glands (Zis and Zis, 1987; Amsterdam et al., 1987; Nemeroff et al., 1992) are enlarged. These are changes that have been identified in populations that are depressed but not necessarily individuals who are diagnosed with cancer.

An important question is whether depressed cancer patients exhibit similar biological alterations in comparison with non-depressed cancer patients. One neuroendocrine change which has been documented in some patients with major depression is an inability to suppress the high amounts of cortisol produced by their adrenal gland. This abnormality is detected using the dexamethasone suppression test whereby 1 mg of this synthetic glucocorticoid is administered to the patient at 11 PM. Blood samples for measurement of cortisol concentrations are obtained at 4 PM and 11 PM the next day. Normally, the elevated synthetic glucocorticoid will down-regulate the cascade of events that culminates in stimulation of the adrenal glands. One-half to two-thirds of depressed patients, however, exhibit dexamethasone non-suppression (Schuckit, 1988).

Pancreatic Cancer

In our work, a high degree of depression has been observed in patients with pancreatic cancer and, based upon their self-reports, they had a very high incidence of depressive symptoms in the month prior to their cancer diagnosis. Using the Quality of Life rating scale it has been shown that depressed cancer patients in comparison with non-depressed cancer patients had other impairments that impacted on their lives. These included difficulties communicating with significant others, difficulty cooperating with their medical care provider, and significant sexual dysfunction. There also is evidence that some of the patients failed to down-regulate their HPA axis following the infusion of dexamethasone. No significant findings have been observed with respect to changes in ventricular size (Musselman et al., 1993).

While preliminary, these observations are potentially important because they suggest that there may be biological events related to the stress response occurring long before the diagnosis of cancer. As such, they may have predictive value in identifying those most at risk for developing certain types of tumors, especially pancreatic cancer. It also appears that pancreatic cancer is different from other types of cancer in that the pancreas is capable of autodigestion due to release and intrapancreatic activation of digestive enzymes (Chiarai, 1896). This can lead to pancreatitis (Kohler and Lankisch, 1987) and the release of pro-inflammatory cytokines which in turn could act within the central nervous system to explain the glucocorticoid, vegetative, and cognitive changes (Lerch and Adler, 1992). In addition to cytokines being produced during the inflammatory response, other chemicals may be produced by the tumor itself. For example, there is evidence that cytokines can be produced by a pancreatic tumor cell line (Yamaguchi et al., 1994). Moreover, pancreatic islet cells produce interleukin-6 when exposed to tumor necrosis factor (Campbell et al., 1989).

References

Abas, M.A., Sahakian, B.J. and Levy, R. (1990). Neuropsychological deficits and CT scan changes in elderly depressives. Psychological Med. 20:507-520.

Amsterdam, J.D., Marinelli, D.L., Arger, P. et al. (1987). Assessment of adrenal gland volume by computed tomography in depressed patients and healthy volunteers: A pilot study. Psychiatry Res. 21:189-197.

Campbell, I.L., Wilson, C.A. and Harrison, L.C. (1989). Evidence for IL6 production by and effects on the pancreatic beta cell. J. Immunol. 143:1188-1191.

Chiarai, H. (1896). Uber die Selbstverdauung des menschlichen Pankreas. Z. Heilk. 17:69-96.

Fras, I., Litin, E.M. and Pearson, J.S. (1967). Comparison of psychiatric symptoms in carcinoma of the pancreas with those in some other intra abdominal neoplasms. Am. J. Psychiatry 123:1533-1562.

Jacoby, R.J. and Levy, R. (1980). Computed tomography in the elderly. Affective disorder. Br. J. Psychiatry 136:270-275.

Joffe, R.T., Rubinow, D.R., Denicoff, K.D., Maher, M. and Sindelar, W.F. (1986). Depression and carcinoma of the pancreas. Gen. Hosp. Psychiatry 8:241-245.

Kohler, H. and Lankisch, P.G. (1987). Acute pancreatitis and hyperamylasaemia in pancreatic carcinoma. Pancreas 2:117.

Krishnan, K.R.R., Doraiswamy, P.M., Lurie, S.N., Figiel, G.S., Husain, M.M., Boyko, O.B., Ellinwood, E.H. and Nemeroff, C.B. (1991). Pituitary size in depression. J. Clin. Endocrinol. Metab. 72:256-259.

Lerch, M.M. and Adler, G. (1992). Acute pancreatitis. Current Opinion in Gastroenterology 8:817-823.

McDaniel, J.S., Musselman, D.L., Porter, M.R., Reed, D.A. and Nemeroff, C.B. (1995). Depression in patients with cancer: Diagnosis, biology and treatment. Arch. Gen. Psych. 52:89-99.

Musselman, D.L., Nemeroff, C.B., McDaniel, J.S., Reed, D., Wingard, J., Seelig, B., Porter, M.R. and Landry, J.C. (1993). Cancer and Depression: Diagnostic Considerations and Biologic Markers. 32nd Annual Meeting of the American College of Neuropsychopharmacology, Honolulu, Hawaii, December, 1993 (p. 123).

Nemeroff, C.B., Krishnan, K.K.R., Reed, D. et al. (1992). Adrenal gland enlargement in major depression: A computed tomographic study. Arch. Gen. Psychiatry 49:384-387.

Pearlson, G.D., Rabins, P.V., Kim, W.S. et al. (1989). Structural brain CT changes and cognitive deficits in elderly depressives with major depression. Am. J. Psychiatry 148:617-620.

Rabins, P.V., Pearlson, G.F., Aylward, E. et al. (1991). Cortical magnetic resonance imaging changes in elderly inpatients with major depression. Am. J. Psychiatry 148:617-620.

Reisine, T.D., Fields, J.Z. and Hamamura, H.I. (1977). Neurotransmitter receptor alterations in Parkinsonis disease. Life Sci. 21:335-344.

Schneider, J.S. (1984). Basal ganglia role in behavior: Importance of sensory gating and its relevance to psychiatry. Biol. Psychiatry 19:1693-1710.

Schuckit, M.A. (1988). Trait (and state) markers of a predisposition to psychopathology. In: Psychiatry. (Michels, R., Cavenar, J.O., Cooper, A.M., Guze, S.M., Judd, L.L., Klerman, G.L. and Solnit, A.J., Eds.) Philadelphia: J.B. Lippincott Co. (53:1-19).

Tolosa, E.S. (1981). Clinical features of Meige's disease. Arch. Neurol. 18:147-151.

Yamaguchi, N., Hattori, K., Masayoshi, O., Kojima, T., Imai, N. and Ochi, N. (1994). A novel cytokine exhibiting megakaryocyte potentiating activity from a human pancreatic tumor cell line HPC-Y5. J. Biol. Chem. 269:805-808.

Yaskin, J.C. (1931). Nervous symptoms as earliest manifestations of carcinoma of the pancreas. J. Am. Med. Assoc.

Zis, K.D. and Zis, A. (1987). Increased adrenal weight in victims of violent suicide. Am. J. Psychiatry 144:1214-1215.

STRESS AND MENSTRUAL CYCLE EFFECTS ON NATURAL KILLER CELL ACTIVITY AND TUMOR METASTASIS: *IN VIVO* STUDIES

Presented by

Shamgar Ben-Eliyahu, Ph.D.

Gonadal Steroids, Surgery and Cancer Survival

The growth of some breast tumors is responsive to gonadal steroids so factors that affect levels of these hormones are likely to have an impact on the progression of these malignancies. Conversely, the impact of sex steroids on tumor development can be exerted indirectly, via the immune system or other mechanisms that control tumor development, and thus would not depend on tumor responsiveness to sex steroids. This seems to be the case in the clinical setting described by Badwe et al. (1991) and Senie et al. (1991): A three-fold increase in long-term mortality rate was reported in women who received surgery for breast cancer during the unopposed estrogen synthesis phase of their menstrual cycle (elevated estradiol/low progesterone levels, days 3-12 after last menstrual period), relative to patients operated during the rest of the menstrual cycle (46% vs. 16% mortality rate, respectively; Badwe et al., 1991). This phenomenon occurred irrespectively of whether or not the excised tumor expressed receptors for sex steroids, but was limited to patients with positive lymph nodes. If generalized to the overall population of premenopausal women in the United States, timing of surgery alone may be responsible for approximately 5,000 deaths each year. However, these clinical findings are controversial. Several retrospective studies have failed to show a relationship between timing of surgery and mortality rate (for review see Corder et al., 1994; Davidson and Abeloff, 1993), and the studies by Hrushesky et al. (1989) and others have suggested that a different, although overlapping phase of the menstrual cycle is characterized by a better prognosis.

It was hypothesized that the observations associating timing of mastectomy with long-term survival are attributable to a decrease in host resistance to surgery-induced tumor metastasis, a decrease caused by suppressive effects of sex hormones on innate immunity. This hypothesis is based on: a) The marked immune suppressing and metastatic enhancing effects of surgery that we and others have demonstrated (Page et al., 1994; Pollock et al., 1984). Such suppression may facilitate metastatic processes previously repressed or under closer control; b) The clinical reports suggesting the involvement of the metastatic process and an indirect effect of sex steroids on malignant cells (i.e., the clinical phenomenon was associated with having positive lymph nodes, but not with tumor expression of receptors to sex steroids. Badwe et al., 1991; Senie et al., 1991); c) The established role of the immune system in controlling metastasis (Herberman and Ortaldo, 1981; Oldham, 1990), along with findings that suggest altered immune competence during the menstrual/estrous cycle (Sulke et al., 1985).

To test several aspects of this hypothesis, an experimental model using F344 cycling female rats and ovariectomized rats treated with sex steroids was established. Mammary tumor cells (MADB106) syngeneic to the F344 inbred strain of rats are injected intravenously at different phases of the estrous cycle (or following hormonal treatment), and the efficiency of the metastatic process in the lungs is then assessed and used as a dependent variable. This particular tumor model was chosen because tumor cells metastasize only to the lungs and their retention in the lungs and the number of consequent lung metastases is controlled by natural killer (NK) cells (Ben-Eliyahu and Page, 1992; Barlozzari et al., 1985). Further, we tested and found this tumor to be negative for estradiol receptors and its *in vitro* proliferation rate was not affected by estradiol or progesterone.

The findings indicated that the susceptibility to metastatic development was higher during proestrous and estrous phases (relative to the rest of the estrous cycle), periods that are hormonally homologous to the high-risk phase reported in women. Two daily injections of 8 µg/kg of estradiol-benzoate (EB), but not one injection of 16 µg/kg, caused similar effects in ovariectomized rats. The administration of these doses of EB has been reported to induce physiological levels of estrogens. Progesterone seemed to attenuate this effect of estradiol (6 mg/kg with the second estradiol injection), but had no effect when administered alone. This latter effect of progesterone was not evident at higher doses and should be thoroughly studied to consider the potential use of this hormone as a prophylactic measure.

Natural Killer Cells

Because NK cells constitute an important immune mechanism in the control of metastatic growth (Herberman and Ortaldo, 1981; Oldham, 1990), and because this tumor model is highly sensitive to the activity of NK cells (Ben-Eliyahu and Page, 1992; Barlozzari et al., 1985), an inquiry of the role of the immune system was undertaken by studying the relations between the estrous cycle and NK cells. During proestrous and estrous phases, although females had significantly more large granular lymphocytes (LGL)/NK cells per ml blood, they did not demonstrate improved cytotoxicity per ml blood. This dissociation between cell number and activity was replicated and was found by other investigators in respect to splenocytes. Thus, the cytotoxicity attributed to a single LGL/NK cell is suggested to be diminished during these phases of the estrous cycle, phases that were characterized by lower resistance to MADB106 metastasis in the above mentioned studies. This suggestion of suppressed NK activity should be tested directly and in other populations of NK cells; although the blood is an important immune compartment in host resistance to MADB106 metastasis, pulmonary NK activity or other immune mechanisms may also play an important role. It is noteworthy that all studies described (including tumor cell inoculation) were conducted during the light phase of the day, a period during which the elevation in the levels of sex steroids occurs.

It is hypothesized that in the clinical setting the surgical procedure induced a physiological condition necessary for the expression of the effects of sex hormones, possibly by immune suppression or by the direct surgical manipulation of the tumor. It is clear from these studies using an experimental animal model, as well as the reports in the clinical literature, that the phase of the reproductive cycle has to be considered as a potentially important variable, not only from the standpoint of experimental design, but also from the standpoint of clinical interventions.

References

Badwe, R.A., Gregory, W.M., Chaudary, M.A., Richards, M.A., Bentley, A.E., Rubens, R.D. and Fentiman, I.S. (1991). Timing of surgery during menstrual cycle and survival of premenopausal women with operable breast cancer. Lancet 337:1261-1264.

Barlozzari, T., Leonhardt, J., Wiltrout, R.H., Herberman, R.B. and Reynolds, C.W. (1985). Direct evidence for the role of LGL in the inhibition of experimental tumor metastases. J. Immunol. 134:2783-2789.

Ben-Eliyahu, S. and Page G.G. (1992). *In vivo* assessment of natural killer cell activity in rats. Prog. Neuroendocrin-immunology 5:199-214.

Corder, A.P., Cross, M., Julious, S.A., Mullee, M.A. and Taylor, I. (1994). The timing of breast cancer surgery within the menstrual cycle. Postgrad. Med. J. 70:281-284.

Davidson, N.E. and Abeloff, M.D. (1993). Menstrual effects on surgical treatment for breast cancer. Cancer Treatment Reviews 19:105-112.

Herberman, R.B. and Ortaldo, J.R. (1981). Natural killer cells: Their role in defenses against disease. Science 214:24-30.

Hrushesky, W.J.M., Bluming, A.Z., Gruber, S.A. and Sothern, R.B. (1989). Menstrual influence on surgical cure of breast cancer. Lancet 2:949-952.

Oldham, R.K. (1990). Natural killer cells: History, relevance, and clinical applications. Nat. Immun. Cell Growth Regul. 9:297-312.

Page, G.G., BenEliyahu, S. and Liebeskind, J.C. (1994). The role of LGL/NK cells in surgery-induced promotion of metastasis and its attenuation by morphine. Brain, Behav., Immun. 8:241-250.

Pollock, R.E., Babcock, G.F., Romsdahl, M.M. and Nishioka, K. (1984). Surgical stress-mediated suppression of murine natural killer cell cytotoxicity. Cancer Res. 44:3888-3891.

Senie, R.T., Rosen, P.P., Rhodes, P. and Lesser, M.L. (1991). Timing of breast cancer excision during the menstrual cycle influences duration of disease-free survival. Ann. Internal Med. 115:337-342.

Sulke, A.N., Jones, D.B. and Wood, P.J. (1985). Variation in natural killer activity in peripheral blood during the menstrual cycle. British Medical Journal 290:884-886.

THE IMMUNOLOGICAL RESPONSES OF BREAST CANCER PATIENTS TO BEHAVIORAL INTERVENTIONS

Presented by

Barry L. Gruber, Ph.D.

During the 1970's, Stephanie and Carl Simonton reported that median longevity was twice as long in advanced cancer patients who had participated in their behavioral therapy program which combined traditional approaches with relaxation, biofeedback, and guided imagery (Simonton et al., 1980). Despite a lack of any scientific evidence, it was generally assumed by the Simontons that the increased longevity had been mediated via changes within the immune system. To evaluate any relationship between behavioral interventions and immune responsiveness, a pilot study was done with metastatic cancer patients.

Experimental Model

A heterogeneous group of metastatic cancer patients with a variety of types of cancer was instructed in the techniques of relaxation, guided imagery and biofeedback. It was a single subject design, with each person serving as their own control in a study that lasted for 18 months. Significant increases were observed with respect to a number of immune parameters, including mitogenic responses to phytohemagglutinin (PHA), Concanavalin A (Con A), and the mixed lymphocyte response (MLR). In addition, interleukin-2 (IL-2), natural killer (NK) cell activity, the E-rosette assay, and measures of IgG and IgM had increased. A number of psychological measures also changed in the expected direction, although not significantly. The limitations of this study included the lack of a control group and the fact that a number of different types of tumors existed within the subject population. Therefore, a more rigorous experiment has been designed which included a wait-list control group which would allow for both between-groups and within-group comparisons.

This second experiment included 13 stage I cancer patients recruited in the local Washington, DC area through newspaper ads and referrals from oncologists. All patients had undergone a modified radical mastectomy and were lymph node negative. None of the patients had undergone chemotherapy or radiation and all were at least three months post-surgery. They were all healthy as well. There were no sleep disturbances or psychotic conditions, and all but one were on a normal American diet. All of the patients were pre-menopausal, aged 34 to 50.

The patients were randomly assigned to one of two experimental conditions. One group began training immediately after the initial three week baseline measures had been collected, while the second group continued to provide baseline data for an extended period of six months before training. After three weeks of baseline blood measures and psychological testing one group was given a nine week sequence of relaxation training, guided imagery, and EMG biofeedback. At the conclusion of training, this group continued to provide monthly blood samples for the next year. Patients assigned to the wait-list control group provided weekly blood samples in the first 12 weeks of the study, corresponding in time to the baseline and training period for the experimental group. They then provided three monthly blood samples before beginning their own training at six months into the project. Weekly blood samples were then collected during their training, and after training they provided monthly blood samples for the next year.

The biofeedback training was designed to reduce muscle tension. The relaxation training consisted of weekly group instruction and two relaxation exercises. They also received a week of imagery training. After four weeks biofeedback training began. Twice weekly sessions were conducted until patients were able to lower their muscle tension to a criterion of 1.75 microvolts root mean square for four minutes on two consecutive sessions. It was felt that this criterion is a reliable index of one's ability to relax muscle tension. By using the same criterion for all subjects it also provided an objective index that something had been learned. In addition, each week patients mailed in postcards which documented the frequency of their practice and their perceived quality of the relaxation and imagery. The patients also used this as a means by which to document any medical, interpersonal or other changes in their lives which might have been pertinent. The psychological inventories employed included the MMPI, the Millon Behavioral Health Inventory, the Sarason Social Support Scale, the Locus of Control, the Affects Balance Scale, and the Mental Adjustments to Cancer Scale. Immune measures included NK cell activity, as well as lymphocyte responsiveness to Con A, and the MLR. In addition, IL-2 and monoclonal assessment of T-helper and -suppressor cells was also performed. The latter included OKT4 and OKT8 monoclonal antibodies, respectively. Measurements were also made of IgG, IgA, IgM, cortisol, beta-endorphin, and thymosin alpha 1. White blood counts and a differential for lymphocyte, granulocyte, and monocyte ratio was also performed. All of the cell assays were performed using fresh blood, although the hormonal assays were performed on samples which had been frozen. All of the samples were collected on the same day of the week and all within about an hour and a half of the same time of day.

Immunologic and Behavioral Correlates

A number of significant changes were observed between the two groups. These are specific to the intervention and include elevations in Con A, MLR, and number of peripheral blood lymphocytes. While NK cell activity is enhanced, there is too much variability in the data to achieve statistical significance. Comparisons have also been made within the groups. During the collection of data during the baseline period there was a great deal of fluctuation about an average point which appeared to be random. But then when training began there occurred an immediate increase in the response of lymphocytes to Con A. This began during the first week of training, returned to baseline the next week before increasing consistently again out to 18 months which was the duration of the study. This was also typical of the pattern of response for other measures as well.

No correlation was observed between the immunologic measures and the hormonal measures, although cortisol increased at the beginning of the study before dropping off. This may reflect the increased anxiety associated with entering such a study. Psychological measures revealed that anxiety declined amongst the experimental subjects. There was also evidence of increased aggression scores on psychological inventories which has been referred to as the 'fighting spirit'. Subjects also had an increase in measures of internal locus of control, although it should be acknowledged that the sort of people who volunteered to participate in this study were already high on this measure.

In summary, these studies showed a correlation between the behavioral intervention of relaxation and guided imagery and changes involving the T-cell population. These changes were also correlated with a reduction in anxiety. It is now five years since the study was initiated and all of the women continue to be cancer-free, although one subject did develop a benign tumor on the other breast. About one-third of the patients continue to practice the relaxation and the imagery.

References

Simonton, O.C., Matthews-Simonton, S. and Sparks, T.F. (1980). Psychological intervention in the treatment of cancer. Psychosomatics 21:226-233.

THE EFFECTS OF PSYCHOSOCIAL INTERVENTIONS ON CANCER SURVIVAL

Presented by

David Spiegel, M.D.

Social support clearly is an important variable in modifying the progression of cancer. But a number of issues need to be accounted for when interpreting the results of such studies. For example, diet and exercise, doctor-patient interaction and treatment adherence, as well as endocrine and immune changes must all be considered. In many of these studies, a correlation between the social support and dependent measure can be demonstrated. However, establishing a cause-effect relationship can sometimes be elusive.

Social Integration and Mortality

There is a strong relationship between social integration and age-adjusted mortality. For example, it has long been known that social isolation is a risk factor for mortality (House et al., 1988). More recently, Reynolds and Kaplan re-analyzed data from the Alameda County study, which reveals an overall relative risk of 2.8 for social isolation and mortality, with a similar relationship for cancer mortality in particular (1990). Thus, social isolation increases risk for cancer mortality, with married cancer patients surviving longer than unmarried cancer patients (Goodwin et al., 1987). There are a number of sub-issues that have to be explored when considering how social support might be beneficial. Psychiatric morbidity amongst medically ill cancer populations is a very important issue. Research at Group Health of Puget Sound has revealed that the rates of major depression are four times higher in medical inpatients than in the general population (Katon and Sullivan, 1990). It is almost 12 percent which is four times the general ECA study rate (Myers et al., 1984). Often, major and

275

treatable psychiatric illness is misdiagnosed or ignored because it is viewed as a sign of the medical syndrome rather than an independent psychiatric illness. This is clearly something that has to be considered in deciding what kind of psychosocial intervention may be beneficial.

Pain

Another important variable is the strong co-morbidity of pain and depression. About 26 percent of cancer patients with metastatic disease and substantial pain meet SCID criteria for major depression (Spiegel et al., 1994). Thus, these data suggest that pain produces a syndrome of major depression in many cancer patients which is something that needs to be taken into account in studies of the relationship between depression and certain kinds of cancer. This may be an important factor in explaining the link between depression and pancreatic cancer. By treating the symptoms of pain, there might be a concomitant reduction in this condition.

It is also necessary to view stress as being inevitable and an adaptive response. At least up to a certain point it is adaptive, although beyond a certain point it can become maladaptive. Stress-induced increases in cortisol in response to surgery can be reduced with the reduction coincided with the induction of the imagery (Manyande et al., 1995). People with cancer are in a very difficult and stressful situation. It is appropriate for them to emote about their circumstances, which in turn frees them to do the other things which are part of the psychosocial interventions, for example, enhancing social support, cognitive restructuring, and coping skills training. In addition, emotional ventilation may also be a very important part of the psychosocial intervention. Such approaches may have physiological as well as psychological benefits.

Social Support and Coping With Stress

Forming bonds of social support and creating new support networks at a time in a patient's life when they may tend to have fewer of them is another important variable. For example, in one study of four patients who died, three had attended their support group within the week of their death. That indicates that they considered the support group as a critical component of their own social and internal lives. They made the effort to be there. In addition, members of the group sometimes will go to the homes of people who are dying. The fact that these people who are so close to death wanted to be with those women they had met in the group indicates that this represents a very important and powerful new social network for them. A third variable involves dealing directly with fears involving disease progression and dying. When people face those fears directly, they handle them better. They move from emotion-focused coping which involves allowing and tapping those feelings, to problem-focused coping in which they can break down the threat into a series of problems that they can begin to do something about. And finally, there are interpersonal issues that are addressed in many of the behavioral interventions. For example, how they manage relationships with family, and communicate with their physicians. Symptom management involving techniques like self-hypnosis, or procedures for pain control also may be very important. In summary, there is a need to address some of the components of psychosocial interventions and then characterize their efficacy in prospective clinical trials.

Social Support and Cancer Survival

In a study designed to assess the efficacy of social support, 86 women with metastatic breast cancer were followed (Spiegel et al., 1981; 1989). They were comparable in age and in most of the prognostic variables that were assessed. The disease-free interval which was three years, was the same for both the social support and control groups. After a period of 20 months, the survival curves began to diverge, and by 48 months all of the control patients in the randomized trial had died, while one-third of the intervention subjects were still alive. The only difference was participating in the behavioral intervention. This difference averaged 18 months. Thus, the women who participated in the support group seemed to live substantially longer (Spiegel et al., 1989). It is particularly surprising since this is rather advanced disease. By the time one dies with breast cancer, a person may have a kilogram of tumor in their body so it is quite surprising that with advanced disease of this nature psychosocial intervention is able to have this effect.

A new clinical trial is currently underway in which potential mechanisms are being addressed. The intent is to assess the biological activity of natural killer (NK) cells, as well as to assess the effects of stressful interactions within the marital relationship. Cortisol levels are also being assessed. Several possibilities will be considered. One is that body maintenance activities are the critical variable. These would include diet, exercise and sleep. Diet is undoubtedly important, although it is interesting that at least one study, the Bristol Cancer Health Center study, reveals that overall survival is worse for patients who participate in diet manipulation than in the control subjects (Bagenal et al., 1990). The methodology is flawed, but the damage has been done with respect to discrediting diet. Another study suggests that dietary fat may be a risk factor for cancer progression, but once again, a number of control variables need to be taken into account (Tretli et al., 1990; Harris et al., 1992).

Modulatory Variables

The doctor-patient relationship is a potentially important variable, along with the type of treatment and the amount of treatment that might be provided as a result of that relationship. Finally, adherence to medical treatment is an important variable, however, none of these variables accounts for the effects of the psychosocial intervention in the described studies. Endocrine status of the individual certainly has to be considered. For certain tumors especially, there is no question that hormones such as prolactin and certain steroids can have a direct impact on tumor cell proliferation (Malarkey et al., 1983; 1991; Bonneterre et al., 1982; Shafie and Brooks, 1977).

Finally, one could postulate that social intervention is impacting directly on the immune system. Studies have revealed differences in both rates of recurrence and survival in malignant melanoma patients who had a six week structured group intervention (Fawzy et al., 1993). This randomized trial with an extended follow-up period showed a reduction in recurrence rates as well as mortality. Furthermore, at six months, patients given the intervention had enhanced NK cell activity. However, the follow-up NK cell differences were not associated with the survival or recurrence differences seen between the groups. Nonetheless, one does have to consider a potentially important role of NK cell activity in this type of experimental model and assess the impact that any type of treatment will have on this component of the immune system.

In summary, there is certainly a correlation between participating in a psychosocial support program and the progression of cancer. In several studies this has been correlated with increased longevity, although in others it has not. In addition to considering the effects of the intervention on longevity, one also has to consider the beneficial effects upon the quality of the person's life which, in many individuals, may be equally important.

References

Bagenal, P.S., Easton, E.F., Harris, E., Chilvers, C.E. and McElwain, T.J. (1990). Survival of patients with breast cancer attending Bristol Cancer Help Centre. Lancet 336(8715):606-610.

Bonneterre, J., Peyrat, J.P. et al. (1982). Prolactin receptors in human breast cancer. Eur. J. Cancer Clin. Oncol. 18(11):1157-1162.

Fawzy, F.I., Fawzy, N.W. et al. (1993). Malignant melanoma. Effects of an early structured psychiatric intervention, coping, and affective state on recurrence and survival 6 years later. Arch. Gen. Psychiatry 50(9):681-689.

Goodwin, J.S., Hunt, W.C., Key, C.T. et al. (1987). The effect of marital status on state, treatment and survival of cancer patients. JAMA 258:3125-3130.

Harris, J.R., Lippman, M.E. et al. (1992). Breast cancer. NEJM 327:319-328.

House, J.S., Landis, K.R. et al. (1988). Social relationships and health. Science 241(4865):540-545.

Katon, W. and Sullivan, M.D. (1990). Depression and chronic medical illness. J. Clin. Psychiatry 51:3-11; discussion 12-14.

Malarkey, W.B., Kennedy, M. et al. (1983). Physiological concentrations of prolactin can promote the growth of human breast tumor cells in culture. J. Clin Endocrinol. Metab. 56(4):673-677.

Malarkey, W.B., Hall, J.C. et al. (1991). The influence of academic stres and season on 24-hour concentrations of growth hormone and prolactin. J. Clin. Endocrinol. Metab. 73(5):1089-1092.

Manyande, A., Berg, S., Gettins, D. et al. (1995). Preoperative rehearsal of active copying imagery influences subjective and hormonal responses to abdominal surgery. Psychosomatic Medicine 57(2):177-182.

Myers, J.K., Weissman, M.M. et al. (1984). Six-month prevalence of psychiatric disorders in three communities 1980 to 1982. Arch. Gen. Psychiatry 41(10):959-967.

Reynolds, P. and Kaplan, G.A. (1990). Social connections and risk for cancer prospective evidence from the Alameda County Study. Behav. Med. 16(3):101-110.

Shafie, S. and Brooks, S.C. (1977). Effect of prolactin on growth and the estrogen receptor level of human breast cancer cells (MCF-7). Cancer Research 37(3):792-799.

Spiegel, D., Bloom, J.R. et al. (1981). Group support for patients with metastatic cancer. A randomized outcome study. Arch. Gen. Psychiatry 38(5):527-533.

Spiegel, D., Bloom, J.R. et al. (1989). Effect of psychosocial treatment on survival of patients with metastatic breast cancer. Lancet 2(8668):888-891.

Spiegel, D., Sands, S. and Koopman, C. (1994). Pain and depression cancer patients. Cancer 74(9):2570-2578.

Tretli, S., Haldorsen, T. et al. (1990). The effect of pre-morbid height and weight on the survival of breast cancer patients. Br. J. Cancer 62:299-303.

BEREAVEMENT, NEGATIVE EXPECTATIONS, AND HIV DISEASE PROGRESSION

Presented by

Margaret E. Kemeny, Ph.D.

Expectations and Survival Time

A profound stressor for HIV positive individuals is the threat of their own mortality. There is a great deal of individual variation in how people confront and deal with the possibility of developing AIDS and then dying, especially with respect to their expectations about their future health. Some people are pessimistic or have negative expectations which might well be manifested as a fatalistic perspective, as well as a feeling of hopelessness and giving up. In contrast, others are very positive about their future and optimistic about their future health.

We designed three studies to assess whether differences in the health and immune system of HIV positive men can be predicted by their expectations about the future. The first study, conducted by Dr. Geoffrey Reed, included 74 men with a diagnosis of AIDS (Reed et al., 1994). Using Kaplan-Meyers survival analysis, we found that there was a nine month difference in life expectancy between men with positive and negative expectancies, with those who were more pessimistic about their future having the reduced survival. A number of variables could account for these differences. For example, the differences could be due to the health status of the individual at the time of the expectancy assessment, their previous CD4 levels, psychological distress, as well as health modulating behaviors of all kinds, including drug use, alcohol use and smoking habits, compliance with medication regimen, neuropsychological status, education, and others. In a series of regression analyses, none of these factors explained the difference in life expectancy, however.

Expectation and Immunity

A subsequent study was designed to address two further issues. One was to expand the assessment of expectations, and the second was to examine a separate sample of the HIV positive men without a diagnosis of AIDS to determine whether expectation can be associated with immunologic processes that can impact upon the progression of HIV. Eight hundred gay and bisexual men were recruited from the Multi-Center AIDS Cohort Study (MACS) to participate in our psychological studies. Initially, a factor analysis was performed using the HIV positive men in this sample to determine the domains underlying their cognitive and affective reactions to HIV. Three factors emerged and one of them appeared to capture expectations about future health (Kemeny et al., submitted). The factor contained items reflecting beliefs and attitudes about one's future health status. This domain was separate from negative mood as well as other kinds of psychological constructs such as coping and social support.

A sub-sample of 127 HIV positive men was selected on the basis of being in the top third of the distribution on the expectancy factor. They included people with very high levels of negative expectation, and people with very low levels of negative expectation, that is, those with an optimistic perspective about their future health. All had been positive for HIV since 1984. The sample was also stratified on the basis of CD4 T-cells. The sample was followed for a period of two to three years to look for changes in their immune system. The immunologic measures chosen were those that are highly related to the course of HIV, and included numbers of CD4 T-cells, the proliferative capacity of lymphocytes, and measures of immune activation. The latter measure is particularly important since there is strong evidence that increases in immune activation are associated with a more rapid progression of HIV (Fahey et al., 1990).

Bereavement

Our prior research has shown that exposure to the death of a close friend or intimate partner can be associated with immunologic evidence of HIV progression (Kemeny and Dean, 1995; Kemeny et al., 1995). In the original study by Dr. Reed, it had been found that the individuals with the shortest survival were those men who had not only negative expectations about their future, but who also experienced a loss to AIDS during the previous year. Thus, the combination of bereavement and negative expectations was associated with the shortest survival time. Consequently, the study of 127 HIV positive men assessed both expectations about the future, as well as bereavement. The relationship of each variable to immune change was assessed separately, as well as the interaction between the two. It was found that the interaction between negative expectations and bereavement significantly predicted changes over the 2-3 year follow-up in the percent of CD4 positive T-cells, the proliferative response to phytohemagglutinin (PHA), as well as serum levels of neopterin and beta-II microglobulin, which are measures of immune activation (Kemeny et al., submitted). In addition, the expectation/ bereavement interaction also predicted changes over time in the expression of the CD38 activation marker on CD8 cells, as well as the HLA-DR marker on CD8 cells. The group of men with negative expectation and exposure to loss showed a greater decrease in CD4 T-cells and the proliferative response, and a greater increase in serum and cell surface activation markers. That is, the group of men who showed the most immunologic change over time - which is consistent with a negative prognosis - were those who had negative expectations about the future while experiencing bereavement. There was no detectable relationship between expectations and the immune system in non-bereaved men. Also, changes in the immune system were not nearly as pronounced in men who were bereaved but optimistic about their health future.

In terms of explanations for these findings, it is possible that pessimistic individuals might be more likely to use recreational drugs or to be non-compliant in taking anti-retroviral medications. Therefore, a number of factors were controlled for, including health behaviors, health status at the time the assessments were made, as well as various general psychological states, such as depressed mood, hopelessness, and loneliness. Even when controlling for all of these factors, the relationship between bereavement and expectation continued to hold as a predictor of immunologic changes. Thus, on a psychological level, the changes appear to be related to the individuals' cognitive expectations about their future health, what they believe is going to happen to them in the future, and whether or not they believe they will go on to develop AIDS, as opposed to general feelings of depression or hopelessness. A subsequent study of previously asymptomatic HIV positive men showed that those with negative expectations and bereavement exposure were more likely to develop HIV-related symptoms over a four year follow-up period (Reed et al., in press).

In summary, these studies of HIV positive men at different stages of disease reveals that expectations are a significant predictor of HIV progression. But this relationship is observed predominantly when bereavement accompanies the negative expectations.

References

Fahey, J.L., Taylor, J.M., Detels, R. et al. (1990). The prognostic value of cellular and serologic markers in infection with human immunodeficiency virus Type 1. New England Journal of Medicine 322:166-172.

Kemeny, M.E. and Dean, L. (1995). Effects of AIDS-related bereavement on HIV progression among New York city gay men. AIDS Education and Prevention 7:36-47.

Kemeny, M.E., Weiner, H., Duran, R., Taylor, S.E., Visscher, B. and Fahey, J.L. (1995). Immune system changes after the death of a partner in HIV-positive gay men. Psychosomatic Medicine 57:547-554.

Kemeny, M.E., Reed, G.M., Taylor, S.E., Vissher, B.R. and Fahey, J.L. Negative HIV-specific expectancies predict immunologic evidence of HIV progression. (Submitted).

Reed, G.M., Kemeny, M.E., Taylor, S.E., Wang, H-Y. J. and Vissher, B.R. (1994). Realistic acceptance as a predictor of decreased survival time in gay men with AIDS. Health Psychology 13:299-307.

Reed, G.M., Kemeny, M.E., Taylor, S.E. and Vissher, B.R. Negative HIV-specific expectancies and AIDS-related bereavement as predictors of symptom onset in asymptomatic HIV seropositive gay men. Health Psychology (in press).

EFFECTS OF A COGNITIVE-BEHAVIORAL INTERVENTION ON HIV PROGRESSION

Presented by

Michael H. Antoni, Ph.D.

This study has been conducted with a cohort of HIV infected gay men over a period of five years. The overall objective of the study has been to introduce a cognitive intervention to bring about psychological changes that might be correlated with immunologic parameters. More specifically, can a behavioral intervention modulate the cognitive and behavioral responses that occur when people are first adjusting to a diagnosis of HIV infection?

Experimental Design

The intervention is comprised of 10 weeks of group therapy. During this time, men learn techniques such as cognitive restructuring, relaxation training, assertiveness training, and instruction on building social support networks. These techniques are designed to address four primary issues: awareness, appraisals, coping responses, and the use of coping resources. The goal has been to make the person a "stresspert". They become more attuned to detecting stressors in the environment and more aware of their symptoms. They also become more aware of appraisals - how they use negative thinking or catastrophic thinking to deal with stressors. Finally, they become aware of their coping responses and the use of coping resources. The men meet in groups of 8 to 10, led by two co-therapists. The typical session includes homework, which is reviewed at the beginning of the session, as well as didactic material in the middle, usually in the form of diagrams on the board, and then a discussion of the stress response. They also have take-home materials and a homework assignment to be completed by the following week. One of the integral parts of the intervention is progressive muscle relaxation training. An adaptation of Jacobsonian relaxation has been employed, and this involves learning to tense and release various muscles of the body. One of the homework assignments is to religiously practice the various exercises. It is recommended that subjects practice progressive muscle relaxation twice a day throughout the study, and that they record their practice of these sessions on small self-monitoring cards that fit in a wallet. This provides a means by which to track not only psychological changes, but also adherence to the treatment that is utilized. At the beginning of the study the subjects are randomized to either the intervention group or to a no-treatment control group. Some of the variables include strenuous physical activities. For this, fitness level and corresponding VO2 max levels are assessed. Men are excluded from the study if they have any symptoms at the beginning that could be related to HIV. Indeed, the men are ignorant of their diagnosis when they first enroll.

Social Support

Five weeks into one of the treatment arms, they are tested for antibodies to HIV and informed of their status by a social worker. Approximately five weeks later they complete the intervention. Thus, the intervention is superimposed over the stressor of first learning HIV diagnosis. Upon learning of their diagnosis, the control group exhibited a significant reduction on the cope-seeking instrumental support scale. However, the men in the intervention group experienced a buffering of this drop in seeking social support (Antoni et al., 1992). Men who already knew the diagnosis prior to the study onset also exhibited some increment in the social support seeking. Seeking emotional support followed a similar pattern. The control group dropped significantly on this measure, while the cognitive behavioral intervention group exhibited a smaller drop. The same trend has been observed with respect to the social provision scale which assesses how much the individual perceives they are actually getting out of the environment (Antoni et al., 1992). Finally, the last measure of social support is loneliness. The control group rose significantly while the experimental group exhibited no change. It should be noted that all of the men were asymptomatic at the time they enrolled in the study. The only difference at the beginning was whether or not they knew their diagnosis of being HIV positive.

Immunologic Measures

Several studies have correlated psychosocial variables with changes in the immune system (for reviews see Antoni et al., 1990; Ironson et al., 1995; Maier et al., 1994). A number of immunologic parameters have been assessed during the course of the studies, one of which is lymphocyte responsivity to phytohemagglutinin (PHA). Although the differences based on the intervention just described are not large, they are statistically significant and reveal that the control group individuals go down significantly in PHA responsivity after learning they are seropositive for HIV (Antoni et al., 1991). On the other hand, the individuals in the intervention group went up marginally. The same trend has been observed with respect to natural killer (NK) cell cytotoxicity. In the context of the psychological changes just presented, these immune data suggest that social support may be able to buffer the immune system from some of the potentially adverse consequences of stress.

It also has been found that denial coping is reduced in the intervention group and remains about the same in the control subjects. Acceptance coping is also changed in the experimental group but not in the controls. Thus, the men appear to respond to the therapy by denying less and accepting more the diagnosis (Antoni et al., 1992). In long-term follow-up studies it has been found that the denial score, and especially the change in denial during the intervention, can be strongly correlated with CD4 counts a year later. The same is true of PHA responsivity. Two years later it has again been found that the change in denial is the strongest predictor of the development of AIDS or symptoms of AIDS (Ironson et al., 1994). In addition, attendance at group sessions seemed to have some predictive value as well.

Consequently, the coping style as well as treatment adherence seem to show the strongest association with disease progression. It is important to realize, however, that more work needs to be done to confirm that this is indeed the case.

There is considerable evidence that viruses that are members of the herpes family may serve as co-factors for HIV progression. For example, the Epstein-Barr virus (EBV), when it infects T-cells, may provide another attachment site for HIV (Kenney et al., 1988; also for review see Antoni et al., in press). There is also evidence suggesting that EBV can affect cell-mediated immunity and that it can transactivate HIV infection (Antoni et al., in press). It has been noted during the course of this study that even though the men are totally asymptomatic and do not know their diagnosis, they nonetheless have significantly higher titers to EBV at baseline compared to their HIV negative counterparts. The control subjects show no change in EBV titers over the 10 weeks of the study. However, the HIV positive individuals who were randomized to the cognitive behavioral group show significant drops over time in the EBV antibody titer. This phenomenon has also been shown in the HIV negative men who did not necessarily start above the laboratory controls, but have been able to bring their levels down over the course of the study. So both HIV positive and negative men show significant declines in antibody titers over the course of the study (Esterling et al., 1992). The only psychological variables that have correlated with the EBV changes are the Reliable Reliance Social Support Score, and Total Social Support Score (Antoni et al., 1992).

References

Antoni, M.H., Schneiderman, N., Fletcher, M., Goldstein, D., LaPerriere, A. and Ironson, G. (1990). Psychoneuroimmunology and HIV-1. *Journal of Consulting and Clinical Psychology* 58(1):38-49.

Antoni, M.H., Baggett, L., Ironson, G., August, S., LaPerriere, A., Klimas, N., Schneiderman, N. and Fletcher, M.A. (1991). Cognitive behavioral stress management intervention buffers distress responses and immunologic changes following notification of HIV-1 seropositivity. Journal of Consulting and Clinical Psychology 59(6):906-915.

Antoni, M.H., Ironson, G., Helder, L., Klimas, N., Fletcher, M.A. and Schneiderman, N. (March, 1992). Stress management intervention reduces social isolation and maladaptive coping behaviors in gay men adjusting to an HIV-1 seropositive diagnosis. Paper presented at the annual meeting of the Society of Behavioral Medicine, New York, New York.

Antoni, M.H., Esterling, B., Lutgendorf, S., Fletcher, M.A. and Schneiderman, N. Psychosocial stressors, herpesvirus reactivation and HIV-1 infection. In: AIDS and Oncology: Perspectives in Behavioral Medicine. Hillsdale, NJ: Erlbaum (pp. 135-168) (in press).

Esterling, B., Antoni, M.H., Schneiderman, N., LaPerriere, A., Ironson, G., Carver, C., Klimas, N. and Fletcher, M.A. (1992). Psychosocial modulation of antibody to Epstein-Barr Viral Capsid antigen and Human Herpes virus-Type 6 in HIV-1 infected and at-risk gay men. Psychosomatic Medicine 54:354-371.

Ironson, G., Friedman, A., Klimas, N., Antoni, M.H., Fletcher, M.A., LaPerriere, A., Simoneau, J. and Schneiderman, N. (1994). Distress, denial and low adherence to behavioral interventions predict faster disease progression in gay men infected with human immunodeficiency virus. International Journal of Behavioral Medicine 1(1):90-105.

Ironson, G., Antoni, M.H. and Lutgendorf, S. (1995). Can psychological interventions affect immunity and survival? Present findings and suggested targets with a focus on cancer and human immunodeficiency virus. Mind/Body Medicine 1(2):85-110.

Kenney, S., Kamine, J., Markovitz, D., Fenrick, R. and Pagano, J. (1988). An Epstein-Barr virus immediate-early gene product transactivates gene expression from the human immunodeficiency virus long-terminal repeat. Proceedings of the National Academy of Sciences USA 85:1652-1656.

Maier, S., Watkins, L. and Fleshner, M. (1994). Psychoneuroimmunology: The interface between brain, behavior and immunity. American Psychologist 49:1004-1017.

ROLE OF CONDITIONING IN THE PHARMACOTHERAPY OF AUTOIMMUNE DISEASES

Presented by

Robert Ader, Ph.D.

Lupus Erythematosus

Classical conditioning is a behavioral intervention capable of suppressing the immune system. The question posed by this observation is whether the degree of immunosuppression is sufficient to alter the course of diseases characterized by an augmented state of immunity. To address this question, studies have been performed using the New Zealand black-white hybrid mouse, which develops a lethal glomerulonephritis at about eight months of age. Traditionally, this animal model has been used to assess various drug regimens that can be used to control the symptoms of this disease. Using this experimental model, conditioned animals receive the immunosuppressive drug cyclophosphamide paired with the taste of saccharin. Non-conditioned animals receive the same exposure to the saccharin as well as to cyclophosphamide, however, they are never paired. Another group of animals receive no drug, but receive all of the various manipulations, including handling and injections. It has been found that in the experimental animals, the taste of saccharin is able to delay mortality in animals that are receiving a concentration of cyclophosphamide which by itself is known to be ineffective (Ader and Cohen, 1982). Consensual validity for this observation was provided by a study conducted by Dr. Reg Gorczynski and his colleagues involving a plasmacytoma (Gorczynski et al., 1985). In this particular instance, re-exposure of the animals to the conditioned stimulus actually accelerates mortality. It has also been demonstrated that conditioned stimuli can delay graft rejection as well (Gorczynski, 1990; Grochowicz et al., 1991).

Pharmacology Studies and Placebos

These data clearly have implications for modulating the symptoms of autoimmune diseases. More generally, these data have implications for the use of placebos in pharmacology studies.

Typically, there are only two groups in any drug study. One group receives the drug and one group does not. No matter how many ways the route of administration, the dose, the frequency, or the duration are varied, whenever somebody in the experimental group receives a drug, it is pharmacologically reinforced, while people in the so-called placebo group go through the same procedures, but they are never pharmacologically reinforced by that particular drug.

It has for many years been argued that the placebo effect is in reality a reflection of conditioning (Ader, 1988). In other words, the response to placebo is essentially a response to a conditioned stimulus, a stimulus that had previously been paired with a drug. If this is indeed the case, then subjects who are in the experimental group who have a large number of conditioned stimuli paired with the drug are, in behavioral terms, on a continuous or 100 percent reinforcement schedule; every instance of taking medication is reinforced. Those who are in the control group are exposed to the same conditioned stimuli but are never reinforced with the drug. From the standpoint of the conditioning phenomenon, one needs to consider the potential benefit of using reinforcement schedules that lie between 0 and 100 percent. There may very well be an advantage to treating people with drug sometimes and placebo at other times, i.e., putting them on a partial reinforcement schedule.

There is very good reason to believe that when people are given placebo initially, it is nearly as effective as the actual drug in about 30 percent of the population. However, when the placebo is the second medication, that is, when it follows active effective drug treatment as would occur in a cross-over design, it may be much more effective. One such study has revealed that when placebo is given first, it is effective in 21 percent of the cases, however, when it is the last drug administered after previously effective drug treatment, it is effective in twice as many instances. Numerous other studies reveal that the effectiveness of a placebo is determined by the experiential or drug history of the individuals in the group (Ader, 1988; 1996).

Clinical Implications

There is now a single case study in which partial reinforcement has been used in an intervention for treating an 11 year old child with systemic lupus erythematosus (Olness and Ader, 1992). The patient was being scheduled for a 12 month regimen of chemotherapy so her pediatric oncologist recommended that she be placed on the same paradigm that had been developed in animals. In this particular instance, cod liver oil was paired with cytoxan, following which she was exposed to an aroma associated with roses. The first three trials involved the taste, the smell, and the cytoxan. For the rest of that year, on some scheduled chemotherapy sessions, only the taste and the smell and the various procedures were used so that in the course of the year she received only 50 percent of the amount of drug that she would otherwise have received.

At the end of that period, this was discontinued. The child did very well and went on to college. No conclusions can be drawn from this or similar observations since it is only a single case report. However, it is a very interesting observation which, when interpreted in the context of the well controlled animal studies, makes a compelling argument that conditioning may have some efficacy in the clinical setting.

In a study of patients being treated for multiple sclerosis using the immunosuppressive drug cyclophosphamide, partial reinforcement procedures were used (Giang et al., 1995). In this study, the patients contract for a series of six chemotherapy trials. However, either the fifth or the sixth trial is, in fact, a sham trial where placebo only is administered. Of the 10 patients who have completed the protocol, eight have shown the same decline in white blood cell count between 7 and 14 days after therapy on the placebo trial as they did in the previous drug trials. That is, they responded to the conditioned placebo. Since this was a preliminary study without adequate controls, it is not possible to conclude that the beneficial effects of the placebo are actually a reflection of conditioned immune changes. Interestingly, upon reviewing the records of the two patients who did not show the changes typical of the other eight, it was noted that they had been previously exposed to the cyclophosphamide or the conditioned stimulus.

Health Benefits of Conditioning

It is quite likely that any disorder which is characterized by excessive immunity, e.g., arthritis, psoriasis, and even asthma, will also respond to this type of intervention. Among the clinical advantages of the conditioning regimen would be a reduction in the total amount of drug required to maintain a particular physiological response and thereby reducing the possibility of side effects thereby increasing drug adherence, attenuating drug dependence, extending the duration of pharmaco-therapeutic effectiveness, and finally facilitating drug withdrawal. Partial reinforcement also provides a means by which to address a critical ethical issue, that is, obviating the need for an untreated control group in clinical studies. If one is able to vary a reinforcement schedule and show a functional relationship, a zero group would have no meaning.

One issue which has to be considered is that of conditioning negative side effects of the drug. This undoubtedly will occur because there is no such thing as a primary and secondary effect as far as the drug is concerned, only as far as the experimenter is concerned. So there is reason to expect that many effects of the drug will be conditioned. However, to the extent that these are negative and noxious or unpleasant, using a placebo cannot be worse than the effects of the active drug because a conditioned response is never as great as an unconditioned response. Therefore, if the patient does have negative effects stemming from re-exposure to the conditioned stimulus, they are not going to be as bad as the effects induced by the active drug.

References

Ader, R. (1988). The placebo effect as a conditioned response. In: Experimental Foundations of Behavioral Medicine: Conditioning Approaches. (Ader, R., Weiner, H. and Baum, A., Eds.) New Jersey: Erlbaum (pp. 47-66).

Ader, R. (1996). The role of conditioning in pharmacotherapy. In: Placebo: The Self-Healing Brain. (Harrington, A., Ed.) Cambridge: Harvard University Press (in press).

Ader, R. and Cohen, N. (1982). Behaviorally conditioned immunosuppression and murine systemic lupus erythematosus. Science 214:1534-1536.

Giang, D.W., Goodman, A.D., Schiffer, R.B., Mattson, D.H., Petri, M., Cohen, N. and Ader, R. (1995). Conditioning of cyclophosphamide-induced leukopenia in humans. J. Neuropsychiat. Clin. Neurosci. (in press).

Gorczynski, R.M. (1990). Conditioned enhancement of skin allografts in mice. Brain, Behavior and Immunity. 4:85-92.

Gorczynski, R.M., Kennedy, M. and Ciampi, A. (1985). Cimetidine reverses tumor growth enhancement of plasmacytoma tumors in mice demonstrating conditioned immunosuppression. J. Immunol. 34:4261-4266.

Grochowicz, P., Schedlowski, M. Husband, A.J., King, M.G., Hibberd, A.D. and Bowen, K.M. (1991). Behavioral conditioning prolongs heart allograft survival in rats. Brain, Behavior and Immunity 5:349-356.

Olness, K. and Ader, R. (1992). Conditioning as an adjunct in the pharmacotherapy of lupus erythematosus: A case report. J. Develop. Behav. Pediat. 13:124-125.

CONCLUSION

Committee Report

Studies of relationships between psychosocial and psychological variables with disease onset and course is the type of Psychoneuroimmunology research that bears most directly on the subject of this conference, *The Psychoneuroimmunological Aspects of Health and Disease.* (For convenience, in this chapter all these variables will be referred to as psychosocial.) Most of the information supporting such relationships has been correlational. Some of the newer work in human populations is predictive, e.g., studies demonstrating that attitudes about illness may be predictive of health outcome. A few studies have also manipulated pathogens by correlating life stress with the response to infection using a 50% effective dose of rhinovirus. Other studies have taken advantage of naturally occurring stressors such as examination stress and assessed health outcome (e.g., upper respiratory infection). Some newer studies have causal implications. There is clearly a need, however, for more research using human populations demonstrating cause.

In most of the research relating psychosocial variables to health outcomes and the mediators of those relationships, the psychosocial variables themselves were viewed as stresses or stressors. There is a need to examine a broader range of predictors of neuroendocrine and immune responses and health outcome. These include the following:

1. Health practices, addictive and coping behaviors.

2. Emotional responses, including valence. For example, is the emotion negative or positive, and differences among types of emotion such as hostility and neuroticism, or anxiety and depression.

3.   Emotional activation -- differences between emotions which presumably do and those which do not generate sympathetic activation or hypothalamic-pituitary-adrenal-corticoid activation.   For example, the difference between the positive emotion of 'joy' which presumably produces activation, and 'calm' which presumably does not.

4.   Cognition -- optimistic and pessimistic outlooks, perceptions and expectancies of control, and of stress or other emotional states.

5.   Environmental characteristics -- for example the effects of stressors, and social networks (as opposed to people's perceptions of those things).

6.   Personality variables and coping style.

To a degree that does not reduce the range of experimental questions to be addressed, standardization of stress and other measures would facilitate research progress.

When the onset of illness is to be studied it is usually necessary to use populations-at-risk to increase the probability of having an adequate base rate of individuals developing disease. Examples of healthy populations-at-risk are the elderly, people with genetic predisposition to a disease, and people under stress such as the those in the Three-Mile Island study. Alternatively, when studying onset, chronic disease flares can be used.

In many studies of the relationships between psychosocial variables and health outcome or the mediators of these relationships, it is necessary to first select one or a few diseases to focus upon. Without such restrictions, disease itself introduces too much variability. Diseases that are most amenable to study are those with clear onset of symptoms. If the onset of a disease or symptoms is known, then the predictors of the disease can be measured prior to the onset of disease without illness induced changes in cytokines or other factors which may influence psychological state or other potential predictors.

The need for additional cross sectional retrospective studies is very limited. The greatest need now is for long-term prospective studies measuring the psychosocial factors before disease onset or the onset of a flare. This is especially important when examining chronic natural stressors which persist over long periods.

It is known that there are changes in neural, endocrine, and immune function and health outcome over the life span and under various normally healthy conditions such as pregnancy. Studies of changes in the interrelationships among these variables are needed as are studies of individual and group - gender, socioeconomic status, and ethnicity - differences in these relationships.

Human subjects are suitable and necessary for some studies examining the biological processes underlying the relationships between psychosocial variables and health outcome. However, there are many questions which cannot be addressed using human subjects; there are too many compartments which cannot be assessed and too many manipulations which cannot be undertaken. A major advantage of using animal subjects is that it becomes easier to design experiments in which it is possible to determine causal relationships between psychosocial variables and health outcome, as well as to assess activity in compartments not accessible in humans. Animal studies which examine the same relationships as are examined in human studies are of particular interest. In this way questions about human subjects can be more fully addressed.

The importance of research that involves health consequences needs to be emphasized. There is a need to concentrate on real disease processes with health outcomes. Host responses to challenges from bacteria, viruses, tumor cells, parasites and autoimmune attack need to be examined and such examinations are needed at every level from the organism to the genome.

Psychosocial variables not only affect disease onset and progression, but disease processes affect psychosocial variables. For example, there is a decrease in energy level and appetite, and an increase in sleep time and body temperature in illness. Such effects are often referred to as "sickness behaviors". Determining the mechanisms underlying such behaviors is also important. It appears that most sickness behaviors are the result of immune system activity. Among the questions which need to be addressed are, "How is information about the immune system communicated to the central nervous system?" "Do peripheral immune products get into the central nervous system?" "Is there an endocrine link or is there communication via the autonomic nervous system?"

When studying potential mediators of relationships between psychosocial variables and health outcome, it is desirable to examine simultaneously in the same subject as many points as feasible in the sequence of biological processes. It is necessary to obtain simultaneous data from multiple systems because there are interactions among the systems which can be seen only when more than one system is observed. The information which is needed is about the whole, not about the sum of the parts. However, the number of observations which it is feasible to make simultaneously is highly limited. Since it is not feasible to obtain complete data, it is important to carefully select the observations to be made to maximize the amount which can be learned.

Considerable research is being and should continue to be done on biological mechanisms. It is important, however, that such studies not be done at the expense of studies demonstrating causal relationships. The latter studies identify the phenomena for which the studies of biological processes are seeking mechanisms. If there is not a phenomenon, there is no reason to look for mechanisms to explain it.

Since the fundamental relationships are between psychosocial variables and disease onset, and since the systems mediating these relationships are at least neural, endocrine, and immune, the need for interdisciplinary research is evident. Collaborations among investigators in different disciplines, however, brings with it its own problems. For example, a statistically significant 20% decrement on some immune measure may be worth pursuing for someone studying relationships between stress and immune function, but be of no interest to a classically trained immunologist. The immunologist might argue that one would need at least a 400% decrement in order to see any health consequences. Neither may have ever actually examined data to determine whether a 20% decrement has functional or clinical significance. Working together and obtaining data about the functional and clinical significance of particular results can be used to overcome such differences and develop a common language. A common language is necessary not only to conduct interdisciplinary (as opposed to multidisciplinary) research but also to evaluate such research.

Intervention studies are paramount for future research. Identifying and characterizing interventions that will enable people to become emotionally and physically healthier is essential for establishing and maintaining a state of optimal health. In addition to providing information about strategies to improve health outcome, research about such interventions can provide information about causal relationships between psychosocial variables and disease onset.

Research on a wide variety of interventions is needed. These include individual and group interventions using psychosocial, cognitive-behavioral, psychopharmacological and other techniques to reduce stress, improve coping and perceived control, increase assertiveness and enlarge social networks. The role of conditioning as an adjunct to pharmacological intervention is of particular interest. The types of interventions being considered here are potentially applicable to most, if not all, diseases. It is important to remember, however, that these interventions should serve as supplements to standard medical care for these diseases, not alternatives.

As noted previously, it is necessary to select one or a few diseases on which to conduct the research to reduce the variability attributable to disease. This is particularly true in intervention studies, because interventions must be tailored to accommodate the particular characteristics of the illness or illnesses. A broad range of health outcome measures need to be considered in relation to the illnesses being investigated. These include but are not limited to incidence of disease, disease progression, survival time, number of flare-ups, quality of life, and cost of care.

It is not clear whether it is better to develop and test comprehensive and complex interventions and subsequently determine the salient components, or whether it is better to begin with a rather simple intervention and build upon it. The more complex an intervention is, the more likely there will be some effect, but at the same time, such studies are difficult and sometimes it is impossible to determine what the salient feature or features are. On the other hand, simpler interventions may not include salient features and may be ineffective.

Regardless of the complexity of the intervention, intervention studies must first address how well an intervention works. Then they can address questions about what constitutes the active component and how the intervention works. Careful consideration needs to be given as to what, if any, biological assessments are to be made. If there are sound theoretical reasons for obtaining particular biological data, the addition of such measures can increase the value of a study considerably. On the other hand, if there is not a sound reason for including a biological measure, the data obtained is unlikely to add substantially to the value of the study. It is clearly undesirable to "throw in a measure of immune function." Usually it is not advantageous to include biological measures in pilot studies determining the effectiveness of an intervention.

Psychosocial interventions should be manualized and there should be checks to determine that the intervention is being applied appropriately. The populations to which the intervention will be applied must be clearly specified and careful attention must be paid to the selection of control groups. Cultural variables must be considered when formulating the specific intervention and outcome assessments. Finally, if the objective of a study is to determine the suitability of an intervention for clinical application (as opposed to determining its mode of action or other characteristics), the cost and benefits of the intervention as well as its practicality must be considered. Because the types of interventions being considered here are not widely accepted and used, to be creditable, the methodological rigor in these studies must be at least as great as that brought to the investigations of standard medical interventions.

There is a need for studies of all sizes. As in other scientific areas, the greatest amount of work must be done in individual research projects. However, there is also a need for small studies to generate pilot data on which to base the larger studies. For clinical trials there sometimes are advantages to using multi-center trials. Multi-center trials have been very useful in evaluating cancer treatments. Such trials 1) make it possible to accumulate more subjects than it would be possible to get in one location, 2) provide an indication of whether the intervention will work in more than one academic center, and 3) serve as a means to educate professionals about the intervention.

Psychoneuroimmunology is increasingly dissolving dualisms of the mind/body, body/environment, and individual/population. The body is more than just anatomy, physiology, biochemistry, or even psychosomatics and molecular biology. The best non-linear communications and systems theory models are needed to describe the interactions and their consequences. Future research is needed to provide data to develop such new models. Such new models may help people to perceive their bodies and their maladies in new ways.

GLOSSARY

6-hydroxydopamine (6-OHDA) - A neurotoxin that selectively destroys sympathetic neurons. It is often used experimentally to induce a chemical sympathectomy.

Acetylcholine - A major neurotransmitter found in the brain, where it has been implicated in regulating memory. It is also the transmitter which activates the skeletal and smooth muscles in the body.

Acrodermatitis enteropathica - A very severe gastrointestinal and cutaneous disease that usually occurs during early childhood.

Acute infectious mononucleosis (AIM) - A relatively short-term infectious disease triggered by the Epstein-Barr virus. It is characterized by fever, lethargy, as well as a large number of immunologic abnormalities.

Addiction - An overwhelming desire or need to obtain and engage in a behavior such as the repeated consumption of a drug.

Adjuvant - A substance that is capable of augmenting an immune or other biological response.

Adrenal gland - An endocrine gland located adjacent to the kidneys which produces corticosteroids that contribute to metabolic activity which acts to reduce inflammation. The gland also produces epinephrine.

Adrenergic - Pertaining to the biological activity of epinephrine or substances with similar activity.

Adrenergic receptors - Binding sites for epinephrine and norepinephrine.

Adrenocorticotropin hormone (ACTH) - A peptide produced by the pituitary gland which stimulates the adrenal cortex to produce cortisol.

Adventitia - The outermost tissue of an organ.

Afferent nerves - Nerves that convey information to or toward the central nervous system.

Agonist - A drug or other compound capable of mimicking a biological response.

Allergy - A hypersensitive state acquired through repeated exposure to a particular environmental substance. It is characterized by activation of the immune system and inflammation.

Alzheimer's Disease - A degenerative brain disease that is characterized by severe disorientation, memory loss as well as motor deficits.

Amygdala - An important component of the limbic or emotional brain. This structure coordinates most of the physiological and behavioral responses to emotional distress.

Antagonist - A drug or compound that is capable of preventing a biological response.

Antibody - The protein product of a plasma cell which is capable of combining with the antigen that triggered its production. They can have multiple functions, but most often contribute to the elimination of antigens from the body.

Antigen - A substance that is recognized as being non-self, and that is capable of eliciting an immune response. It also is capable of combining with antibodies and/or T-cells.

Anti-serum - Serum containing a specific type of antibody.

Anxiety - Extreme apprehension and nervousness often producing physical symptoms including sweating and increased heart rate.

Autoantibody - An antibody that attaches to self-antigens. Such antibodies can sometimes trigger tissue damage and specific forms of autoimmune disease.

Autoimmunity - An immune response directed against a person's own healthy cells or their constituents.

Autonomic nervous system - The component of the nervous system that regulates internal organs. It is comprised of the sympathetic and parasympathetic branches.

Axon - The part of a neuron through which information is transmitted to other cells.

B-cells (B-lymphocytes) - Lymphocytes that serve as the precursor of antibody-producing plasma cells.

BCG (bacillus calmette-guerin) - An attenuated form of *Mycobacterium bovis*.

Catecholamines - Organic compounds that contain a benzene ring with two adjacent hydroxyl substituents (catechol). In the context of the nervous system, the term generally refers to dopamine and its metabolites, epinephrine and norepinephrine.

CD4-positive cells - Those lymphocytes that bear a surface marker that is primarily characteristic of T-helper cells.

CD8-positive cells - Those lymphocytes that bear a surface marker that is primarily characteristic of T-suppressor cells.

Cell-mediated immunity - A form of defense characterized predominately by lymphocytes and phagocytic cells.

Central nervous system - The brain and spinal cord.

Chemotaxis - A process characterized by cells migrating to a particular site as a consequence of specific chemicals; e.g., phagocytic cells migrating to the site of an invading pathogen as a consequence of specific chemicals.

Circadian rhythm - A cyclic change in physiological or behavioral variables that lasts approximately 24 hours.

Classical conditioning - Learning that occurs when a stimulus that is capable of naturally producing a particular response is paired with a neutral stimulus. The neutral stimulus subsequently becomes capable of eliciting the same response as the naturally occurring one, e.g., a dog salivates to the sound of a buzzer which has previously been paired with food.

Concanavalin A (Con A) - A plant product which is capable of stimulating predominately T-lymphocytes.

Corticosterone - The predominant glucocorticoid produced by the adrenal gland in murine species. At high concentrations it has been found to inhibit immune function, although at low concentrations it is necessary for lymphocytes to function. It is released during the stress response and serves to mobilize glucose stores.

Corticotropin releasing factor (CRF) - A neuropeptide that is capable of stimulating the release of adrenocorticotropin horomone (ACTH) which, in turn, stimulates glucocorticoid release.

Cortisol - The major glucocorticoid produced by the human adrenal gland. At high concentrations it has been found to inhibit the immune system, although at low concentrations it is necessary for lymphocytes to function. It is released during the stress response and serves to mobilize glucose stores.

Cytotoxic - Substances that are capable of causing damage to cells.

Delayed-type hypersensitivity - Sometimes referred to as cell-mediated immunity, this is a T-lymphocyte-mediated reaction to an antigen. It usually requires 24-48 hours to develop fully and is characterized by the release of a large number of lymphokines as well as the accumulation of monocytes and macrophages.

Deprenyl - A selective inhibitor of monoamine oxidase B.

Efferent nerves - Nerves that convey information away from the central nervous system.

Endocrine organ - A gland that is capable of secreting chemical substances directly into the bloodstream to regulate cellular activity at distant sites. The substances secreted by endocrine glands are referred to as hormones.

Endorphins - Neurotransmitters that are capable of producing biological and behavioral effects similar to those induced by morphine.

Endothelium - Layer of cells that line the inside surface of blood vessels, lymph vessels, and serous cavities of the body.

Endotoxins - Toxins produced by the cell wall of gram-negative bacteria (i.e., lipopolysaccharide). They have both toxic and pyrogenic effects.

Epinephrine (also called adrenalin) - Hormone secreted primarily by the adrenal gland. Epinephrine is capable of stimulating the sympathetic branch of the autonomic nervous system and is a powerful vasopressor. It also increases certain metabolic activities such as glucose release.

Epstein-Barr virus (EBV) - A member of the herpesvirus family which is believed to be the causative agent of infectious mononucleosis.

Glucocorticoids - Steroids that are capable of mobilizing glucose. Cortisol is the primary form produced in humans while corticosterone is the primary form produced in rodents.

Granuloma - A mass of lymphoid tissue with actively growing fibroblasts that is associated with the inflammatory process triggered by infectious disease.

Growth hormone - A protein produced by the anterior pituitary gland which controls the rate of skeletal and visceral growth. It also directly influences the metabolism of proteins, carbohydrates, and lipids.

Helper T-cells - A type of T-lymphocyte that facilitates the biological activity of other lymphocytes, including antibody production by B-cell derived plasma cells.

Histocompatibility - Literally, the ability of tissues to co-exist. In the context of transplantation immunology, identity between the tissue and identifying characteristics of the host so that the tissue will not be rejected.

Homeostasis - The events that enable the body to maintain a consistent internal environment.

Hormones - Chemical signals produced by endocrine and exocrine glands to regulate distant cells.

Humoral immunity - Pertaining to soluble molecules such as antibodies.

Hypothalamic-pituitary-adrenal (HPA) axis - The domino-like cascade whereby corticotropin releasing factor (CRF) from the hypothalamus stimulates the release of adrenocorticotropin hormone (ACTH) from the pituitary and subsequently glucocorticoids from the adrenal gland.

Hypothalamus - A structure located beneath the cerebral hemispheres of the brain which is responsible for regulating many endocrine functions as well as the autonomic nervous system.

IgA - A type of immunoglobulin or antibody found in saliva, synovial fluid and other non-vascular fluids within the body.

IgD - A type of immunoglobulin found on human B-cells where it contributes to the activation of these cells in response to an antigen.

IgE - The type of immunoglobulin that in humans is primarily responsible for immediate hypersensitivity reactions.

IgG - The primary type of immunoglobulin or antibody produced in humans in response to a variety of antigens such as bacteria and viruses.

IgM - A relatively large immunoglobulin produced early during the immune response.

Immunoglobulin - The combination of proteins that forms the structural basis of an antibody.

Immunosenescence - Deleterious effects upon the immune system associated with the aging process.

Innervation - The distribution of nerves to a particular tissue.

Interferon - Anti-viral proteins produced by a number of different cell types, especially those of the immune system.

Interferon-gamma - An anti-viral protein produced by lymphocytes that is also capable of modifying the immune response.

Interleukin-1 (IL-1) - A chemical product of primarily macrophages which stimulates short-term activation of T-cells. It also has pyrogenic and sleep-inducing properties.

Interleukin-2 (IL-2) - A predominantly T-cell product that stimulates the long-term proliferation of T-lymphocytes.

Lateral ventricle - A cavity in the brain located deep within the cerebral hemispheres and which contains cerebrospinal fluid.

Limbic system - A collection of brain regions that regulate emotion and memory.

Lipopolysaccharide (LPS) - A large molecule found in the membrane of gram-negative bacteria which is capable of stimulating B-cell division in laboratory rodents.

Lymphadenopathy - Disease of the lymph nodes.

Lymphocyte - A mononuclear cell that responds in a relatively specific manner in response to antigens.

Lymphokines - Soluble products of lymphocytes that exert numerous biological functions during the course of an immune response.

Macrophage - A large phagocytic cell, usually associated with fixed tissues in the body.

Metabolite - The altered product of a chemical reaction.

Metastasis - The migration and subsequent growth of malignant cells at sites distal to their origin.

Mitogen - A substance that is capable of inducing lymphocyte cell division.

Monoamine oxidase - An enzyme that converts catecholamines to aldehydes. It is found in brain tissue in two different types, A and B, based upon their specificity for substrates and their sensitivity to various inhibitors.

Multiple Sclerosis - A neurologic disorder that occurs following the destruction of the myelin sheath of some neurons.

Mycobacterium - A genus of microorganisms that exist as slender rods and are gram-positive.

Natural killer (NK) cells - A type of cytotoxic cell that plays a potentially important role in destroying tumors and viral-infected cells.

Neuroendocrine - The process whereby the brain regulates the biological activity of various endocrine glands throughout the body.

Neuroimmunology - The study of brain-immune interactions. Traditionally this term was used to describe pathologic states within the brain that were caused by immunologically-mediated events.

Neuron - A nerve cell capable of transmitting information.

Neuropathy - Functional or pathological changes in the peripheral nervous system.

Neurotransmitter - A chemical produced by neurons that transmits information between cells.

Noradrenergic - Pertaining to the biological activity of norepinephrine.

Norepinephrine (also called noradrenalin) - A neurotransmitter released in the brain, the sympathetic branch of the autonomic nervous system and as a hormone by the adrenal medulla.

Parasympathetic nervous system - The component of the autonomic nervous system that functions to conserve energy and resources during relaxation.

Parenchyma - The functional elements of a tissue or organ as opposed to the structural framework.

Parenteral - Administration through some route other than the alimentary canal (i.e., intravenous, intramuscular, subcutaneous, etc.).

Parkinsons Disease - A neurological disorder characterized by muscular rigidity, tremor, and hypokinesia. The symptoms are the result of a deficiency of dopamine in the substantia nigra.

Peptides - Sequences of amino acids that can serve as hormones as well as neurotransmitters.

Peripheral nervous system - Network of sensory and motor nerves that lie outside the brain and spinal cord.

Phagocytosis - The internalization of pathogens into leukocytes. This process usually results in the destruction of microorganisms.

Phytohemagglutinin (PHA) - A plant product capable of stimulating predominately T-lymphocytes.

Pituitary gland - The master endocrine gland located in close proximity to the hypothalamus. Its hormones regulate a large number of endocrine glands throughout the body.

Plasma cell - A fully differentiated B-cell capable of producing and secreting antibody.

Pokeweed mitogen (PWM) - A plant product capable of stimulating both B- and T-lymphocytes.

Prolactin - A hormone produced by the anterior pituitary gland that stimulates lactation in post-partum mammals. It has also been found to stimulate certain measures of the immune system.

Psychoneuroimmunology (PNI) - The study of the inter-relationships between the brain, behavior and immunity.

Pyrogens - Substances that are capable of producing fever.

Rheumatoid factor - An antibody directed against IgG found in the serum of individuals who suffer from rheumatoid arthritis.

RU-486 - An anti-progesterone steroid that binds to the progesterone receptor as well as to the glucocorticoid receptor.

Sensitized - A synonym for immunized. Prior exposure of the immune system to an antigen.

Serotonin - A vasoconstrictor found in many body tissues as well as the brain where it functions as a neurotransmitter. It has been implicated in a number of brain mediated activities including a form of depression.

Severe combined immunodeficiency (SCID) - An abnormality of the immune system characterized by deficiencies of both B- and T-cells. This type of disorder usually occurs during a very early stage of stem cell differentiation.

Stem cell - A precursor cell that gives rise to the effector cells of the immune and other systems.

Suppressor T-cell - A type of lymphocyte that reduces antibody production by B-cells or the activity of T-cells.

Sympathectomy - Destruction of the sympathetic nervous system, usually by means of pharmacologic or surgical manipulation.

Sympathetic nervous system - The division of the autonomic nervous system that is capable of mobilizing the body's energy resources. This usually occurs during periods of stress and arousal.

T-cell (T-lymphocyte) - A cell dependent upon the thymus gland for its maturation and which participates in a large number of immune reactions.

T-cell rosette - The 'rosula' or circular pattern resulting from the attachment of cells to the surface of a T-lymphocyte.

T-helper 1 (Th-1) - A type of T-helper cell that produces cytokines that favor cellular immunity.

T-helper 2 (Th-2) - A sub-population of T-helper cells which produce cytokines that favor humoral immunity.

Thymosin alpha 1 - A thymic peptide that stimulates T-helper cells and activates certain neuroendocrine circuits.

Thymus - A bi-lobed endocrine organ located beneath the sternum which regulates the development of T-lymphocytes.

Titer - The quantity of a substance required to cause a reaction.

Vaccination - Administration of attenuated antigens for the purpose of conferring protection against infectious disease.

ADDITIONAL READINGS

Ader, R. (Ed.) (1981). Psychoneuroimmunology. New York: Academic Press.

Ader, R., Felten, D. and Cohen, N. (Eds.) (1991). Psychoneuroimmunology, 2nd Edition. New York: Academic Press.

Blumenthal, S.J., Matthews, K. and Weiss, S.M. (Eds.) (1994). New Research Frontiers in Behavioral Medicine: Proceedings of the National Conference. National Institutes of Health. Washington, DC: U.S. Government Printing Office.

Bridge, T.P., Mirsky, A.F. and Goodwin, F.K. (Eds.) (1988). Psychological, Neuropsychiatric, and Substance Abuse Aspects of AIDS. New York: Raven Press.

Buckingham, J.D., Gillies, G.E. and Cowell, A.M. (Eds.) (1994). Stress, Stress Hormones and the Immune System. London: John Wiley & Sons.

Carlson, J.G. and Seifert, R.A. (Eds.) (1991). International Perspectives on Self-Regulation and Health. New York: Plenum Press.

Cohen, S. and Syme, S.L. (Eds.) (1985). Social Support and Health. New York: Academic Press.

Cooper, E.L. (Ed.) (1984). Stress, Immunity and Aging. New York: Marcel Dekker.

Cotman, C.W., Brinton, R.E., Galaburda, A., McEwen, B. and Schneider, D.M. (Eds.) (1987). The Neuro-Immune-Endocrine Connection. New York: Raven Press.

Cousins, N. (1979). Anatomy of an Illness. New York: W.W. Norton.

Cousins, N. (1989). Head First. New York: W.W. Norton.

Fisher, S. and Reason, J. (1988). Handbook of Life Stress, Cognition and Health. New York: John Wiley & Sons.

Friedman, H.S. (Ed.) (1990). Personality and Disease. New York: John Wiley & Sons.

Glaser, R. and Kiecolt-Glaser, J. (Eds.) (1994). Handbook of Human Stress and Immunity. San Diego, CA: Academic Press.

Groppel, J.L. (1995). The Anti-Diet Book. Orlando, FL: LGE Sport Science, Inc.

Hadden, J.W., Masek, K. and Nistico, G. (Eds.) (1989). Interactions Among Central Nervous System, Neuroendocrine and Immune Systems. Rome-Milan: Pythagora Press.

Hall, N.R.S. and Goldstein, A.L. (1986). Thinking well: The chemical links between emotions and health. The Sciences. New York Academy of Sciences, pp. 34-41.

Hall, N.R. and O'Grady, M.P. (1991). Psychosocial interventions and immune function. In: Psychoneuroimmunology, 2nd Edition. Felten, D., Cohen, N. and Ader, R. (Eds.) New York: Academic Press, (pp. 1067-1080).

Hall, N.R., Anderson, J. and O'Grady, M.P. (1994). Stress and immunity in humans: Modifying variables. In: Handbook of Human Stress and Immunity. Glaser, R. (Ed.) New York: Academic Press, (pp. 183-215).

Hobfoll, S. (Ed.) (1986). Stress, Social Support, and Women. New York: Hemisphere Publishing Corp. In: Biorhythms and

Stress in the Physiopathology of Reproduction. Pancheri, P. and Zichella, L. (Eds.) New York: Hemisphere Publishing Corporation, (pp. 35-36).

Husband, A.J. (1991). Behavior and Immunity. Boca Raton, FL: CRC Press.

Husband, A.J. (Ed.) (1993). Psychoimmunology, CNS-Immune Interactions. Boca Raton, FL: CRC Press.

Kurstak, E., Lipowski, Z.J. and Morozov, P.V. (Eds.) (1987). Viruses, Immunity, and Mental Disorders. New York: Plenum Medical Book Company, (pp. 65-80).

Kvetnansky, R., McCarty, R. and Axelrod, J. (Eds.) (1992). Stress: Neuroendocrine and Molecular Approaches, Volume 1 and 2. Philadelphia: Gordon & Breach Science Publishers.

Lewis, C.E., O'Sullivan, C. and Barraclough, G. (Eds.) (1994). The Psychoimmunology of Human Cancer: Mind and Body in the Fight for Survival. New York: Oxford University Press.

Locke, S., Ader, R., Besedovsky, H., Hall, N., Solomon, G., Strom, T. and Spector, N.H. (Eds.) (1985). Foundations of Psychoneuroimmunology. New York: Aldine.

Loehr, J.E. (1994). Toughness Training For Life. New York: Plume/Penguin.

McCubbin, J.A., Kaufmann, P.G. and Nemeroff, C.B. (Eds.) (1991). Stress, Neuropeptides, and Systemic Disease. New York: Academic Press.

Miller, A.H. (Ed.) (1989). Depressive Disorders and Immunity. Washington, DC: American Psychiatric Press.

Mind and Brain: Readings from Scientific American Magazine. (1993). New York: W.H. Freeman.

Plotnikoff, N.P., Faith, R.E., Murgo, A.J. and Wybran, J. (Eds.) (1991). Stress and Immunity. Boca Raton, FL: CRC Press.

Sapolsky, R.M. (1994). Why Zebras Don't Get Ulcers: A Guide to Stress, Stress-Related Diseases, and Coping. New York: W.H. Freeman.

Spiegel, D. (1993). Living Beyond Limits. New York: Times Books.

The Defending Army: Journey Through the Mind and Body. (1994). Alexandria, VA: Time-Life Books.

The Enigma of Personality: Journey Through the Mind and Body. (1994). Alexandria, VA: Time-Life Books.

Thompson, R.F. (1985). The Brain: A Neuroscience Primer, Second Edition. New York: W.H. Freeman.

Watson, R.R. (Ed.) (1993). Alcohol, Drugs of Abuse and Immunomodulation. New York: Pergamon Press.

Weiner, H. (1992). Perturbing the Organism: The Biology of Stressful Experience. Chicago: University of Chicago Press.

Williams, R. and Williams. V. (1993). Anger Kills: Seventeen Strategies for Controlling the Hostility That Can Harm Your Health. New York: Random House (Times Books).

The following journals specialize in publishing articles pertaining to the brain and immune system:

The journal, ***Advances: The Journal of Mind-Body Health***, is available from the Fetzer Institute, 9292 West KL Avenue, Kalamazoo, MI 49009-9398.

The journal, ***Brain, Behavior and Immunity***, edited by Robert Ader, is available from Academic Press, 1250 Sixth Avenue, San Diego, CA 92101.

The annual review journal, ***Exercise Immunology Review***, edited by Roy J. Shephard is available from Human Kinetics Publishers, 1607 N. Market Street, Champaign, IL 61825.

The journal, ***NeuroImmunoModulation***, edited by S.M. McCann & J.M. Lipton is available from S. Karger Publishers, P.O. Box 529, Farmington, CT 06085.

Proceeds from the sale of this book will be used to support research programs at the Institute for Health and Human Performance, Orlando, Florida and educational programs through the Psychoneuroimmunology Research Fund, Malibu, California.

An educational discount is available when purchasing multiple copies of this book for use as a textbook. Please direct inquiries to:

Health Dateline, Inc.
9757 Lake Nona Road
Orlando, FL 32827

Phone (407) 888-3384
Fax (407) 438-6667